Praise for *Happily Ev* ||||| D1048354

"What a comfort to know that while no one wants to 'need' it, there is a book that will help widows in a unique, compassionate, and contemporary way. Encouraging a smile while tackling tough subjects and providing necessary support and education, this book will be invaluable to those so badly in need."

—Lee Woodruff,
contributor to *CBS This Morning* and *New York Times*
bestselling author of *In an Instant* and *Perfectly Imperfect*

"Learning to live happily after the experience of devastating loss is among the most important lessons that can ever be taught. Carole Brody Fleet not only teaches this lesson, she dares to answer the questions that many are afraid to ask, wrapped in warmth and hope for a brighter future."

—Marci Shimoff,
New York Times bestselling co-author of *Chicken Soup for the Woman's Soul*
and author of *Love for No Reason*; featured teacher in *The Secret*; host of
Happy for No Reason (PBS)

"Yes, even after the loss of a beloved, when all seems bleak and hopeless, it is possible to find your way out of despair. Filled with compassionate understanding, practical guidance, and honest reassurance that a meaningful life awaits, *Happily Even After* is a worthy companion for your journey."

—Judy Ford,
author of *Every Day Love: The Delicate Art of Caring for Each Other*

"Chock-full of personal questions and powerful answers, *Happily Even After* is full of compassionate and heart-healing advice. With a wisdom garnered from experience, Carole Brody Fleet's comforting, hand-held approach will help you move through the anguish of being 'half' and into the life-inspiring solace of feeling whole again."

—Lori Bryant-Woolridge,
author of *The Power of WOW: A Guide to Unleashing the Confident, Sexy You*

"Not just another grief book. I like this because it has spunk and because it is practical and not preachy. Carole Brody Fleet's lists of things that can wait for a while and of things that *can't* wait can be put to immediate use, for example. Her suggestions for establishing a routine are healthy. And since emotions do not go away, it is important not to skip any steps in healing. I also like the author's assurances that everyone is unique, that you are in charge, and that if you can't find it, then create it. Carole's idea about celebrating Valentine's Day anyway shows the sort of creativity that she encourages. *Happily Even After* offers a strong list of referrals and itself is a powerful guide to navigating a tough course. Carole has written what I consider the widows' bible. She shows us the way to 'good grief,' and I will be recommending this book for years to come."

—Linda Hawes Clever, MD,
author of *The Fatigue Prescription*

"It's all in here—the emotions, the financial details, the scream you want to scream, and the hand you want to hold—all served up with the kindness and humor that can make a gal feel a lot less alone."

—Lenore Skenazy,
syndicated columnist and author of *Free-Range Kids*

"The author of *Widows Wear Stilettos* has done it again! *Happily Even After* fills a critical gap that aims to support the widowed mother, thereby supporting her children. By speaking honestly and from experience, Carole Brody Fleet conveys her respect and understanding of the uncharted territory of widowhood. This book is a beacon of hope in a sea of darkness. A true survivor's survival guide."

—Jill Starishevsky,
author of *My Body Belongs to Me* and co-author of *A Tiny Step Forward: Providing Children a Positive Way to Cope with Grief*

"Bravo to Carole Brody Fleet! As a young widow with five children, I feel connected to *Happily Even After*. Each chapter gives voice to the different scenarios that a widow encounters. This book is a heartfelt and concrete road map that can guide widows through an emotionally challenging and chaotic time."

—Charlene Khaghan,
co-author of *A Tiny Step Forward: Providing Children a Positive Way to Cope with Grief*

happily
even
after

happily
even
after

a guide to getting through (and beyond)
the grief of widowhood

carole brody fleet

foreword by lisa kline

VIVA
EDITIONS

Published in the United States by Cleis Press, Inc.,
2246 Sixth Street, Berkeley, California, 94710.

Printed in the United States.
Cover design: Scott Idleman/Blink
Cover photograph: ooyoo/Getty Images
Text design: Frank Wiedemann
First Edition.
10 9 8 7 6 5 4 3 2 1

Trade paper ISBN: 978-1-936740-13-0
E-book ISBN: 978-1-936740-23-9

Library of Congress Cataloging-in-Publication Data

Fleet, Carole Brody.
 Happily even after : a guide to getting through (and beyond) the grief of widowhood / Carole Brody Fleet.
   p. cm.
  ISBN 978-1-936740-13-0 (pbk.)
 1. Widowhood. 2. Spouses--Death. 3. Grief. I. Title.
 HQ1058.F56 2012
 306.88'3--dc23
                    2012005845

dedication

This book is lovingly dedicated to:

All of the courageous widows, widowers, and their loved ones, whose letters and postings comprise this book and who so willingly shared their thoughts, trials, and experiences. Though you may not realize it, you are helping countless people in their grief recovery and I salute your spirit, your generosity, and your selflessness in giving of yourselves.

My mother, Eilene,
who believed that Widows Wear Stilettos was possible;
my incredible daughters, Kendall Leah and Michelle Louise,
who made my dreams believable;
and to my husband, Dave Stansbury,
who helped those dreams become "do-able."
Thank you all for putting up with ridiculous schedules, more cold leftovers than hot meals; and for celebrating the triumphs, helping me through the challenges, being my "sparkle," and for simply loving me.
The four of you are my heroes and I love you all so much.

My father, Elvin "Clink" Clinkenbeard, of blessed memory.
February 2, 1923–May 23, 2001
Daddy, time tempers the rawness of pain, but never the missing of your presence with us, or the hole in our hearts left by your absence. I miss you and I love you.

And, as always, to the late Michael Alan Fleet, Sr., of blessed memory.
July 21, 1945–December 19, 2000
May our work and our continued mission always be to your honor, your legacy, and to the fulfillment of your final wishes that our journey and experience together as a family would serve to help others in need. With my love forever.

table of contents

foreword

AS A FELLOW WIDOW ON MY OWN JOURNEY OF HEALING, I FELT THE MOST
important point in Carole Brody Fleet's *Happily Even After* is that you start to
know yourself now that you've lost your husband. Carole makes you think,
cry, and laugh as she guides you on your path to a new life. Carole lights up
your darkness like a fairy godmother; holding your hand while being honest,
funny, and realistic. It is how you choose to deal with your loss that directs
the journey into your new life. This is how you begin to heal and move
forward.

Carole teaches you that widowhood doesn't define you, but it will play a
role in shaping you. *Happily Even After* will remind you to never forget the
past but also to enjoy the present and to not be afraid of the future, which
you can control and enjoy without any guilt.

Carole is a driven and passionate person in all that she does. Her infec-
tious and caring personality has helped so many across the country while on
her mission to help the widowed get through their loss. Her guidance lets you
know that you are not alone and will give you the strength to carry on. Rich

with experience, her goal is to reach out and to teach from her heart and soul. Carole is delightful and inspiring; she's a true angel.

Lisa Kline
host of Bravo's *Launch My Line*

preface

(Or, "Let's Get It Started"!)

ONE DAY, MY AGENT AND I WERE TALKING ABOUT THE WONDERFUL SUCCESS that Widows Wear Stilettos had become and how excited we were at the prospect of mobilizing millions of widowed in need. I made a passing remark regarding all of the letters that I receive on a daily basis that many times ask the same questions—questions about money, questions about children, questions about emotions, family challenges, dating, love, intimacy—you name it and I've seen it. Other letters begin with a prelude akin to, "I know that I'm the only one in this situation…" and whatever the situation was, I had seen at least ten other letters from others in the identical situation yet; the authors of these letters were convinced that they were each all alone.

My agent listened for a few minutes and then announced, "That's your next book."

With that declaration (or direct order, I'm not sure which), I began to work on the book that you are now reading—a book that was written in large part by *you*, treasured members of the widowed community. The questions in the book are taken from actual letters written by widow/ers to me, as well as from message board postings by the thousands of visitors at www.widow-swearstilettos.com. The answers that you will see are the actual answers that I provided to the authors of the letters along with additional observations and commentary.

You may also recognize advice offered in the book that is also on the CD and with good reason: it's valuable advice that bears repeating and advice that everyone needs to know. We're not just here to help you with your attitude (because *everyone* has an "attitude"). Instead, we are here to help you with your "widow-tude," Widows Wear Stilettos's very special way of describing your approach to moving into a "new normal" or your life post-widowhood.

You will find that the questions and answers in the book cover a broad range of subjects. In other words, I can all but guarantee that if you have a question about your widowhood or your Healing Journey, at least one other widow has had that question too. The great news is that you will not simply find questions in this book, you will also find *answers* to those questions as well.

It is with great pleasure that I invite you to begin (or continue along on) your healing journey. Let's now take that first step together.

prologue

Whatever path I choose to take on my healing journey,
it is my path to choose and to take.
My path is unique because I am unique
and is therefore not subject to opinion.
I accept that I will make mistakes on this journey
for which there is no map and no direction;
no easy or quick way "out" or "through."
I will have difficult days.
I will fall short of my expectations
and perhaps the expectations of those whom I love.
I will lose my way.
But I will find my way back.
I will chart my course and direction.
I will recover and learn from my mistakes.
I will have wonderful days that counter the difficult.
I will exceed my expectations

while discovering that those whom I love
also love me in return and without condition;
expecting nothing more from me than I am able to give.
And while I know that the healing journey is a process,
as long as I am moving forward
slowly,
determinedly,
resolutely,
and with purpose,
the healing journey is not simply a process;
it is also
a promise.

—Carole Brody Fleet
June 2001

I FONDLY RECALL THE FIRST THREE-QUARTERS OF 1998 AS A WONDERFUL, halcyon time in our family. I had just retired from a fifteen-year career in the legal profession to embark upon a career in the cosmetics industry, a career for which I felt "to the manner born." If anyone had any doubts as to my potential for success in this industry, a quick glance at either my face or in my cosmetics drawer (yes, that's *drawer*, not "bag") would put those doubts immediately to rest, and happily, I realized the very success that I used to spend nights envisioning.

After a phenomenal twenty-eight-year career as a police officer and narcotics investigator, my husband Mike was looking forward to his retirement with a mixture of wistfulness and eager anticipation. He loved the work and the people with whom he worked, both of which he would miss terribly, but after twenty-eight years of bad guys and bad takeout food, crazy schedules, and constant call-outs, he was ready for a well-deserved rest. In stark contrast to me and my city-girl personality, Mike was a cowboy of the old school; longing simply to ride horses, throw a rope, stare at stars, and generally live a more leisurely life than the "mean streets" had offered. He was completing his illustrious career on an incredible high note; setting records in the seizure of drugs and drug money and spending the last three years of his career as part of an elite task force on which any police officer would be anxious to work.

Our daughter Kendall was nine years old at the time and was very busy being a nine-year-old girl. As with many of you, I spent a lot of time shepherding her from one activity to another: swimming lessons on Wednesday afternoons, gymnastics on Saturday mornings, Hebrew school twice a week, and religious school on Sundays; the usual kid stuff in which most mothers are involved. In short, we were living life pretty much just like everyone else.

Until one day—one horrible, awful, terrible, gut-wrenching, forever-life-altering day.

Exactly two weeks after his much-celebrated retirement, Mike was diagnosed with amyotrophic lateral sclerosis (also referred to as ALS, or what is more commonly known as Lou Gehrig's Disease). With that diagnosis came the beginning of a new journey; one that we always referred to as the journey of our lives.

Mike's valiant battle with ALS came to a peaceful end on December 19, 2000, and with that ending came a new beginning; a scary and uncertain beginning called "widowhood."

To quote the Beatles, the journey known as widowhood is without a doubt "The Long and Winding Road."[1]

After Mike's death, as the weeks turned into months, and as I slowly rejoined the human race and began the arduous task of building a new life with a then preadolescent daughter of eleven years, I also embarked upon a search for answers to the many questions that all widows have, and I couldn't find those answers. While wonderful books all, absolutely *none* of the grief books that I had read were addressing any of the very perplexing questions that were running around in my head; it seemed that the only thing that anyone wanted to talk about was grief and *only* grief. Talking about grief

---

1 "The Long and Winding Road," written by Paul McCartney, performed by the Beatles, original release date 1969 by Apple Records.

is fine and even necessary for a while; however, I also knew that *focusing* on grief was going to keep me in a place of sorrow and I just couldn't envision living that way for the rest of my life. Worse still, the more time that passed after Mike's death, the more questions I had—questions that badly needed answering and many of which I was afraid to even ask.

Years later, it finally occurred to me: If you can't find it, then you *create* it! And with that decision Widows Wear Stilettos was born.

It's now time to answer the wide array of questions that I know you have. Since our philosophy at Widows Wear Stilettos is "What Now and What Next," let's begin our question-and-answer journey together.

chapter one

THE "WHAT NOW?" OF WIDOWHOOD

"WHO AM I?"

"What do I do now?"

As I lay on my couch the day after Mike's funeral, in my stunningly attractive penguin-printed flannel pajamas with the feet in them, these two questions repeatedly turned over and over in my mind. They were burned into my brain; they were etched into my "soul with a hole." Day after day, I continued to just lie there, pondering these two questions. I didn't open the blinds. I'm not entirely sure that I ate anything. I just lay there thinking: "Who am I?" and "What do I do now?"

Not only are these understandably daunting questions, these are by far the two most frequently asked questions by widows. The funeral is over with and everyone has gone home and returned to their lives, yet for *you*, the reality of widowhood and the building of a new life has just begun. You are left without any sense of direction, and in many cases, without even a sense of self. You are simply left...alone.

You may be surprised to learn that the "What Now?" of widowhood isn't limited to only those who have been recently widowed. You may have been widowed for quite awhile and feel as though you are still trapped in the "Who Am I?/What Do I Do Now?" phase of your Healing Journey, wanting oh-so-much to move forward and not having an inkling as to how to begin.

Let's then examine the questions and concerns regarding the "beginning"—this most important part of your Healing Journey—as well as some of the ways that you can begin to *slowly* refocus and rebuild into a promising new life of your own. Whether your loss happened last week, last year, or last decade, let this very moment be a new start for you. It is time for your Widowtude Adjustment to begin.

"WHAT DO I DO WITH MYSELF NOW?"

> *"What do I do now? I'm so scared and feel like I'm going crazy."*
>
> *"There are so many things you have to do in the beginning and you don't even know in what direction you're going most of the time."*
>
> *"I really don't know what to do with myself. I'm trying to find a way to move on with my life and be happy again."*
>
> *"I lost the love of my life and facing the rebuilding of my life has left me anxious and exhausted."*

One of the reasons that you may feel "zombie-like" or like you're "going crazy" right now is that you may have been dealing largely in a *re*active manner: you're *re*acting to the death, you're *re*acting to everyone's opinions regarding what you should be doing and how you should be doing it (and there are a lot of those opinions, aren't there?), and you feel like you have absolutely no control over anything. When you begin to take *pro*active measures, that is, taking control of as much of your situation as you possibly can, you will naturally begin to feel much stronger and far more centered and grounded than you are feeling right now.

How do we begin to take these first proactive steps? First, commit to establishing a very basic and easy routine in your day-to-day life. The sooner that you resume a daily routine, the sooner you will rid yourself of anxiety and feeling as though you are completely "lost." We always feel better when there's routine in our lives because "routine" equals "control." We can't control life and death, but we can begin to take control over our reactions to it. I strongly encourage you to establish your routine with the very most important thing in your life—your health. When the body suffers a shock, the immune system suffers as well.

WHAT ARE YOU EATING AND WHAT'S "EATING" YOU?

Now, trust me when I tell you that I am *not* an over-the-top health nut. I don't weigh and measure everything that goes into my mouth (do *you* have that kind of time?). I don't obsess excessively over food labels (mostly) and with the possible exception of marshmallow fluff or the white stuff inside of Ding-Dongs (neither of which I believe actually qualifies as "food"), I believe that in moderation and as long as our doctors say that it's OK, there is room in our lives to enjoy just about any food that we wish. However, I also know that when you make the effort to eat well, you will physically feel better and your body will treat you kindly in return.

If you have suffered a serious loss of appetite and eating is proving difficult for you, don't worry about "three squares" a day or succumb to the pressure to eat that you may be feeling; both of which can be totally overwhelming. Eat when your body asks you for food and make your calories count. Minimize the fast food and junk food and choose lean proteins, fresh or frozen vegetables, and whole grains. Organic soups or any soup that is low in sodium also make great easy meals any time of the day—yes, even at breakfast—and you can always add items like fresh vegetables and cooked pasta to them if you wish. One of my favorite "quick and easy's" is a grilled cheese sandwich and tomato soup, which is nutritious, easy to prepare, and easy on the stomach.

Rather than worry about sitting down to large meals or overwhelming amounts of food at one time (which can cause you to mentally overwhelm and shut down), concentrate instead on eating several small meals during the day to keep something in your stomach and your blood sugar stabilized. Don't get hung up on the word "meal" either. A small meal can consist of something like string cheese and a handful of almonds, a hard-boiled egg and baby carrots with veggie dip, or a small container of yogurt with a teaspoon of wheat germ or granola on top.

We also have the opposite end of the spectrum of emotional eating, which is turning to food for comfort, peace or, let's be honest, just because it makes us feel good. However, if you find yourself constantly turning to fast food, junk food, sweets, and/or snack-type foods that are decidedly unhealthy and that habit is translating into weight gain, the time to get hold of it is right *now*. This has nothing to do with vanity and everything to do with a body that needs to be able to fight this trauma that you have sustained. This is your health we're talking about and poor eating habits or binge eating and resulting weight gain can be just as dangerous to one's health as not eating enough and excessive weight loss. Remember, where your health is concerned, there is no compromise.

Instead of hitting the drive-through for the third night in a row or constantly phoning the pizza delivery that's on speed dial, reread the section above concerning healthy eating. It's really nothing extraordinary or that takes hours to prepare (because I'm not that person either). Simply focus your daily eating on good, healthy, wholesome foods. That doesn't mean don't *ever* periodically treat yourself to the drive-through or Pizza Dude Delivery (without both of which I would probably perish), just don't let it become your daily routine.

Lullaby and Good Night?

Without a doubt, the most difficult part of the day is bedtime. The house is quiet, there's nothing to distract you and worse yet, there's that enormously empty hole in the bed next to you. However, if you don't get sleep, your body will eventually turn on you and you're going to wind up getting sick. It is inevitable.

Try to aim for a regular nightly bedtime and a regular rising time in the morning. Don't exercise, don't start cleaning the house, don't start paying the bills, or otherwise engage in any physical or mentally stimulating activity right before bed. Give yourself a "cut off and calm down" period before bed, sending a message to your body that it's time to go to sleep. Treat yourself to a cup of herbal (decaffeinated) tea, read quietly, or write in a journal. In other words, use your actions to "tell" your body that the time for rest has arrived.

One of the things that I found very helpful at bedtime was listening to soothing music while I was drifting off. I set a timer and the quiet music distracted my brain, which admittedly even now tends to race in absolute dark and quiet. Another wonderful aid that I found was "soundscape" CDs, which are sold at many discount and specialty stores. All I have to do is listen to the sounds of the ocean for ten minutes and I'm out like a light.

If your body needs a nap during the day and you can manage one, by all means grab a nap, *without* feeling guilty for doing so. Although you need to take care that a nap doesn't disrupt necessary, restorative evening sleep, I also believe that if your body is telling you to lie down someplace, you need to lie down someplace! It's kind of like what they teach you right after you have a baby, i.e., "When the baby sleeps, Mommy sleeps." Keep your nap short (thirty minutes or less) so that your evening routine is not interrupted and chances are excellent that you will feel much fresher and better equipped to face the rest of your day.

PAYING ATTENTION TO YOU INCLUDES EXERCISE, PAMPERING, AND SOCIALIZING TOO!

OK, before you run away screaming or throw this book across the room, exercising does *not* have to mean spending two hours a day in a gym someplace. Most women don't have that kind of time under the best of circumstances and I'm no exception. I don't work out obsessively and I guarantee that you will not find me on the cover of any fitness magazines in full makeup and big hair wearing teensy stretchy pants and drinking fancy water. (I'm more the no-makeup-during-workouts, sloppy ponytail, worn-out sweats, Crystal Lite type.)

Exercise can be something as simple as walking around your neighborhood for a few minutes every other day. Just a few moments of fresh air outside will truly do wonders for your soul and for your widow-tude. If it's cold, bundle up; if it's hot, wait until evening, but commit to moving around just a little bit. Get outside of the four walls that you have been staring at for far too long, if only for just a little while. At this moment in time, it's not about lifting weights or cardio or jumping around to the latest video craze. It's about moving, changing up your scenery, and giving you an opportunity to take a few deep breaths.

On the other hand, if working out has been a regular part of your daily routine, and the thought of working out right now isn't overwhelming to you, by all means, continue to work out in whatever way(s) you think best. From high-intensity spinning to the quieter pursuits of yoga or Pilates, continuing your regular workout routine will not only keep your body strong, it will help you mentally as well. One word of caution: The body is more prone to injury after having sustained emotional trauma. Do not choose this moment in time to embark on anything new or extraordinarily strenuous; in other words, unless you've been working at it for a while, now would not be the time to begin triathlon training. For the time being, stick with the routine to which you (and your body) are already accustomed.

Here's a word you may have not used or heard in a while: pampering. Remember pampering? It's what you used to do before all of this turmoil and upheaval came barreling into your life. As with exercise, this does not need to be time consuming, expensive, or especially girly, if that's not your style. Pampering can be twenty minutes in a tub with bath salts that you can get at your local drugstore. It can be an afternoon of scent sampling and coffee or a fun makeover at a department store cosmetic counter or with an in-home beauty consultant, and scent sampling and makeovers are often free of charge. If you're not into doing the "girly thing," you can still pamper and pay attention to yourself. Pampering can also consist of a few quiet moments at night or in the morning, perhaps spent with your faith or with other meditative pursuits. Do something to renew and revive *you*.

I realize that you may not feel particularly social right now and that's absolutely fine; you don't have to go out clubbing on a Saturday night. Instead, grab a trusted friend, someone who lifts your spirit and makes you feel better just by being around her. Put on an outfit that makes you feel wonderful. It doesn't have to be over-the-top or designer-fab. It just has to make you feel great. Then go and get out of the house for a couple of hours.

Do you have interests or hobbies or activities that you have had to either backburner or that you've let fall by the wayside altogether? Now is a great time to get back to what it is that you love to do—it's OK to do that. Don't feel guilty for taking some time to enjoy yourself in a creative, spiritual, or athletic pursuit. Nowhere does it say that you have to be "gloom and doom" twenty-four hours a day and the boost to your mental and emotional well-being will be phenomenal.

When you implement just a few of these suggestions into a very easy and low-key daily routine, you have just assumed control of your situation. When you are *pro*active and in control, the feelings of feeling "crazy," being "lost," or lacking direction will soon begin to diminish.

Your Body Is Trying To Tell You Something—*Pay Attention*!

I strongly advise and will continue to remind you that if you have suffered or are suffering any of the following symptoms, *please* contact your doctor immediately:

Serious loss of or unusual increase in appetite
Sudden / rapid weight loss or weight gain
Dizziness
Heart palpitations
Inability to sleep
Sudden weight loss or gain
Hair loss
Headaches
Fatigue (to the point that you are unable to work or otherwise function normally)
Digestive problems
Feelings of hopelessness or despair
Suicidal ideation

Don't assume that you're just in a "phase" that will eventually pass. A strong body will allow you to better cope emotionally and that's the goal right now. If you are having any kind of potentially serious symptoms, *get help right away.*

"OLDER" VS. "YOUNGER"—"WHO AM I?"

> "I'm sixty-six years old. I have joined [several] different support groups but they were not for me. I'm nothing like the women I've met."

> "I'm forty-eight years old. Am I a young widow? Because I really don't fit in with the older widows that I've met [at support groups]."

> "I am not sure that I qualify as a young widow as I'm fifty-four years old, but I feel like I have more in common with young widows."

> "I am so incredibly sad. I am fifty-one years old and have never lived alone in my life. Am I too old to be a 'young' widow?"

> "I am fifty-two years old and my husband was sixty-three years old. I might not 'technically' be a young widow, but I feel too young to be going through this."

Reading these questions reminds me of those alleged fashion "experts" that tell us that after a certain age, we can't have long hair or wear miniskirts or tank tops or high heels or anything with spaghetti straps, and these so-called experts get to decide on the magical age cutoff for us. Never mind what makes *you* feel comfortable or what *you* think is appropriate or in what styles *you* look and feel terrific. Forget about the fact that you exercise, you eat healthy foods, you look amazing; when there is one more candle on your birthday cake tomorrow than there is today, all of a sudden you're expected to cut off all of your hair. You're not supposed to be wearing miniskirts or tank tops or spaghetti straps, and while we're on the subject, you had better go out and buy some sensible shoes.

Sorry folks, that's just ridiculous. Besides, I never was any good at taking orders, listening to "experts," or following the crowd—just ask my mother or my agent.

Consequently, I'm delighted to inform you that neither widowhood nor Widows Wear Stilettos works that way. In particular, "qualifying" as a younger widow isn't like qualifying for the Olympics or qualifying for a home loan. In your mind and inside of your heart, if *you* feel that you are a "younger widow," then you are indeed a younger widow. Period.

It is true that the first book targets many issues geared toward women who are generally younger *chronologically* because the issues that these women face are particular to their situation. As opposed to a widowed sisterhood who may be somewhat chronologically older, many younger widows were left with young or adolescent children still to raise. These are women who perhaps planned to have more children or were denied the opportunity to have children at all. Rather than approaching retirement or enjoying an already-retired life, these women either still have careers or are going to be reentering the workplace after having been stay-at-home mothers. These are women for whom marriage was supposed to be for a much longer period of time than what they actually experienced. The largest and saddest common denominator is that virtually none of the younger widows' chronological peers will be able to relate to that with which the young widows are coping.

However, it didn't take us very long to discover that Widows Wear Stilettos (in all of its forms) not only appealed to widows of *all* ages, but that the insights, opinions, advice, and education was absolutely applicable to widows of all ages as well. Therefore, if you have failed to find support or people that relate directly to your grief and your pain; if you feel completely out of place at support groups whose membership might not include those who still have children to raise, a career to attend to, and perhaps love wearing those high heels, then you absolutely belong at Widows Wear Stilettos. The year reflected on your birth certificate *does not matter* and what other people think *certainly* does not matter—it's your emotional health and well-being with which we are and will always be concerned.

Let me add an excerpt from one of my favorite letters that I have ever received:

"I found [Widows Wear Stilettos] after reading a story about you in *Woman's World* Magazine and I'm so happy that I did. I am a widow who tried support groups and hated them. They were all full of old stodgy people who didn't want to live anymore. I feel like I finally found a place where I belong and where people understand me. I don't care that I am eighty-five years old and have six grandchildren and two great grandchildren...I feel young inside and [your] website is the only place that I feel like I belong."

Take a lesson from the very wise author of this letter: clearly it is what's on the *inside* that counts! Remember, if you are receiving comfort, support, community, solace, or whatever it is that you are seeking to get you through one of the greatest challenges that you will ever face, then Widows Wear Stilettos is where you belong. We pride ourselves on welcoming all ages and offering support and education that is relevant to the entire widowed population and *that* will never change.

"Why Don't I Feel Better Yet?"

"I lost my husband to an accident. It has been two months and the pain just keeps getting worse."

"I lost my husband a week ago and I haven't a clue how to live life now."

"My husband died from a heart attack a month ago. I have such terrible feelings of sadness, loneliness, and hopelessness. I cry at the drop of a hat. The weekends are endless. How do I move on and get over the future that will never be?"

"It has been eight months since my husband passed. I want so much to go on in life and not be so weighed down with depression, sorrow, insecurity, and sadness, but I don't know how to move [forward]. Is the mourning and grief supposed to be like this after eight months?"

"I lost my husband two weeks ago in an accident. I have been trying very hard to go on with my life, but I'm still in so much pain."

There's little that hurts my heart more than hearing a widow say, "It's been three weeks" or "It's been six months" and they cannot figure out why they don't yet feel better. Why don't you feel better? Because it's only been three weeks or six months; of *course* you're still sad.

The fact is that the great majority of widows have completely unrealistic expectations of themselves as to their recovery and can't figure out why they're still crying more than laughing after a few weeks or even months have passed. This is likely compounded by the possible presence of a person (or people) who have decided on your behalf that you should be "over it and moving on," regardless of how much (or more to the point, how *little*) time has passed since your husband's death. You *must*, right *now*, get *realistic* about what you have been through and that from which you are recovering.

Many of you already know that the very first thing I encourage when loss

12

is recent is to "baby" yourself. Your loss is brand new and truly, you are still in the "shock" phase. Right now, even though it might not be the most comfortable place, it is perfectly fine to be in that phase, a sort of "fog" if you will. Regardless of whether or not the death of your husband was expected, you are still trying to get your head around what has happened to you. That "fog" is your body's cushion against the shock that you have sustained. Allow yourself to be cushioned because it's OK to actually be just plain *sad*.

Resist the very natural urge to make any huge decisions right now. A "huge decision" is defined as one that has or may have long-term ramifications, i.e., selling a house because it's "too difficult" to be in it; changing your career; radically changing your appearance, etc. The only decision making that carries any kind of urgency are those decisions that concern filing for any survivor benefits to which you are entitled (for example, through your husband's employer and/or the government) and taking care of any kind of dispositions that may be set forth in a will. Other than that, everything else can wait.

As a person, I have many strong suits. Patience is not among them. Patience is a virtue that has long since eluded me and in fact, is a trait that is admittedly lacking in most of the female members of my family. However, I quickly learned and embraced the fact that neither the grieving-and-recovery process nor the ensuing healing journey was going to be fast or easy or something that I could cut short or circumvent altogether. You *must* be willing to take time and patience with you. Please remember that recovery is a baby-step process. Be willing to allow yourself the *time* to do so.

> *"I was doing okay but I feel my body stressing. Once again, I'm not able to keep food in and I don't sleep. Is this common?"*

If you had a sore throat or a broken leg or a horrible cough that wouldn't go away, you would go to the doctor, right? This is no different. When grief starts to affect you physically (inability to sleep; inability to keep food down or in; sudden weight loss or gain; hair loss; headaches; etc.), your body is telling you that it needs HELP! You can't permit your physical health to deteriorate; you need to be physically healthy to continue on your healing journey. Reread the symptoms listed earlier and do *not* allow any kind of symptoms to continue or worsen. See your doctor *immediately*!

"Why Don't I Feel Better Yet?"—The Sequel

"My husband died [a few] years ago and I'm in more pain now than I was the first week after he died. I've remarried, but this pain won't [go away]."

"I have been a widow for [several] years now and it is still very devastating."

"I am just 'going through the motions.' It has been years and I still can't see the light at the end of the tunnel."

"I feel like I'm going backwards. You think that in time it will get easier but it just 'gets different.'"

"The first year was hard but I found the second and third years even worse. It seems like the longer they are gone, the more you miss them."

Have you ever had any kind of dental work? Of course you have. What happens after the dentist is done drilling or pounding or extracting and that anesthetic starts to wear off? It hurts—a bunch!

One of the reasons that you may feel worse as time passes or as though you're "going backward" is that the fog that we just talked about—the "anesthetic" that has cushioned you against the shock of your loss—has begun to wear off. Just as happens when that dental anesthetic begins to wear off, the anesthetic that has numbed you against your loss begins to wear off as life slowly begins to resume. The fog begins to lift and the pain becomes more acute—more real. Furthermore, things like legal and financial matters, transitioning your children into a life without Daddy, and returning to work can all serve to postpone the facing of your own grief, with which you may just now be starting to cope.

Another reason that you may be feeling your emotional pain even more acutely with the passage of time is that you did not allow yourself adequate time to heal initially. There is no shame in that of course, but as my mother used to tell me, "If you skip over any part of your life, at some point in time, you will go back to retrieve it." This is what you may be experiencing now.

(This is also the explanation used to rationalize ninety-year-old men with bad comb-overs wearing diamond studs in their ears, shirts unbuttoned down to their navels with obligatory gold chains, and driving fire-engine-red sport cars).

For whatever reasons, at the time of your loss—whether it was too difficult for you to be alone; a friend or relative told you that you should be "over it" and you believed them; you busied yourself to distraction with work, children, or both—you were not permitted to truly grieve and accept that which had happened to you.

Ever hear the phrase, "back to basics"? This is what I'm going to encourage you to do now—go back to the "basics" of healing. Even though you may be further away from your husband's death in terms of chronological time, you may very well need to revisit the very basic first steps of healing in the ways that I described earlier. Reestablish your basic routine; pay attention to your health and start your recovery processes over again.

If you have since remarried or otherwise re-involved yourself in a serious relationship, you need to share your feelings with your partner. Don't keep them guessing by playing the "What's Wrong / Nothing" Game because that's unfair to both of you. Let them know that you still don't feel as though you are quite past your loss and that you're going to need love, patience, and understanding while you attend to this very important emotional growth period in your life. I assure you that anyone who truly loves you and is committed to you and is aware of what you have been through is going to understand and support you all the way through your pain.

Finally, if you feel that all else has failed and that despite all of your best efforts to seek support, take advice, and implement suggestions, you just can't seem to move forward in a healthy and positive way, *get help*! This truly does bear repeating over and over again because you don't *have* to do this all by yourself. While continuing to surround yourself with the tools and the support that you need, you should consider consulting with your doctor as to therapies and different alternatives that will best serve you and your needs right now. Emotional wounds and symptoms are every bit as serious as physical symptoms and your doctor is in a position to either help you or direct you to a specialist who *can* help you.

Our widowed friend put it so well earlier when she observed that, "It doesn't get easier; it just 'gets different.'" This observation is actually one of the first things that I teach all widows. Will life be the same as before? No, it won't. Will life once again be wonderful? If you open your mind and your heart to that possibility, it certainly can be.

The "Square Peg" Syndrome

> *"My husband passed away [after a work-related accident]. We were married [for many] years [and] I have two adult children. I feel so alone in whatever I do. I have only a few close friends because I stayed at home for years. My fear is losing the quality of life my husband and I had built."*

There doesn't have to be a loss of the "quality of life" that you and your late husband built together. You now know that life is going to be different, but given time to heal and an open heart to new possibilities, you will get there. Here are a couple of suggestions:

1) Stay close to those close friends. Plan "girls nights out" with them— movies, dinner, whatever you'd enjoy together. Will they relate directly to your pain? No, not unless they themselves are widows. But if nothing else, you will be back out in the "Land of the Living" and enjoying yourself once again. Remember to take baby steps here; this doesn't mean going out every night.

2) Meeting new people who have the same values and "quality of life"

is as simple as putting yourself where those people are. Get busy at church or synagogue, volunteer, whatever your passion is that helps to enhance your particular set of values.

"I became a widow in my early forties. I don't fit in with the fifty-to-seventy-year-old widows. I don't know how to 'fit in' anywhere. I don't know what to do anymore."

Like you, I felt like I didn't have much in common with widows in the somewhat-older age groups, except for the fact that I too had lost my spouse. So it's natural that you don't feel as though you have anything in common with our chronologically older widowed counterparts. That's completely understandable. My feeling is that if we are indeed a collective "square peg," we are wasting our time trying to fit into round holes. I decided to start punching out some square holes, that's how (and why) Widows Wear Stilettos came to be. So while I understand the feeling of not fitting in anywhere, you must now realize that you *do* fit in somewhere—you fit in with millions of women *exactly* like you.

"I don't even know where to look for single friends."

"Recently, I have wanted to get out and do things, but where is everyone? They have their own lives with husbands and children and I'm on my own."

"I've practically begged people to do things with me, like going to a movie or something, but they all have stuff going on. Do I need to make new friends instead of the friends we were 'couples' with?"

You can certainly keep the friends that you and your husband had as a couple; realizing that yes, they are going to have their "couple" activities going on but what's wrong with making new friends as well? What are you doing to facilitate new relationships, new adventures, and new possibilities?

If you want to go out with the "girl half" of your couple friends, pick up the phone with your datebook in hand and ask, "What are you doing on Saturday (or on Sunday, or on the seventh, etc)?" Don't just say, "Let's go to a movie sometime" or "We should get together for lunch someday soon." "Sometime" and "someday" are not days of the week. Book a date, a time and a place to meet, and *go*! I assure you that no matter how busy they think they are, no one has "stuff going on" every single hour of every single day.

> *"I'm a widow [in my forties and] I don't fit in with widows [in my age group] that have children."*

I know that you feel like you don't fit in with those of us who have children, but the fact is that quite often, children whose parents are in your age group (forty years old and above) are grown or almost grown. My own daughter is a young adult, lives on her own, and leads a very busy and active life. Translation: I don't see a lot of her now. Further, as she continues to move forward in her burgeoning career and continues to grow into adulthood, this fact of life is not going to change. So you may have more in common with the forty-year-old and fifty-year-old widows with children than you think. Give them a chance. While you may think that you have nothing in common with these women, remember that a great many of them, including yours truly, are coping with the "Empty Nest Syndrome" on top of widowhood and would be only too happy to have a friend like you.

"Who Am I?" (for the "Technical" Widow)

> *"My husband and I were as one. He was my better half and now I feel like I'm just a 'half.' I'm lost."*
>
> *"I'm moving on with my life because I know that is what he would want me to do but I am not whole. He was a huge part of who I am and now I am trying to find out who and what I am supposed to be."*
>
> *"I can't focus. I keep taking the first steps but [find myself] back in the same spot again. I want to move forward but I don't know*

how. I don't know who I am."

"I have been a widow for [many] years. My three children [are now] adults and don't need me anymore. I have done what I had to do [in raising the children] and now I am lost."

One of the first and most difficult parts of beginning—or continuing—your healing journey is the question of "Who am I *now*?" and subsequently finding an answer to that question. After all, you weren't planning on being single at this point in your life, correct? Let's add in that since about the time we entered the world as females, we have been traveling in "packs," as it were. There isn't much of anything that we do by ourselves, right? Now, top it all off with the fact that since we were approximately three years old and were given our first Bridal Barbie complete with Tuxedo Ken, we have been conditioned to think in terms of being one-half of Mr. & Mrs. Happily-Ever-After living in White-Picket-Fence-Land.

Except that when it came to Happily-Ever-After, you got cheated. Big time.

When you have been one-half of a couple for any significant period of time, it is indeed a disconcerting feeling when all of a sudden it's just you. As frightening as the prospect may be, you must be willing to take the *time* to get to know who you are as a woman on your own.

Too many widows make the mistake of jumping into a new relationship way too soon after their husband's death. You'll meet some of those women later in the book who made this mistake by their own admission. The rationale is simple and quite human. It's easier to "plug a hole" and "fill the void" than to face the pain of being alone or the pain of the first holidays or the pain of trying to rediscover who it is you are and what it is that you want out of life. However, it's an absolute guarantee that pain avoided is pain that will come back around to bite you at some point; remember, we just learned that if you "skip over" a part of your life, you *will* go back to retrieve it. Once you address, focus on, deal with, and move forward from the pain of grief, you are then free to focus on this new, wonderful, fascinating creature called *you*.

Take your time here. Take the *time* to figure out who it is you are and just as importantly, what it is that *you* want from life now. Since you lost your husband, it is quite likely that you've not once taken the time to ask yourself those two simple questions. The time has now arrived.

What is it that you've always dreamed of doing and have never done? Are there places to which you have dreamed of traveling and have never been? What passion or pastime have you perhaps given up to which you would love to return or maybe have never even explored? Now is the time for *you*! Now is the time to begin to cultivate your interests and your passions and your dreams—that's how you're going to get to know this awesome woman called *you*! While you may feel like you don't "know yourself" right now this minute, trust me when I tell you that you *are* going to resurface, and you're going to resurface stronger than ever.

It is all right to be a little afraid. Actually, it's all right to be a *lot* afraid. The biggest fear in life is the fear of the unknown but don't let that fear stop you from moving forward into a life filled with hope and promise. In other words, don't let the fear of being alone *keep* you alone!

P.S.: Just because children become adults doesn't mean that they don't "need" you anymore. I'm an adult and I still need my mother, just as my adult daughter occasionally needs her mother as well (even if only to kill spiders and nurse her through the flu).

"Who Am I?" (for the "Not-So-Technical" Widow)

"My husband and I were married for [many] years and divorced for [several] years. During the years of divorce we remained the best of friends, had daily contact, and were a support system for each other. We were talking of reuniting again. He recently died of a heart attack and I'm not sure if I'm a widow or not."

"My boyfriend of [many] years was killed in an accident. I am not 'technically' a widow because we were never married. However, I feel lost because I have no 'title' to explain the depth of our relationship to people. When people hear that my 'boyfriend' died,

even though our relationship was [long term], they do not equate it to someone saying that their 'husband' died. I feel upset when I feel that I have to make a case for the degree of my loss and the grief that I have endured."

"I lost my fiancé [in a terrible accident]. It felt so wrong picking out funeral flowers at the florist while surrounded by wedding bouquets. We were together [for many] years. I don't know how to be alone since I never have been [alone]."

"I met the love of my life and he asked me to marry him. We never got to have the wedding that we wanted, since he passed away six months later. People have told me that it should be easier for me since we never married, but I feel like we were married."

"I got engaged to my then-boyfriend. He was in the service and shortly after our engagement he was deployed [and was subsequently] killed in action. Since we had yet to be married, I was wondering if I'm still considered a widow."

I have received an exceptionally large number of letters that have all asked essentially the same question: "If I would not be considered 'widowed on paper' but I'm still a 'widow of the heart,' do I 'qualify' as a widow?"

The answer is no—and yes.

You are usually not considered a widow for purposes of any kind of survivor benefits that are issued by governmental entities. However, since laws vary widely from state to state and from country to country, it is very important to check the laws where you live regarding your entitlement to any survivor benefits issued by any government agencies. Speaking generally however, if you are unmarried, you can benefit financially only if your partner made written provision for you to do so, typically through a will or a life insurance policy.

Otherwise, you are absolutely going through and have gone through many, if not all, of the same emotions that your "technically" widowed sisterhood experiences. You may not technically be a widow but since when is love governed by technicality? Devoted love, abiding love, committed love is love, regardless of what is or is not on paper. And if indeed love is love, it naturally follows that loss is loss. In your heart, your loss is no less than mine or anyone else who has lost a spouse. Your loss should not be diminished or in any way trivialized simply due to the lack of a marriage license. In other words, whomsoever says or believes that it should be "easier" for you because you were never married is woefully incorrect. No one gets to dictate how you "should" feel or how much "easier" your recovery should be. *No one.*

As I pointed out earlier, as far as your emotional recovery is concerned, there are no "qualifying" requirements here. I would strongly encourage you to continue to seek support at and with Widows Wear Stilettos as the very special sort of "widow of the heart" that you are. Trust me, regardless of your technical marital status, you will always be supported and welcomed with open arms.

> *"I have been divorced for [several] years and now my [ex] husband has passed away. Can I refer to myself as a widow?"*

As are many of the answers surrounding this particular widowhood journey, yours too is a "yes and no" situation. Technically speaking (and be aware that this is *only* technically speaking), since you were divorced from your husband, you are not "technically" widowed. This pretty much pertains only to things like filling out forms at doctor's offices where you would indicate your marital status as "divorced." However, as we all well know and as previously discussed, the heart is not governed by technicality or paperwork and it is perfectly normal for you to be experiencing the same kinds of emotions that a "technical" widow feels. Don't let anyone tell you otherwise, i.e., "Well, you were divorced," as though it were no big deal.

Another important aspect is that depending on factors such as the length of your marriage and any children that you may have as a result of the marriage, you may still be entitled to Social Security benefits as a widow designee. Please be sure to visit their very helpful website for additional information.

A WIDOW BY ANY OTHER NAME—PLEASE!

"It's so hard to transition to being 'single.' I don't know which word I hate more, 'widow' or 'single.'"

"I can't stand being called a widow."

"It is very hard for me to say that I am a widow."

"I hate the word 'widow.'"

"Is there anything worse than being called a widow? I don't think so."

There is an excellent reason that you hate being referred to as a widow. Aside from the fact that it means that you have lost your spouse, when you hear the word "widow," what is the very first image that enters your mind? Chances are excellent that the image in your mind is the same stereotype that we all likely once had—the image of a woman who is older. Perhaps she has graying hair and lots of grandchildren. Maybe she's shrouded in black all of the time and talks to her cats. Whoever she is, whatever the image that plays in your mind, this you know to be a fact…she is *not* supposed to be you (although I actually *do* talk to my cats).

I too used to hate the word "widow" exactly because of the very connotation that the word brings. Let's be honest, we just don't fit that word, do we? We don't fit the image of the "widow" that everyone has in their heads. This is a stereotype that I am ardently committed to breaking wide open, in the hopes that people will quit looking at widows like we have two heads and a back hump.

But is the *word* "widow" really that horrible?

I know, that sounds like a truly stupid question. While I will grant you that the *experience* of widowhood is pretty danged awful, I want you to carefully consider this: Do you realize that the word "widow" is really a badge of honor?

I'm *honored* to be the widow of my late husband. I'm *honored* to pass along the legacies that he left to our daughter. I'm filled with pride when other police officers recognize Mike's name and smile while they tell me of the lessons that they learned under Mike's tutelage, or fondly recall funny experiences or happy times that they knew with him. I'm *honored* to have been married to my husband for "forever," even if "forever" wasn't very long for us. Has it ever occurred to you that you too were married or committed to your spouse for "forever"? How many people can lay claim to being together "forever" in this day and age?

No one actively seeks out widowhood and I grant you that ours is not an enviable situation in which to be. However, don't confuse the *word* "widow" with the *experience* of being widowed. Rather than cringe at being referred to as a widow, I would instead encourage you to take pride in the fact that you were married "till death did you part."

A "FLEET-ING" THOUGHT

By proper definition, a "single" person is one who has never married. You are therefore not single. Should someone inadvertently refer to you as "single," don't get huffy or insulted. However, permission is granted to *gently* (please hold onto that word!) correct anyone who refers to you as "single" by saying, "I'm not single, I'm widowed." Or if someone asks if you are single, simply nod your head, while replying, "I'm widowed, yes."

"How about us widowers? You left us out and we need help too."

Many have asked me if I was intentionally leaving widowers out in writing the first two books and of course, nothing could be further from the truth. I chose not to write about widowers' feelings directly because I felt that it might have been an insult to widowers. I'm not a man and I obviously can't write from a man's perspective. Men are different than we are and their reactions are different than ours. Think about how you feel when someone who isn't a widow or widower tells you that they "know how you feel." I believe that widowers might have felt the same way if I had tried to write from a widower perspective and rather than feeling left out, I would likely receive letters from widowers asking, "How could *you* possibly know how *I* feel?"

All of that being said, and as you have likely discovered, much, if not most, of what we address and teach absolutely applies to widowers as well as widows. We are proud and delighted to count several hundred widowed men in our membership.

LIVING SINGLE IN A "COUPLES" WORLD

> *"My husband was killed in [the war]. I have a[n infant] child and I am expecting our second child soon. I want to know how to get to know people without them judging me. All they see is a single mom who is pregnant again and does not know what to do."*

Trust me when I tell you that people are not going to "judge" you or your family. They are going to have so much respect and admiration for you and how you are taking steps to move forward, both for yourself and for your children. Don't be afraid to get to know people, or to let them know who you are and what it is that you're going through. You may also want to contact other military widows that you know and join a support group. In addition to Widows Wear Stilettos's support groups both online and in-person, an excellent resource for military widows is the American Widow Project, a wonderful organization founded by a military widow. The AWP has all kinds of resources, support, and education for your particular widowhood journey and further information is included in the Recommended Resources section in the back of the book.

> *"I have never felt so alone, and out of place in my life. People my age do not become widowed. I feel like such an outcast."*
>
> *"I have become an outcast. All of my friends are 'couple' friends [who] are having babies and dinner parties."*

The fact that you feel like you don't fit in or you feel like an "outcast" is completely logical or what I like to call feeling like the cruise director on Noah's Ark. It seems like everyone else in the entire world is paired off, doesn't it? Making matters worse, there has historically been minimal support for those who don't have grandchildren and didn't get to be married for decades. We are indeed the "square peg" that we discussed earlier.

While you should not avoid your "couple friends" altogether, you also do not have to attend every gathering or dinner party where you might wind up feeling like the proverbial "fifth wheel." How about grabbing the "girl half" of some of these couples for some Girlfriend Time—go shopping, go to a movie, or out to dinner. Couples today are not bound at the hip and generally have their own circles of friends, independent from one another.

When you are feeling a little stronger (and you will), think also about cultivating new friendships with other single women as we discussed earlier. There are definitely plenty of singles out there. Get involved in volunteer work, participate in a 10K charity walk/run (which are a blast), sign up for an adult hip-hop or tap class, check out different kinds of classes at your local community college (they offer everything from foreign language classes to tennis lessons to cake decorating). There are lots of ways to connect with other single women. Will they be widows like you? Some may be widowed and others won't be widowed but a widowed marital status should not be a prerequisite to a new friendship.

I also want to once again encourage you to continue to get to know another absolutely fantastic woman—you! I know that the prospect of going out alone anywhere that isn't the grocery store or the local mall can be an intimidating prospect indeed, so start out small. Take yourself out for a coffee or for a salad. Go to an afternoon movie. Take in a concert in the park. You will slowly learn to enjoy your own company and guess what? Despite how insecure or conspicuous you may be feeling, no one is going to point and stare at you (assuming that you're not going out wearing a sandwich board that reads, "I Am Widowed").

I also want you to begin thinking carefully about what it is that *you* want. This indeed may be something that you simply haven't had the time or inclination to ask yourself. It's OK for you to have wants, needs, goals, and dreams outside of your job or your children, because you are ultimately going to be much more productive in the long run when you begin to move into your own fulfilled life.

"Is it natural to feel envy for my friends and coworkers that have spouses, families, beautiful homes, or boyfriends?"

Of *course* it's normal to feel envious. You once had what you perceive everyone else as still having and it is not fair. You feel like everyone else in the world "has it all" when everything that you once held near and dear has been taken away from you. That's completely and a hundred percent normal as well. What you need to realize, however, is that you are comparing your momentary "weakness"—the grief of loss and loneliness—to the "strength" of being paired off. You are in a very vulnerable place right now: a place of loss, healing, and gradual rediscovery and that is indeed a very uncertain place in which to be.

You must realize that the friends and coworkers whom you envy are also human, complete with human frailties. They may *appear* to have beautiful homes or "perfect" spouses and boyfriends (is there *really* such a thing?). But guess what? Behind the closed doors of the beautiful homes, those same friends and coworkers are also having fights over the mortgage that is attached to that "beautiful home" and whose turn it is to clean up after the dog or to wash the dishes. They're dealing with orthodontist bills and kids with the flu and cars that break down and husbands that hog the remote and boyfriends that forget birthdays and other challenges that they don't share and that *you can't see.*

There's an old saying—if we all stood in a circle and threw our troubles into the air, we'd all run to catch our own. In other words, envy is normal but you also don't really know that what it is you're envying is worth having. So let's instead concentrate on how you can best augment, complement, and enrich your own life and I would not be surprised if one day soon, *you* became the envy of some of these friends and coworkers.

THE "PLURALITY" OF LOSS

> *"My 'widowhood' started when my husband was diagnosed and the loneliness and awkwardness with friends started at the same time. When your spouse is diagnosed with a terminal illness, and you know what's coming, the grief starts immediately. It's very hard for people to understand that during the time the person you love is gravely ill, your relationships change drastically, especially when you are trying to prepare young children for the death of a parent."*

> *"My husband bravely fought his illnesses [with a variety of different treatments]. Six months [later], he passed away. I feel so cheated. We did everything we could to make him better and then he died anyway. I just feel that we deserved another chance."*

> *"My husband was supposed to live. These treatments were supposed to take care of the [illness]. Since he died, I keep asking myself, 'What was the point?'"*

> *"My husband and his illness have been my one and only focus for the last year-and-a-half. And then poof! Everything is gone."*

> *"The only thing I concentrated on was my husband. Since he died, I don't know what to do to fill up the time and the empty hours."*

You might be surprised to learn that when you lose a spouse after a long-term or lingering illness, you are also experiencing several other losses of which you may not even be aware. After dealing with a lengthy and catastrophic illness, you are also likely experiencing losses of purpose, as well as a loss of hope or positive expectancy.

From the moment of diagnosis, your husband's illness literally dictated every moment of your day, from when (or sometimes if) you ate a meal to when you could leave the house. Then one day, the illness—along with your sense of purpose—is gone. The very thing that has governed every movement and every decision that you made on a daily basis is no longer there, and now you have no idea what to do with yourself. Days that were once filled to overflowing with the "business" of illness and care-giving now seem to stretch out endlessly in front of you. Sometimes it's difficult to even recall what life was like before illness struck and took over your household.

If the illness with which you were dealing involved treatments, surgeries, time spent in physical rehabilitation, and so forth, that means that on some level, conscious or otherwise, there was a reasonable expectation that your husband would recover, or at the very least, be around for a good while. When that doesn't happen, in *addition* to dealing with the loss of your husband and the loss of purpose, you are also wrestling with a loss of hope and positive expectancy; or, as our friend essentially said in her letter, a feeling of "What was the point of going through all of this if he was going to die anyway?"

Even if you were dealing with an illness where there was absolutely no hope for any recovery or healing, you nonetheless automatically believe in the best possible outcome. For example, with ALS (the disease with which Mike was afflicted), the average prognosis from diagnosis to death is anywhere between two and five years. When Mike was diagnosed, I believed with all of my heart and without any doubt that he would defy the odds and be around for a very long time or that, at the very least, he would make it to that magical "five-year mark." In sad point of fact, he survived for less than half of that period of time and even though we knew that his was a terminal illness, the positive expectancy that he would be with us for a much longer period of time was dashed.

You must accept the pluralized loss with which you are dealing, that yours is truly a multifaceted loss that encompasses more than the physical loss of your husband alone. Next, you must remember that where there is life, there is *always* hope and that means that even where catastrophic or terminal illness is concerned, if there's a fight to be had, you *fight*! You fight with everything that you have until that fight comes to its end. No treatment or surgery or reasonable effort to preserve life should ever be considered a "waste of time" or a "wasted effort." You, your husband, and your family were correct in fighting his illness with all of the strength and courage that each one of you possessed.

Did any of us realize the happy outcome that we were seeking? Sadly, no. That said, would you do it all over again in the same way? Would you fight with every fiber of your being? I'll bet I know the answer to that question.

"When It Rains…"—The "Pancake Tragedy" Phenomenon

> *"I lost a baby and almost died. My husband and I were married shortly thereafter and [a very few months] after we were married, he passed away."*

> *"I lost my husband, leaving me with five children. I lost my mother, my father, and my brother [while in my teens]. After my husband's death, I met and fell in love with a man who also died."*

> *"My husband died tragically after [an accident]. After [approximately one year], I met another wonderful man who cared for me greatly and I loved him deeply. He [subsequently] suffered a heart attack and died [the day after the attack]."*

> *"My fiancé took his life and I spent [several] years deeply depressed. I finally felt like I [recovered] and I met the most amazing man. He [was] killed in an accident. I feel so horribly lost. Once again, I am faced with the relentless, 'You will find someone else.' I will just be scared to death that if [I meet someone else], they will end up dead too."*

> *"I lost my husband [to] a stroke. I lost my dad [a short time later]. Why is everyone in my life leaving me?"*

When I share the story of our family's journey with audiences and with the media, I generally share only one-third of the entire story. You see, ten days prior to Mike's death, our uncle very premeditatedly committed suicide. In fact, Kendall and my mother were at his memorial service while I was with Mike in the intensive care unit at the hospital, where he was nearing the end of his life. A mere three *weeks* after Mike's death, I was on an out-of-state business trip when I collapsed. I was immediately flown home, taken off of the airplane in a wheelchair, rushed to the hospital and on an operating table twelve hours later, undergoing major abdominal surgery. Six weeks later, I had no sooner recovered from surgery when I received a phone call from the hospital, informing me that my father had been admitted. He was diagnosed with metastatic liver cancer within twenty-four hours and passed away nine weeks after the diagnosis.

All of these events happened within a time span of four *months.*

Reeling from shock? Completely numb with disbelief? Totally. I am sure that for a while there, I wasn't answering the phone with "Hello?" I was answering by saying, "What *now?*"

Welcome to the phenomenon of "Pancake Tragedy"—the trials and challenges that come one on top of another on top of another still.

You first wonder exactly what you did that was so horrible that you deserve these tragedies that are stacking up just like pancakes. You next wonder exactly how you're supposed to get through today and tomorrow and the day after that. You are, without a doubt, afraid of leaving your house or answering your phone or opening your door for fear of what's going to happen next.

Why are you being made to endure so many tragedies? We know that we cannot answer the "Why me?" We can deal only with the "What now?" First, it's important to realize that even though losses may be coming one on top of another or in close proximity in terms of time, relationship, or both, each loss is *individual.* Too many think that because they have grieved one loss (or two or ten) that they are not entitled to grieve another loss, that somehow there is a "statute of limitations" on the amount of grieving that you're permitted to do.

It is also vital to recognize that your relationship to each loss is completely different. For example, I lost my husband and my father—the two most important men in my life—within four months of one another. However, I was a spouse to one and a child of another, making the loss *perspective* entirely different and completely individual. I never once felt that I wasn't entitled to grieve my father's death as a separate and distinct loss simply because I was still mourning the loss of my husband.

Next, return to those "basics" that I keep talking about by taking care of you in the best way possible. That will always be how you are going to best enable your recovery from multiple tragedies. Continue to surround yourself with love and support; people want to help you and I encourage you to let them do so.

You may feel as though you are continually getting knocked on your backside and that you don't have any "fight" left in you. Guess what? You have a lot of fight in you. Get ornery, get stubborn, and get determined to keep going! I know what it's like to have bruises on your butt from getting knocked down so much—get up, brush yourself off, and get just cranky enough to decide that all of these tragedies combined are *not* enough to stop you from moving forward. Please also take comfort and trust in the knowledge that eventually—even though it seems like it may take awhile—the storm clouds do pass.

Anyone who has either heard me speak or has known me personally for longer than ten minutes knows that one of my favorite questions to ask is as follows:

"What is it in your life that is *so* big, that it has the right to keep you from your dreams and your happiness? What is it that is so huge that it either has the ability or the power to keep you from living a life of abundance? What is it that you are allowing to stop you from having all of the joy that you deserve?"

I want you to find the strength to answer: ABSOLUTELY NOTHING!

This resolve must also extend to include any additional misfortune that has befallen you since your husband's death. Do not let anything, including the loss of your husband and/or any other tragic events subsequent to his death, become so gargantuan that it prevents you from living a life filled with abundance and peace; you have earned that right.

"[Several] years ago, I was widowed and was starting to move on with life. I rekindled a relationship with my ex-husband. The anniversary of the death of my late husband came and my ex offered to take me to his grave. Two days later [my ex] was killed. Shock is hardly the word for what I'm feeling. I can't help but feel like a 'black widow.' After two deaths, I feel like perhaps I am meant to be alone."

You know, after my husband's death, someone actually told me (at his funeral no less), "Perhaps you're just meant to be alone" and that this was the perfect explanation as to why I was widowed at such a young age. I have previously addressed this rather insensitive observation and I believe this to be true: If you were "meant" to be alone, you would be living in a cave someplace.

If I were "meant" to be alone, I would have never married and I am confident that I would not have compounded that by making a little person, who eventually turned into a big person and who virtually ensured that I would *never* again be alone or ever again permitted to lock a bathroom door or enjoy private domain over clothing, shoes, hair products, or appliances. Some people may *choose* to be alone; however, none of us were ever *meant* to be alone.

Similarly, you obviously did not *choose* to be alone. You met, fell in love with and built a life with another person. When that life came to an end, you wisely moved forward and were beginning to build a new life with your ex-husband when a comparable tragedy befell you. This in no way defines you as a "black widow," nor is it some kind of "sign," divine or otherwise, that you should be alone. It simply means that you have loved and known the love of two wonderful men whom you sadly lost far too soon. That's it. If you learn nothing else, please know this:

While widowhood will definitely shape you, it does not have to *define* you.

I'll take it one step farther. Once you have traveled far enough along on your healing journey, I would encourage you to open your heart to the possibility of loving once again. You do not *have* to be alone. There aren't any quotas or limits on the amount of love to which we are entitled in our lives and you are unquestionably entitled to love and to be loved in return once again—without fear, without reservation, and without feeling like the "Ghost of Christmas Yet to Come."

IT'S A "WRAP"...STILETTO-STYLE!

By now, you have discovered that the "What Now?" of widowhood encompasses many different aspects, from learning how and where you fit in to how you can begin to change your widow-tude toward the word "widow." It's time now to move on to the many different emotional aspects of widowhood and your healing journey. This is a great time to grab a highlighter or pen and play a little game with yourself. How many of the following situations, emotions, and issues have happened to you too? Don't be surprised when you find yourself nodding or even laughing along!

chapter two

EMOTIONS—
EVERY SINGLE LAST ONE OF THEM

THERE IS A VERY FAMOUS DOCTOR, WHO WROTE A VERY FAMOUS AND oft-quoted book concerning the "five stages" of grief. These stages are generally described as denial, anger, bargaining, depression, and, finally, acceptance.

With much respect paid to the good doctor, I have found that it's not always that cut-and-dried simple and it certainly isn't necessarily chronological. Not only are there a whole heck of a lot more emotions with which you may be dealing, but many widows are surprised at some of these emotions once they crop up and seemingly take root.

And what of the people around you? The people who may want to help but instead wind up causing you even more worry, guilt, grief, or for that matter denial, anger, bargaining, and depression. Let's now have a look at virtually every single emotion (along with a few "other people" situations) that many, if not most, widows are coping with at some point on their healing journeys, and what to do with those emotions and people if and when they all show up.

The "Art" of Grieving—*Your* Way

> *"I wonder how I will ever get over the grief. I feel empty and so alone, even with family around me. I feel as though I am stuck in the grieving process."*

> *"I have always been so open about my loss that I didn't realize till now that I was never really open about my grief."*

> *"I cry every day. I'm just having a hard time accepting that he died."*

> *"I am trying to do what he would have wanted, but it's just so hard. I don't know how to live without him and there are days where I don't do anything but sit and cry."*

The first question that comes to mind is, how long has it been since you lost your husband? As you have learned in Chapter One (The "What Now?" of Widowhood), grieving is neither quick nor is it easy. Though we wish it did, recovery does not and will not happen in hurry-up fashion. Knowing what you now know about the grief process, are you truly being realistic about your current emotions and reactions considering the amount of time that your husband has been gone? In other words, have you given yourself that permission that we talked about, the permission to be genuinely sad and in mourning?

If it has been at least one year since your husband's death and you're feeling "stuck," I'm going to ask you what may sound like a very stupid question, but, as always, I ask you to hang in there with me:

HAVE YOU ACTUALLY MADE THE *CHOICE* TO HEAL AND MOVE FORWARD?

I know that probably sounds completely and stupidly obvious. Who *wouldn't* choose to move forward in a positive way? The answer is—a lot of people. Many people actually *prefer* to stay miserable rather than learn how to take the baby steps to begin to move on. It's easier to stay miserable. It's easier to stay right where you are, even if where you are is in a place of pain. That's why people *choose* to stay in destructive relationships or at jobs that they hate or remain unhappy in general because they *choose* not to do anything proactive about it. It's just easier to whine and complain and stay in the house with the blinds drawn and in the penguin-pajamas with the feet in them (that last one was me).

A fantastic mentor of mine taught me years ago that we will remain the same until the pain of remaining the same becomes *greater* than the pain of change. So it's a choice. You can go ahead and permit grief or bitterness or anger to consume you, which changes absolutely nothing, or you can make the *choice* to begin—*truly* begin—your healing journey. So make a conscious choice that you are right now, *today,* going to take your first steps toward a new life. Yes, there are going to be good days and challenging days, but you are going to continue forward no matter what. You are going to be like those clown punching bags that we had as kids—you hit them and they bounce back up. We've *all* been knocked down and knocked down hard, but we do not have to *stay* down.

If you still feel that despite genuine efforts, you have made little or no progress, the time may be at hand to seek additional help. This can be in the form of a support group, counseling, coaching, or therapy. Whichever you choose, realize that there is help waiting for you, you need only ask.

THE "ART" OF GRIEVING ACCORDING TO THE REST OF THE WORLD (AND HOW TO HANDLE IT)

"My sisters seem to think it's about time I moved on, that I've done enough moaning and groaning."

"So many of my friends and family have been so insensitive. Their main thought is that I should just get over it because [my husband] is not coming back."

"You will never know how very much you helped me through those days of disgust and horror as I was bombarded with [insensitive] remarks. I thought that I would lose my mind, and I wanted to

> *just die. I regret to say that I still get those remarks made to me when I least need [to hear] them."*

> *"I have been dealing with the dumb questions and comments from friends and family since we found out about my husband's [illness]. I know they all mean well and they are trying to understand what I am going through. However, each one has their own idea of what my grief 'should' be, so it is tough to say the least."*

> *"I get comments from friends and family that I should be 'over everything' by now because it's been [a few] years since my husband died."*

> *"My husband died [and] I have never felt so alone. At the time, I remember saying many times that I am blessed to have so many wonderful family and friends, and I truly believe that. However, they all act like I should be 'over it' by now."*

Isn't it so incredibly easy for other people to decide not only in what manner, but for how long, you should be grieving? Well, guess what? *You* are the boss here. This is *your* healing journey. No one gets to decide for you when to grieve, how to grieve, and/or how long it "should" take to grieve. And yes, people *do* say seemingly stupid and unbelievably insensitive things at exactly the wrong time.

For what others are putting you through, I am so sorry, but you can also clearly see that you are not alone in that experience. Believe me, I am doing my best to educate the entire world on what to say during times of grief, tragedy, and life difficulty or more importantly, what *not* to say.

Out of all of the friends and family who are telling you that you should be "over it" because it's been "x" amount of time, i.e., whatever time parameters that *they* have designated appropriate for your grieving, how many of them are also widowed and have endured the suffering, the pain, and the loss in the same way that you have? I'm going to take a wild guess and say none.

In fact, *no one else* is qualified to dictate to you when you should be "over it" and that includes other widows! As we have already learned, people want you to be "over it" because (a) death in general is an uncomfortable subject and (b) it's easier for *them* if you are "over it." *They* are uncomfortable with your grief. It is very easy for everyone else to tell you that "Time is all it takes" when they're not in your position.

It is true that time helps the pain take its proper place in your heart, but the *experience* doesn't ever truly leave, and who wants it to? There is a very special place in my heart that will always belong to my late husband. It obviously doesn't mean that I didn't have the room, the desire, or the capacity to love another (because we all have that ability), but I don't ever want to "get over" my late husband and the life that we shared together. Instead, as you will learn shortly, you don't get "over it," you *move forward* from it. Given time and patience with yourself, the pain, the grief, and the experience of widowhood will take an appropriate place and perspective in your life and the smiles will slowly begin to outnumber the tears.

You also have to remember two things:

1) Most of the people who are saying these things to you generally mean you *no intentional harm*. Most people are not sitting around somewhere, conspiring and thinking up ways to mess with your head, wound your heart, and deliberately hurt your feelings. Yes, you will have to exercise patience as you endure these comments, but try the best that you know how to remember that deep down, most want for your recovery and your return to happiness.

2) That said, you must again remember that this is *your* healing journey. *You* are in charge. *You* are the boss. No one else gets to tell you when or how to be "over it." Besides, you now know that being "over it" is a myth.

One more thing—I absolutely believe that there is such a thing as "staying in the sadness" for too long but only *you* can make that determination. Listen to your own internal "clock," not to the opinions of others. As I've said before, if you feel that even with the passage of time and with legitimate effort made on your part, that you are not moving forward in the way that *you* would like, then (and *only* then) you should seek help or additional support.

> *"[My husband] was in a coma and then I had to withdraw life support, [which] was his expressed wish. It's been, well, as you know…hell. I get hit hard with setbacks. Plus I have a very controlling and odd situation with [my husband's] family. I still face constant confrontation from [a family member]. I only want to begin to move on peacefully, to regain happiness and a sense of stability. I am not great [with] confrontation and I'm still very broken and healing."*

I'm a very outspoken, strong, spunky person with a whole lot of moxie, but I don't know of many people who like confrontation less than I do. I can't even watch reality television because I can't stand confrontation or people intentionally being mean or hurtful or snarky to one another. At what point exactly did *that* become "entertainment"?

That said, if I'm backed into a corner by *anyone* for *any* reason, watch out. I will come out swinging and it will not be pretty.

You must now consider yourself backed into a corner of sorts. A family member or friend who stays in touch periodically, sharing fond memories while helping you heal and move forward is one thing; deliberate confrontation or the insinuation of their decision to live in the past while insisting that you do the same is quite another. They may need to seek professional help in coping with the loss of their loved one and there's nothing wrong with that at all; however, they do not get to either make you or keep you miserable in the process.

You may not like confrontation and I completely agree that you've been through quite enough without having to deal with the prospect of a confrontation, particularly with a family member. However, it's time for you to take charge. Nothing will change if you don't assert yourself and put a stop to this behavior. It's time for you to find your voice. It's time for you to get a little cranky and a lot determined to take back *your* life and *your* healing journey. You can be controlled only if you *permit* the control to be assumed.

Is there another family member that you can speak with about this situation? If so, that might be an avenue for you. If not, it's time to "disconnect." Change your telephone numbers and email address if you must, but the time for inaction has to come to an end. Quit giving away the power that you're giving to this person; it's keeping you from moving forward to that place of peace you're seeking and that you rightfully deserve.

"How Can I Help?"

> *"My sister was tragically and suddenly widowed. She has two young children and she has been doing really well so far. Of course she has her moments, but she has been so strong. I love her so much and want to know if there is anything I can do to make things easier for her. Is there anything I can do at all to take some of this pain away for her?"*

You are an awesome sister! It's wonderful that you are taking such a proactive interest in helping your sister through such a terrible time.

Your sister needs to feel community and sisterhood with other women who are in a similar position. There are literally millions of widows out there; however, I can assure you that right now, your sister feels completely alone. Get her into an environment of widowed community support just as soon as you can. Equip her with as many "healing tools" as possible because the more tools that she has at her disposal, the easier her healing journey will be. You will find a wonderful list of Recommended Resources for widows in the back of this book.

Since it is a well-known fact that we who have children tend to neglect ourselves, you should next make sure that she's taking care of herself. Offer to take the kids periodically so that she can get out, or get sleep, or have a bubble bath, or engage in any activity for just a little while, from which she won't be distracted by the children.

I'm sure that your sister is quite strong, but I also know that she doesn't feel that way all the time. Continue to create an environment that will allow her to break down or get mad or be quiet or just be downright sad without having to worry about what other people think, which is a primary concern among widows.

I know that you're frustrated that you can't "take the pain away" entirely. However, we can all help her find a way *through* the pain. You are a wonderful and caring person and your sister is fortunate to have you in her corner.

> *"My mother is widowed. [She] is not doing well, and is treating the people in her life very badly. We are struggling to help her [but] she does nothing to help herself. I'm afraid that if something doesn't change soon, she will drive everyone away. I love my Mom very much, and I miss my Dad too. I know the pain is not the same, but we are tired of the emotional abuse she is putting us through. Do you have any advice?"*

You are very wise in your immediate recognition that Mom's grief is different than yours. As mentioned earlier, I lost my husband and my father within four months of one another and while the grief is overwhelming in both cases, the "complexion" of the grief is quite different.

Mom is first going to have to want to help herself and that may require a bit of tough love on your part. Yes, it's sad and awful that your father is gone, but none of you signed up to be whipping posts either. You are going to have to lovingly but firmly let her know that the time has come for healing and that you will be more than happy to support her in any way possible but what you will *not* do is allow yourself to be "beaten up," so to speak. No one is obligated to put up with any kind of abuse from anyone for *any* reason. You are also correct in assessing that she will drive everyone away if she doesn't choose to change her ways and that choice can be only hers.

Most of all, remember that you can lead a horse to water, you can push its head down to the water, heck, you can splash the water all over the horse's face, but until that horse opens its mouth, it is not going to take a drink. This may not be the most sensitive metaphor, but it is certainly applicable.

You have been and are doing all of the right things for your mother, but unless *she* decides to help herself, it is a certainty that she will drive everyone away. Furthermore, if you and others around her allow her to continue to abuse you, well, we call that enabling and it's not helping her either. Perhaps she is striking out because she feels isolated as a younger widow. When you direct her to Widows Wear Stilettos and other widow communities, she will find thousands of women who are dealing with the same loss and pain as she and it will further help her to see that support is available and that she is not all alone in her grief.

"I work with someone who just lost their husband after a terrible ordeal for the whole family. I would like to send a thoughtful gift to her and her daughters. My dilemma is that I don't know her very well, but I really want to send her something that she will remember because I feel so bad for all of them. Do you have any suggestions?"

"My neighbor just lost her husband. I'd love to get something for her and her family that will let her know that I'm thinking of them, but I don't want to get them more flowers. Can you help?"

If you do not want to go the flower, plant, or fruit basket route, the following are some great suggestions and the best news is that all of them are extremely affordable.

NOT-SO-ORDINARY SYMPATHY GIFTS INCLUDE:

1. A gift card to a moderately priced restaurant, which will help get all of them out of the house for a nice meal. Also appreciated are gift cards to a local coffeehouse or bakery, or a gift certificate for a one-time housecleaning from a bonded and reliable service so that they can relax in a clean environment.

2. A gift card for a manicure or pedicure or a mini-massage; even

youngsters can enjoy having their fingers and toes painted.

3. A gift card to a grocery store to put groceries in the house for a day or the week. Better yet, if it's practical for you to do so, go to the store, purchase and deliver the groceries yourself. I promise that you'll get a grateful smile in return.

4. A beauty basket filled with spa products—bath salts, beads, or bubble bath; an eye gel mask that can be chilled in the refrigerator for eyes that are tired, swollen, and puffy from crying and lack of sleep; moisturizing lotion and body mist; a loofah; a terry cloth headband; a bath pillow; and an aromatherapy candle. All of these items can be purchased at a drugstore or discount retailer quite inexpensively. You might even include a bottle of wine or sparkling apple cider.

AND DON'T FORGET THE VERY BEST GIFT:

Remember, the best gift of all is a kind and willing ear to lend. Invite your friend out to lunch or in for coffee, sit down with her and *listen*. This is the sort of "gift" that she may appreciate most of all.

> *"Just after my friends' wedding anniversary, he was diagnosed with [a terminal illness]. I am no stranger to grief, but this is a completely different situation when it comes to loss. Can you give me any advice as to how to help my friend now and after her husband passes away?"*

What a fantastic friend you are to be reaching out on behalf of your friend who is facing such an enormously sad challenge in her life.

My first piece of advice to the friends and loved ones surrounding a caregiver is that as long as there is life, there is hope, especially in the minds of the patient and the immediate family. If he is still undergoing any kind of potentially curative treatment, and even though everyone else may feel that it may be for naught, the patient and his family still have the hope and the positive expectancy that the treatments will do some good. If nothing else, treatment may at least prolong his life for a while.

There are those who actually might be inclined to ask the patient or his family, "Why go through this? It's hopeless" (yes, people can be *that* unthinking), when really, all the patient and family need right now is unconditional love and support, even if the treatment is simply palliative (comfort) care. In other words, and to put it bluntly, people should not bury the breathing. If you hear anyone making such comments or implications, quietly take them to one side and politely ask them to stop.

See to it that your friend is eating regularly (even if it's not a lot) and that she's eating as healthfully as humanly possible. Ironically, hospital cafeteria fare is not always the healthiest on the planet. Offer to run errands for her, like trips to the grocery store, the dry cleaners, the bank, etc. Bring over a precooked meal for her. When the appropriate time arrives, you can tell her about the various widow resources that are available to her and direct her to tools of support that are offered. She will immediately find that she is not alone as a widow and that sense of community will comfort her as well.

I applaud your efforts to make this time in your friend's life as comfortable as possible. Many tend to shy away from such an uncomfortable situation (ask me how I know), yet you are instead jumping right in to be a source of strength, comfort, and information.

THE ETERNAL QUESTION (AND ANSWER) TO "WHY ME?"

"I keep asking God, 'Why did this happen?'"

"I don't understand why this happened to me. What did I do to deserve this?"

"I have always had a very strong faith, but I do not understand how something like this could happen to me."

"I am pregnant with our first child. [My husband] died suddenly and now I'm left to wonder why this happened to us."

I believe this to be not just a simple question, but also the rally cry for the widowed everywhere. Why, oh *why* did this happen to me? What did *I* do? I'm a good person. My husband or wife was a good person. Why is this tragedy happening to *me?*

I began singing what I call the "'Why Me?' Blues" almost immediately after my husband was diagnosed. I initially didn't bother much with being sad. I went straight to being flat-out *angry.* My husband had dedicated twenty-eight years of his life to service in the community as an award-winning police officer and completed two tours in Vietnam prior to that. We were good people in a good marriage, raising a good family, doing all of the "right" things that "good people" do, and the reward for all of it was an illness that was going to eventually take my husband, along with all of our plans and dreams for the future. Someone needed to explain *this* to me.

One day, while I was railing away and crying "Why me?" to my rabbi, he responded with an answer that I didn't much like, and you won't like it either. The rabbi looked at me, and in a very matter-of-fact tone asked me, "Why not?"

(Told you that you wouldn't like the answer but hang in there with me on this.)

I looked at this man—a wonderful and brilliant religious leader and educator, a trusted friend, counselor, and confidante—like he had two heads. How *dare* he utter such apparently insensitive words to me! Why *not?* I had just given him a laundry list of "why not"! We're wonderful people. My husband was a fantastic human being. Our life as a family is being destroyed. Our beautiful nine-year-old daughter gets to watch her daddy die. I'm pretty sure that we don't deserve to have this happening to us.

After patiently listening to my rant, the rabbi then posed a very interesting question:

"If not you, then to whom should this be happening instead? Think of all of the good, decent, giving, loving people like yourselves and determine, if not you, then to whom should this destiny befall? Tell me, who *does* deserve this?"

You know what? As much as I hated—truly *hated*—to admit it, he was absolutely right.

The fact is that none of us deserve to be in this position. Period. None of us did *anything* to deserve this fate. Widowhood is not some form of retribution, divine or otherwise, nor is it any kind of punishment or sentence.

So why you? Why any of us? Some would say that it's because only the strongest are called to such a position in life. Think about this—has it occurred to you just how strong you are to have made it through the untimely death of your spouse? Whether you lost him last week, last month, last year, last decade, or the last millennium, you are *here*, seeking strength and support. You are *here*, learning from the experiences of others. Perhaps you have even shared your own experiences, so that others may learn from you. You are not giving up, even though you may have thought about doing so approximately one million times.

No one will argue that you were dealt a horrible hand when your husband was taken from you, irrespective of the circumstances that surrounded his death. Even the most spiritual among us will have more than a few moments of anger, along with a whole bunch of unanswered questions; the first of which is usually, (say it with me), "Why me?" However, the bigger tragedy would be to stay angry or in perpetual mourning or in any state that prevents you from moving forward into a life of abundance and happiness—the life that you have not only earned, but richly deserve as well.

I want to invite you to shift your thinking just a little bit. Instead of spending a whole bunch of time on the "Why me?" let's instead focus on "What now?" Let's alternatively ask ourselves: "What am I going to do today and tomorrow to help myself (and my children) heal and move forward?"

Continuing with a "Why me?" mindset will do nothing to change the situation or further your healing journey. Deciding instead to work on the "What now?" will!

"Closure"—The Word That Would Not Go Away

"It seems like every time I think of his death and try to 'understand' what happened, I get sick. How do you ever have closure with sudden death?"

"My husband was murdered and after a [very long] trial process, the [responsible person] was found guilty and sentenced to prison. People keep telling me that now I'll have closure. Even though everything is finally over with, I don't feel like I have closure and I don't feel like I ever will. What's wrong with me?"

"I [was] hoping that [my husband's memorial service would] give me some closure [so] I could start moving on. I just didn't think that it would be this hard to accept."

"People keep talking about 'closure' and I keep waiting for it, but it hasn't happened for me yet. How long does it take?"

There are words in the English language that I completely *hate* to see and/or hear. Included on my personal "Hit Parade" are the words:

"No"
"Can't"
"Low-carb"
"Guilt"
"Overlimit"
"Some Assembly Required"
"Size" and "zero" used in the same sentence.
(Don't even get me going on size "double-zero.")

48

However, as much as I hate these words, few words make me angrier than the word "closure." This is a subject that is so very important that although I have previously discussed it at length, it merits discussion once again, if for no other reason than to reassure every single widow out there that there is absolutely, positively *nothing* wrong with you.

As used today, "closure" refers to that enigmatic component that apparently we are all assumed to be frantically seeking on this journey called widowhood. "Closure" has become some kind of idyllic goal for which we should be striving. This alleged goal is somehow achieved when we wake up one morning and *voila!* The pain, the loneliness, the anger, and the grief have suddenly and magically disappeared. A funeral service, a guilty verdict in a trial, the mere passage of time—these are supposedly the catalysts that are supposed to help you achieve this mystical "closure." How many times have you been told, "Now you'll have closure" (or words to that effect) since your husband's death? Once? Twice? Eight million jillion basquillion times?

I'm hoping to save you a great deal of time and frustration in the search for closure by once again revealing the huge secret: There is *no such thing* as "closure." Quit searching for it.

As defined by most, closure means that you have either the desire or the capability to put "it" behind you. "It" of course refers to the death and the events leading up to the death of your husband. In fact, many people will expect a "closure achievement" attitude from you, a "Glad that's over, now let's get on with life," dust-off-your-hands mindset. Essentially, closure has just become an alternative and more diplomatic way of saying, "Get over it," because people either are uncomfortable with or do not care to deal with the concept of his death and your grieving.

You know what? That's just too damn bad.

(Remember how patience isn't one of my strong suits? Neither is diplomacy.)

The loss of your husband is a life-transforming event. You are *forever* changed as a result. There will never be "closure," nor will there be any escaping that fact. Yet, when this elusive "closure" doesn't happen, you begin to wonder if something is wrong with you; as did the widows who wrote these letters. How is it possible that you cannot put this experience "behind" you when everyone is clearly expecting you to do just that? Because you will never put this experience behind you. Ever. Furthermore, why would you even *want* to?

I want you to think back to that season in time when your husband died. It felt like you were crying continually and that you couldn't even mention your husband's name without bursting into tears. Then you found that as time passed and you began moving steadily through your healing journey, the overwhelming part of the grief lessened and that slowly but surely, a sense of normalcy returned to your life.

However, the *experience* that was the loss of your husband remains with you always. It is something that you carry with you every day. You cannot "close" it, nor should you be made to feel as though you have to. It becomes a component of you, just like a body part. I invite you to embrace this experience called widowhood and make it a part of you.

Rather than think of your healing journey in terms of achieving "closure," I encourage you instead to think of this as a life-altering event from which you *move forward.* Do you want to leave the horrible feeling of daily grief and anguish behind? Most definitely. But "slam the door" on your past? Absolutely not!

"Strength"—Their Perception and Your Reality

"I am pretending to be strong, but I feel like I'm dying inside. Since I have been told that I am a strong person, I am not sure how to let go of my pain."

"Only my late husband understood that I am not so strong. I lost the only person who let me be who I am."

"Everyone tells me what a strong person I am, but I want to scream at them that I'm not. I feel like I am trying to be the person they think I should be. Behind closed doors I cry my heart out."

"I was one of those 'incredibly strong' people who everyone admired since I went on with my life and supposedly didn't sink into depression. If they only knew."

"People don't understand why I act like I do. I put on a good front, but when I am alone, I cry, scream, and I don't like my life anymore."

"Everybody [tells me] that I am doing 'really good' and that I am 'really strong.' I just want to tell everyone, 'You have no idea!'"

I know too well how it feels when everyone keeps telling you how strong you are and you just want to look at them and say, "Um, you're kidding, right?" I know that you're feeling like if one more person tells you how strong you are, you're going to scream, out loud, in their face. It does get frustrating after about the zillionth time you've heard how "strong and amazing" you are, and after hearing it a zillion times, you feel as though you're not allowed to be weak or frail or all of the things that you may be right now and have every *right* to be right now.

However, what all of those people are *really* saying to you is, "I can't imagine having to go through what it is that you're going through and I admire you so much." Graciously thank them for the compliment, as your strength is perceived as an asset, but also feel free to let people know that you are hurting inside.

Since I know that sometimes all we need is permission, here it is. I am telling you that it *is* OK to be in grief. It *is* OK to let people know that you are not feeling particularly strong. It is *definitely* OK not to be strong every single minute of every single day. The pain that you are experiencing hurts and it hurts tremendously; however, I'm going to encourage you to quit fighting. Quit fighting the grief. Quit fighting the sorrow. End the tug-of-war with that two-headed monster named Pain and just let go of the rope.

Those of you who are familiar with Widows Wear Stilettos and my own backstory also know that I grew up in Southern California. As such, beach going and swimming have always been and are still a huge part of my life—from backyard pool parties as a kid to lifeguarding and swimming competitively in my teens; to the all-too-infrequent forays to hotel swimming pools and beachside resorts on vacation as an adult, I'm a true "water baby" (which I think may be a prerequisite listed somewhere in the Constitution of the State of California) and going to my "happy place" generally means that I'm in, near, on top of, or under a body of water.

One of the first lessons that you learn about swimming in the ocean is that if you get caught in a riptide, you are to let the tide carry you out and then swim parallel to the shore until you hit calmer water and can swim back in. Trying to fight a riptide is not just dangerous; the only thing that fighting will accomplish is wearing you out, ultimately leaving you unable to save yourself.

Use the same train of thought now. Quit fighting this riptide called Grief. It's stronger than you and just like the riptide in the ocean, fighting the "grief riptide" will also wear you out. Give yourself permission to be sad or in grief or in pain; it's all right to be sad and it's all right to *take the time* to be sad. Instead of fighting the grief, go along with the grief. Go with this tide; swim parallel to the shores of peace that I know you to be seeking. Make the grief a part of you. Acknowledge out loud if you have to: "I'm sad, and it's OK to be sad right now."

The sooner you quit fighting the grief or worse, trying to avoid the grief altogether, the sooner you will start to move through this most painful part of the healing journey and you will hit those calmer waters. You'll soon come to find that the better days will outnumber the rough days, slowly and surely.

By the way, every single last one of you *is* strong even though you may not always feel like it. You're getting up and going to work every day; you're managing a household on your own; many of you are raising children; and you're all taking positive steps to move forward with life. Sounds pretty danged strong to me! At what point did grief and sadness become synonymous with weakness? Guess what? It isn't.

Whatever Happened to "Gone But Not Forgotten"?

"It's only been a few weeks since my husband's death. I am having trouble dealing with everybody's willingness to forget him—how is this possible? I think people don't want to acknowledge their own vulnerability to death but I just wish they were more sensitive to my feelings."

"The daily phone calls are beginning to subside and I know that as time goes on, everyone will get back to their busy lives. But how can they forget about him so fast?"

"I thought everything was going well, until 'friends' started to disappear. Many people have told my [children that], 'We'll do this or that' and not one of them has ever done anything with or for them. People have just left our lives."

"What I am having the most trouble dealing with is everybody [forgetting my husband]. I know this may not be how they perceive their [behavior], but it makes me so angry when people flinch when I mention [my late husband's] name."

People haven't "forgotten" your husband; however, it is going to be much easier for everyone else to move on with their lives than it is for you. Why? The fact is that others are not going to be affected in the same way as you are. They aren't the widow and no one is going feel this loss in the same way as you do. People may "flinch" at the mention of your husband's name because it's a general fact of life that people are (a) uncomfortable with the topic of death, and (b) simply don't know what to say to you.

(When it was that people forgot that the words, "I'm so sorry" are truly sufficient, I do not know.)

Generally speaking, friends and family really haven't "disappeared." They've gone home and gone on and that's not unreasonable. After the funeral, everyone's lives go on, and we are left to pick up the pieces of a shattered life all by ourselves. I know that it can feel horribly lonely and that it feels very strange to see everyone going about their daily business when your world has come to a screeching halt. Many people want to give you space and time to begin healing or perhaps just let you get some well-deserved rest. These same people are not going to want to bother you with daily phone calls or visits, instead leaving it up to you to contact them.

If you are feeling lonely or as though everyone has abandoned you, why not pick up the phone and call someone for a cup of coffee or for dinner or for a walk around the neighborhood. Take the initiative and let others know that you wouldn't mind a bit of company. If people have made promises to your children that haven't come to fruition, pick up the phone and make the arrangements. I know that this should absolutely fall to others to do; however, think about this: Have you ever said to a friend, "We have to get together for lunch," and then it never happens? Here's the thing—if it's not written down on a certain date at a certain time, it's not going to happen. Remember what we learned in Chapter One: "Sometime" and "someday" are not days of the week. Make the plans.

Above all, please do *not* be afraid to talk about your husband. You may be the one that needs to put others at ease (as we so often are), because people think that they will upset you by bringing up the subject of your husband's obvious absence. If you want to talk about him, go ahead and talk about him! People will take their cues from you and if you're fine talking about him, especially if you're smiling while you're doing it, they will be comfortable with talking about him as well.

> *"I'm feeling really alone right now. I had great support for the first year and then everyone went back to their lives. I'm still here struggling every day with the loss. Even my own mother can't support me the way I'd like her to; she's still mourning the death of my father [that took place many] years ago. I [have a degree as a therapist] and I know what to tell others but I am having a difficult time myself. Any advice?"*

As you have learned, and as you know by your particular profession, it's perfectly normal for people to "go home and go on" with their lives. Remember, they are not the widow and they weren't the ones left behind to "pick up the pieces" and begin anew. *No one* is going to feel this loss as acutely as you do. You are also correct in that if Mom is still in deep mourning years after the loss of your father, she cannot be the support that you need; in fact, she may well be trying to "out-mourn" you and playing a game of, "Who's Hurting The Most." These are just two of the reasons that I'm so pleased that you found Widows Wear Stilettos. You are in a place where people truly understand what you've been through and you have access to so much education and support to help you on your healing journey.

I'm very proud and impressed that you too dedicate your life to helping others in need. However, let me assure you that just because you "…know what to tell others but are having a difficult time," it does not negate your education or your ability to help others. Let me put it another way. I hold a Certificate in Paralegal Studies and I'm an extremely experienced paralegal and settlement negotiator in my own right. However, if I need legal assistance, I am certainly *not* about to represent myself. I'm going to seek help, wisdom, insight, and advice from another who is qualified to help me. Surgeons don't operate on themselves; hair stylists get someone else to do their own hair; and you're doing the same thing here by seeking help from others in a position to help you. What a fabulously positive step forward you have taken.

GUILT BE GONE!

"We always said 'I love you' every day, but we were fighting the day that he died and barely said one word to each other. I still feel very guilty and horribly regretful that we did not talk that day. How do I get over this guilt and regret?"

"My husband died unexpectedly. We had an argument before he left the house, and I thought he had gone somewhere to cool off and

> *would come home later. The police came the next morning to let me know that my husband was gone [deceased]."*

Guilt is both an art perfected by many of our mothers and unfortunately, one of the many unpleasant realities of widowhood. In addition to the tremendous and obvious sorrow expressed in each of the thousands of letters that I receive, surprisingly at the heart of many of these letters is guilt—guilt that *none* of you have any business shouldering.

The fact that you and your husband fought on the day that he died means only one thing: You and he are human beings. You have absolutely nothing to feel guilty about. People quarrel. People don't always get along. People are not living their lives thinking, "I'd better not get mad at him or her; what if they died today?" It is true that the maturity that comes with time and experience teaches us to "pick our battles"; however, the fact of the matter is that we are going to have disagreements with our loved ones—*all* of our loved ones—at some point in our lives and likely more than once.

My husband was ill for a little over two years and we were on the roller-coaster ride of tests, diagnostics, and specialists for an entire year prior to his diagnosis. During that three-year time span, we laughed, we cried, we made meals, we went out to dinner, we helped with homework, we paid bills, we went to family functions, and yes, we argued. What married couple on the planet *doesn't* argue? In fact, it was the daily striving for the "normalcy" of marriage in *every* respect that kept Mike's mind off of illness, focused on the day-to-day as much as possible and in his own words, "...keeps me feeling normal." I refused to "tiptoe" around him (and vice versa) or treat him other than who he was—my husband who occasionally made me cranky, as I know I likewise did to him and quite expertly too.

There is no denying that it was a very sad coincidence that your husband died the same day that you had a disagreement, but this in no way means that you should have to bear any kind of guilt or supposed responsibility for the rest of your life. I instead encourage you to look back over your entire marriage, whether that marriage was for ten years or for ten minutes. Revel instead in the marriage that you enjoyed, the love that you shared, and the life that you led, rather than in the passing anger of one unfortunate moment in time.

> *"I feel that maybe if I had not left him to take [our child to school], he would have been fine. I have never had to deal with pain like this."*

> *"I should have taken better care of him."*

> *"If I'd gotten to him sooner, he might still be alive."*

> *"He always neglected his health and never would go to the doctor. I wish I had bugged him more about getting a physical because he might be alive now."*

> *"If only I hadn't 'let' him [as in "let" him race cars, ride a motor-cycle, go skydiving, or otherwise participate in an activity that led to an accident resulting in his death]."*

The times that I've heard, "If only I…" are literally countless. I know this guilt. I *did* this guilt on several levels. I was in the last category; my lament being, "If only I hadn't 'let' him go to the stable that day, then he wouldn't have had the riding accident that *might* have triggered the illness that led to his death two years later." The only problem is that as adults, we cannot and should not control one another and it wasn't up to me to "allow" or "disallow" my husband to do anything, as if that would have even been a subject up for debate.

We would all like to believe that we have *that* much control over destiny; that we can prevent illness and death just by our very presence and that we have the power within ourselves to change an outcome. The fact is that we simply don't have that kind of power. This fact must be combined with the reality that it is impossible to be with our loved ones twenty-four hours a day, keeping a watchful eye over them. It is impossible to forbid another adult from pursuing a hobby or getting into a car or traveling for business or doing whatever it is that they wish to do for fun or need to do in their line of work. You must accept the fact that your presence or lack thereof did not affect the outcome that was your husband's death.

If you are as I was and you were widowed after your husband's extended illness, the thought process is indeed generally along the lines of, "If only I'd taken better care of him…" Better than what? Better than the absolute best that you had to give? You did the very best that you could do. Taking care of your husband did not mean that you were going to be able to heal him, as many widows mistakenly believe. It meant that you were the one who made him comfortable and peaceful throughout his illness and no one can ask more of you than that.

There are those who believe that they might have acted in such a way that they actually hastened their husband's death; perhaps with the sort of medical treatment involved or the decision to discontinue medical treatment altogether (including life support). Let me assure you at the outset that you did *nothing* to hasten your husband's death. It is illegal to do so and no member of the medical profession would permit it.

Journey with me back to December 18, 2000—the day before Mike's death.

Mike was acutely aware when the end of his life was near and since it was his specific wish to die at home, we brought him home from the hospital for that expressed purpose. Once we had arrived home, we had wonderful assistance from hospice personnel, who carefully instructed me how to administer palliative or "comfort" medication to my husband. They were very precise as to the dosage as well as the frequency with which I was to give the medication. They were also very gentle and kind in conveying these instructions to me, comforting me all the while.

However, these compassionate and well-meaning people were also trying to communicate with someone whose mind was completely muddled and whose body was grossly sleep-deprived and flu-ridden; yes, both Kendall and I had the misfortune of coming down with horrible cases of the flu at the exact moment in time that Mike's life was coming to an end.

Given my physical and mental state, it then naturally followed that what

I heard the hospice personnel saying was, "Go into that room and end your husband's life."

It took a while, and several family members and loved ones having a number of heart-wrenchingly difficult discussions with me before I realized that I was not "ending" Mike's life at all. I was simply making him comfortable, so that the end would not be spent as the last ten days had been spent, in horrible agony. With the help of hospice and our loved ones, I was able to turn my guilt into the realization that what we were doing was simply alleviating pain and suffering. We were *not* "rushing" what was actually the inevitability of his death.

> *"I can't begin to describe the hurricane of emotions that I have gone through, including guilt for feeling relieved because I wouldn't have to fight his illness anymore."*

> *"His illness took everything out of me. It drained me emotionally, my own health isn't that great, and it financially wrecked our family. Am I terrible that I feel relief that he's not here anymore?"*

The reason for feeling guilty at your relief that the illness has come to an end is quite simple. You are confusing "relief" with "wishing." You think that because you're *relieved* that your husband is no longer suffering, and that you are not being challenged on a daily basis to the very depth of your being in every way possible, that this somehow equates with *wishing* that your husband would pass away.

You couldn't be more mistaken.

Mike railed against his illness like a warrior going into battle but then we were all warriors against that illness, every single one of us. The doctors, the nurses, the physical and respiratory therapists, the professional caregivers, the family caregivers, the close friends—we were all one great big collective boxing glove. And at the center of the battle was Mike. Never one to give up anything without a fight, Mike fought with everything that he had, even eschewing hospice at one point in his illness, stating that he wasn't ready to, "just curl up in bed and die." That wonderful man fought until his body simply could not fight any longer.

When Mike passed away, there wasn't one of us who wasn't in over-whelming grief and pain at this tremendous loss. At the same time however, there was also a great sense of *relief* that Mike didn't have to suffer anymore in *any* respect. The illness had taken such an enormous physical and emotional toll on Mike and on the rest of us that it was only natural to experience a sense of relief that the suffering had come to its end.

Feeling relief that suffering—*everyone's* suffering—has come to an end is absolutely normal and nothing about which to feel guilty; for as we know, the patient is not the only victim of illness, so too is the family. The physical, emotional, and financial suffering that accompanies catastrophic, long-term illness, and/or terminal illness (for everyone concerned) defies description. Who *wouldn't* want to see that come to an end? However, this should in no way ever be misconstrued as some kind of "wish" or desire that your husband should have departed this earth even one second before he did. It simply means that a horribly sad and difficult chapter in your life has reached its conclusion, and you are rightly relieved at having reached that conclusion. Your husband is no longer in pain or suffering. You are now able to begin healing in all respects. This is indeed a welcome (and guilt-free) relief.

> *"My husband committed suicide and I just can't get past the guilt of not being able to stop it. I just thought he was moody once in a while. I'm so stupid that I didn't see how depressed he was and now he's gone."*

> *"My husband committed suicide [years ago]. Even after all this time, I can't help but feel responsible for his dying because if I had known that he was in trouble, I could have stopped him from doing this."*

If you are widowed as a result of a suicide, you may have unwittingly convinced yourself that you could have done something to prevent the situation from occurring; that there were signs that you should have seen or steps that you should have taken or attention that you should have paid. Well, sometimes there aren't any clear signs. Sometimes there are no blatant clues given. You are not a mind reader, you do not have superpowers and you are most certainly not "stupid" or "responsible." A person who commits suicide is deeply troubled and the resulting action likely had little, if anything, to do with you. You want answers that you may never receive. You may never understand the thought processes that led your husband to a tragically permanent decision.

The most important thing that I want to convey to you is that you *were not* and you *are not* responsible in any way for your husband's death or his decision to end his life. It was *his* decision and completely beyond your control. This wasn't your fault or your doing. Do not lay blame on yourself, nor should you allow anyone to do that to you and sadly, there are those that may try out of anger, out of need, and yes, out of lack of common sense. You have the control here. Please take it.

I also want to point out that you've made an important choice as well—the choice to live. The choice to move forward with your life. The choice to seek out support and positive reinforcement. Continue to move in that direction, free from any guilt that you may feel at being a "survivor."

> *"I had to make the decision to remove [my husband] from life support [in accordance with] his wishes. I was initially led to believe that he was going to get better, until the doctor said that he would not [recover]. I am not sure that I made the right decision."*

> *"I [took] my husband off of life support. The last week that I had with him was the hardest week ever. I had to sit and listen to the doctors give [me] no hope and bad news. My mind was constantly on what was best for my husband. [People] forget that I am a human and I had to sit there and watch [medical personnel] take him off life support and watch him take his last breath."*

I do not believe that there could be much worse in this life than to be left to make the horrendously difficult decision to end life support for a spouse. What amazing strength you have shown.

While it is perfectly normal to second-guess such a decision, the facts are these: First, doctors would not have permitted the cessation of life support unless there was absolutely, positively no possibility of medical recovery. Despite what people may think or what television dramas and daytime soap operas may lead you to believe, we don't have the power to simply shut off a switch if or when we feel like it. Second, and more importantly, you honored your husband's wishes. Do you understand just how courageous you are to have made that decision? Do you understand that you did *exactly* what your husband wanted you to do? No one—absolutely *no one*—wants an existence that includes machines breathing for them and being fed through or with tubes. It's not living.

You know, when Mike was initially diagnosed, I did what anyone else would do in this day and age. I jumped onto the Internet to find out what we could do to prolong his life. I discovered that with the introduction of a ventilator/respirator and placement of a feeding tube, my husband would never die. I was thrilled with this information, that is, until my husband quite calmly informed me that he had absolutely no intention of allowing any such intervention on his behalf. This declaration led to a rather spirited (and really loud) argument, which he ultimately won.

However, two years later, when we had reached the most critical part of his illness, and when he was so obviously suffering, I fully understood his decision not to have any kind of life-support intervention; for you see, at that point, he could no longer eat. He could not speak and be understood. He could barely swallow or even breathe on his own comfortably. However, and as awful as it was for me and for everyone who loved him, I respected his wishes fully and to the letter. To have done otherwise would have not only gone against his wishes, it would have been an incredibly selfish act.

You did the most difficult thing in the world by putting your own grief and feelings second and honoring your husband's last request. Yours is not to feel guilty or to wonder if you made the right decision. Despite what anyone else may say to you, or how others may second-guess your medically informed decision, you need to rest in the knowledge that you were lovingly and coura-geously there with your husband until the end and that you did *exactly* what you were asked to do by the person who loved you the most and whom you loved in return.

> *"[My] letter was posted [at the former 'Dear Carole' column on the website] and your response made such a difference in my life. I had to make a life support decision that I was having a hard time dealing with. Your CD also helped me to begin to forgive myself and understand that my husband's wishes came first. I am still spending most of my time alone, but I am working on trying to go on."*

I remember well your letter and since there are so many others who have had to make that same awful decision that you have, we knew that your letter would be a shining example of courage and comfort to others, and it was. The responses from women who were in the identical position of having to make the "life support decision" were overwhelming and without exception; each expressed tremendous relief and comfort at discovering that they were not alone in their feelings or their experience. Isn't it wonderful that just by asking your question, you were able to help so many other women reach peace with the same decision(s) that you had to make.

However, permit me to tweak your thinking again, just a little bit. You mention beginning to "forgive yourself." Forgive yourself for what? What did you do that needs forgiving? You respected your husband's wishes. You demonstrated courage and strength that I daresay not many people possess. So exactly *what* needs forgiving? I said it on the CD, I've said it here, and I'll say it one more time: Do you *understand* just how amazing and brave you are? If you don't, I'm happy to remind you.

Just the fact that you are taking proactive steps to move forward means that you are doing better every single day. Remember, we only need to worry about forgiveness when a wrongdoing has occurred and I don't see that here.

"I lost my husband two years ago in an accident and I was in the accident with him. People say that I'm lucky to be alive, but I don't feel lucky to be alive at all. In fact I would have rather died right along with him. I have a hard time being positive about anything but I'm hoping to eventually find some peace in my life."

"My husband and I were in a car accident and he was killed. I feel like my life is over but I'm still alive. I don't want to be here anymore."

One of the many reasons that Widows Wear Stilettos was born is because my late husband demanded that I go forward with my life and that I find a way to take our experiences and use them to help others in need. What legacy did your husband want you to carry forward? Regardless of whether or not the two of you had children, irrespective of whatever else was going on in your life as a couple, and whatever his specific wishes, this I know to be true: He wanted you to keep on living and loving and growing as a woman.

So when I hear widows say things like, "I wish I'd died with him" or "I wish I died instead of him," I truly want to cry. Then, after I get past wanting to cry, I want to scream out loud. Admittedly, I tend to jump from sad to angry pretty quickly and when I hear comments such as these, I want to ask, what on *earth* would your not being here accomplish?

Yes, it's terrible that your husband is gone and no one will ever argue that fact. However, I want you to stop and take a really good look around you. Look at your loved ones, the family and friends that are standing by you. Look into the eyes of your children, whatever their ages. Look at the legacy that your husband has left for you to carry forward. The loss of a loved one is always difficult, regardless of the circumstances or at what age death occurs. However, the one thing that I want you to remember, right now and forever after, is that *you're still here.*

I know what you're thinking. You're thinking, "So what? I'm not sure I even want to be here right now." I also know that especially if you are a recent widow, the concept that "You're still here" may be a difficult concept for you to embrace. It might even be difficult for those of you who have been widowed for a longer period of time. The fact remains, however, that you are still here, you are alive, and there is still a life out there to be truly *lived*, not just simply slogged through.

The process of feeling better or feeling joyful or feeling like anything other than heavy with sorrow is not an overnight process. You will not wake up tomorrow morning or return to work on that first day back feeling magically healed. I have always used the word "process" because that's *exactly* what it is. I use the words "healing *journey*" because that's *exactly* what it is. You will first make the *choice* to heal and your recovery will take place slowly, surely, and over a period of weeks and months. Over time, you will begin to notice welcome changes—you aren't crying quite as much; you're enjoying activities more; in fact, you'll find that you *want* to be involved in activities. Best of all, when you think of your husband, you will eventually do so with more smiles than tears, and that's OK too.

While I understand that at this moment in time, you may feel guilty at having survived the tragedy that took your husband's life, and as though you're doing nothing more than picking up the pieces of a life that has been devastated, I want you to stop and think about this:

After what you have been through and have experienced, what is the world going to throw your way that you *won't* be able to handle?

Do you realize that most people in this world never get to truly find out just how strong they are? Most will never discover the real depth of their strength, their commitment, their courage, and their mettle. Now while I realize that this is a discovery process for which none of us volunteered, nevertheless, we have learned just how truly strong and resilient we are. Even if you don't feel especially strong right this minute, you will soon realize this fact, as well as just how empowering that knowledge can be.

Life may not feel good or seem good right now and that's all right for the time being, and even for the immediate future. Nevertheless, there will come a time that life is again going to hold the gifts of promise, excitement, hope, warmth, and peace for you. How can you best honor your beloved's memory? By continuing to heal and by moving forward.

You *are* still here. You will find peace with the fact that you are still here and in spite of—and especially *because of*—what you've been through and endured, you *are* entitled to live a life filled with happiness, contentment, and peace. Along with that, you must also acknowledge that *you are still here* and that you are open and willing to doing what it takes to s-l-o-w-l-y make your return to a happy life.

Though there are obviously many different kinds of guilt from which you might suffer, you have just learned that at the heart of all guilt is the one commonly held belief that:

"I could have changed the outcome. I could have created a result other than my husband's death."

This is simply not the case and what a tremendous burden you have placed on yourself by living this way.

Without exception, every single widow, including me, feels or has felt guilt concerning her husband's death and it doesn't even matter *how* she lost her husband. I honestly don't know of one widow who has not experienced guilt on some level, for some reason. *All* kinds of guilt.

But now, it is time to leave the guilt behind. *All* of it.

We're all done with the guilt portion of the program. It's time for peace now; you have earned it. It's time for healing; you've earned that as well. It's time for you to live in the light and the knowledge that you were a wonderful, loving, supportive wife and that you did everything possible for your husband while he was here with you. Whatever circumstances took your husband, you did the very best by him that you could at that moment in time. You must find comfort and peace in that knowledge and I know that you will.

THE ANATOMY OF ANGER

"There's so much pain and anger inside of me and I just want it to go away."

"I was so angry at him for 'leaving.' The logical part of me knows it wasn't by choice but I can't be logical when I think about it. I'm still angry at him for 'leaving' and whenever I think about him, it's with anger."

"My husband killed himself [without prior warning]. [I have] much anger toward him and my self-esteem is virtually nonexistent."

"Did you get mad at God? I am a Christian, but I have not been back to church."

I remember sitting with Mike in the doctor's office, us on one side of the colossal mahogany desk and the doctor on the other. The doctor rose from his chair, came around the desk, sat down on the edge, and placed a compassionate hand on Mike's shoulder. He then ruefully looked into Mike's eyes and pronounced his diagnosis of an incurable and subsequently terminal illness.

Mike was going to die.

That was it.

No surgeries, no treatments, no "experimentals," no reassurances, no promises…no hope.

The future was finished.

Over.

There was nothing for us left to do, except pray that he would be around for a longer period of time and as cruel fate would have it, that hope was ultimately destroyed as well.

Naturally, the doctor said all of the typically uplifting things to us, such as, "We're going to fight this; we're not giving up so don't you give up," but no matter what the doctor said or how cheerful a façade he tried to put on, we all knew what that wretched diagnosis meant:

My Michael—my husband, my best buddy of almost twenty years, and loving daddy—was going to die. And it was going to be sooner rather than later.

After feeling like we had each been hit in our stomachs with wooden planks, we left the doctor's office clinging to each other tightly, as if to hold one another up. Slowly and silently, we walked outside, heading to the car and not looking at one another; each lost in the hazy hell that was our shock. As we made our way back to the parking structure for the agonizingly long drive home, I remember waiting for the signal light to change and stopping to take a good look around me. The tableau that greeted me was one that I will never forget.

The sky was a brilliant blue that day and the weather was absolutely perfect. It was one of those typical autumn Southern California days; the kind from which cheesy souvenir picture postcards are made and that makes everyone in the world want to live here. There were people scurrying about the vast medical complex, rushing to get to work, perhaps late for an appointment; while others were sitting in lush green courtyards enjoying a morning coffee and conversation. Car horns were honking, signal lights were changing, people were laughing...and I couldn't absorb it.

It was almost obscene to me. How could life go on in such normal, mundane fashion when our lives had just come to a complete standstill? How could people be carrying on conversations and eating their morning muffins and hurrying to cross the street and yelling at the traffic when I had just been told that one of the most wonderful human beings on the planet was going to lose his life? Why hadn't the entire world come to a halt? Because *our* world certainly had.

As coincidence would have it on this horrible day, we were also nearing the conclusion of the Jewish High Holy Day period, meaning that I was to be in synagogue that very evening. Usually a time of year that I especially enjoy, on this night I instead sat in the synagogue with my arms firmly crossed and with an expression on my face that could only be described as stone-like.

I was livid.

I...was...*enraged.*

There I was sitting in the synagogue, where I was supposed to be in a prayerful place in my mind and heart; trying to spiritually renew myself for a new year and the only thing that I felt was pure, unadulterated, organic *anger* through and through. The worst part was that there was *no one* to yell at. There was *nowhere* to place blame. I had *no one* on whom to take out my rage and my feelings of utter and complete hopelessness.

So I blamed God. I got well and truly mad at Him. Boiling mad. The British call it the "red mist" and that's precisely what I was—"red mist" *mad.* I blamed God for absolutely everything connected with and to Mike's illness and the complete wreck that this illness had made and was going to make out of all of our lives. Not only did I get mad at God, I *stayed* that way for almost two years before I finally got the tools and the help that I needed to move past the anger that threatened to consume me alive.

So what exactly are you supposed to do with all of this anger?

Just being able to admit that you are angry is a necessary and courageous first step. It's an emotion that we are conditioned to suppress (for better or worse) from a very young age and being able to admit that you are just flat-out angry is a very brave thing to do.

Next, let's try to isolate the anger. At what or at whom exactly are you angry? Is it the "Why me?" factor that we discussed earlier? Is there a person or people on whom you can reasonably place blame? Or, as with this author, perhaps the most maddening part of the whole thing is that in reality, there may be absolutely no one or nothing at which to direct your anger.

Let's now take note of what you do *not* get to do with your anger:

1) You do *not* get to take your anger out on yourself, on your children, or on your pets by indulging in emotionally or physically abusive behaviors (and yes, there are those who have committed any one or all of the above).

2) You do *not* get to use anger as an excuse for destructive behaviors (drinking to excess; abusing drugs; unsafe or compulsive sexual behavior; driving too fast; self-mutilation; compulsive gambling; and so forth.)

It goes without saying that if any of these behaviors is something with which you either struggle or are tempted, you *must* seek help from a doctor or other mental health expert *without delay*.

What helps to allay anger? Physical activity immediately springs to mind. As we learned earlier, this does not mean hours in a gym or running miles around a track. This means just getting out and breathing fresh air around your neighborhood. In other words, work on raising your heart rate rather than your blood pressure.

Next, take advantage of wherever it is that you live and go get yourself some scenery. For example, as I shared earlier, my "therapy" has always been the beach. Once I see or even so much as smell the ocean, I can feel my shoulders immediately drop and relax. Where do you live that has wonderful scenery to offer? No matter where you live, there is always somewhere that you can go to think, reflect, or just commune with nature.

Continue to surround yourself with support and encouragement, particularly from those who understand what it is that you're going through and also understand what you mean when you say that you are angry. If you feel that you are "stuck" in a place of anger or as mentioned above, that your anger is either taking over your life or causing you to behave in a destructive manner, get help!

Through your anger, and though it may at times be difficult, please always remember that your husband did not willingly "leave" you[2]. He did not make the choice to depart this earth prematurely and he certainly didn't have hurting you in mind when he did. Strive for a willingness to move past your anger into a place of peace. It takes time, but it can be done.

---

2 For those of you who are suicide survivors, please take note: I also fervently believe that your spouse did not "choose" to leave, although the death may have been by their own hand. Generally speaking, a suicide victim sees no other way out of their own personal pain. In other words, it's not that they wanted to "leave," rather, they felt that there was no way to stay.

WALKING THROUGH THE "VALLEY OF THE SHADOW" ALONE

"I have gone from extremely anxious to extremely depressed."

"I have sought treatment for depression, but haven't found any miraculous medical cocktail that can take away the pain."

"Facing rebuilding my life has left me anxious and exhausted."

"I have been a widow for the past several years. I do not know where to turn to start a new life with new friends."

As you begin and progress through your healing journey, you are going to encounter and deal with a plethora of emotions, ranging from fear and anxiety (which we discuss next) to anger, depression, and exhaustion. The first thing that you must realize and accept is that experiencing any one or every single one of these emotions is absolutely and one hundred percent *normal*. This fact should bring you comfort in and of itself. Accept and embrace these different emotions as they occur, understanding that this is a normal state of the grieving process. However, normal though it may be, it is not fun to be in a state of fear, anxiety, depression, or exhaustion. How do we move through these emotions in a healthy, productive way?

Let's first visit our old familiar nemeses: Fear and Anxiety. I've said this before and I will say it again—*pro*activity is one of the best weapons against these feelings. As we discussed in Chapter One (The "What Now?" of Widowhood), taking control over a situation where you have had virtually no control is essential in conquering fear and anxiety. Realize that courage does not come in the "wishing." Courage comes in the *doing*.

If you are feeling "anxious and exhausted" at the prospect of rebuilding your life, don't look at the entire rebuilding process all at once, which can certainly be overwhelming. If I had been looking at my prospective entire lifetime all at once thinking, "OK, how do I fix *this* mess?", I'd have been anxious and exhausted too.

So, rather than completely overwhelm yourself by looking at everything all at once, let's instead, look at the "first floor" of your rebuilding process, starting with organization. I am all about organization and lists for one main reason—it gets everything out of my head and onto paper. When you "empty the garbage," (that is, get everything out of your head and onto paper), you will automatically experience feelings of calm and control.

"EMPTY THE GARBAGE"

Start your list with any "have to's" that you are facing. These may include:

1). Anything involving immediate generation of income to your household (filing for benefits, etc.).

2). Seeing to the disposition of assets and/or items as set forth in your husband's will.

3). Seeing to the financial and legal transition of your assets.

4). Beginning the going-through process of your husband's personal belongings (if you feel ready to do so).

As you compile your "have to" list, it is important to remember that not everything on the list needs to be accomplished in one day, or in one month or in six months. This is simply a means of prioritizing and helping you to establish a calm and a badly needed balance in your life.

Now I want you to compile a "want to" list. Many widows look at me quizzically when I mention a "want to" list, but this list is every bit as important as your "have to" list. This is the list that is going to be the blueprint for your entry into your new life. Think about it for a few minutes. What do you *want* to do? I'll bet it's been quite a while since you've asked yourself that question!

> ## Widows Just Wanna Have A Life!
>
> Your "want to" list might include things such as:
>
> 1). A return to activities that you enjoy—anything from attending church or synagogue to your spinning class at the gym.
>
> 2). Starting something new or trying something that you've always wanted to try and haven't yet attempted.
>
> 3). Rekindling friendships or starting new ones. If the thought of making new friends is a little scary, remember, there are thousands just like you at the various widow communities listed in the Recommended Resources in the back of the book and thousands of friendships have been made and continue to flourish in those communities.
>
> 4). Traveling—and it doesn't have to be around the world!

As a widow moves through her healing journey, she may also add items such as selling the home or changing a job or career to the "want to" list; however, I will continue to caution that these are things that carry long-term ramifications, both financially and emotionally. Life-altering decisions require careful consideration and should not be done hastily or immediately after suffering a loss.

Let's now move from our nemeses named Fear and Anxiety, to our all-too-common enemy: Depression.

Shortly after Mike died, I was talking to my mother and confessed a deep dark secret that I had been harboring. I revealed that I thought I "might be depressed." She looked at me with a raised eyebrow and said, "Well, let's see, you've just lost your husband after two years of illness. You've just undergone major surgery and your father is in a coma. You 'think' that you're depressed? Carole, you would be weird if you *weren't* depressed!"

Leave it to Mom to point out the obvious. After all, isn't that what mothers are there to do?

Whether you lost your husband suddenly or over a period of weeks, months, or years, the fact remains that you have suffered one of the most profound losses that you will ever know. After the loss of your husband, your heart, your soul, and your spirit have taken such a collective "hit," that it would be highly unusual if you *weren't* depressed.

However, we also know that there is a difference between "situational" depression and "clinical" depression. If you have any question whatsoever as to depression, if you find that you are having dark thoughts, suicidal ideation or if you are either tempted to or already are coping in a destructive manner, once again, you *must not hesitate* to seek immediate medical attention.

If you have or are seeking help for depression, I congratulate you; however, if you feel the same as our good friend, who wrote that she hadn't found any "miraculous medical cocktail that can take away the pain," that certainly doesn't mean that there isn't medication and/or therapy that can help you. It just means that you need to find what is going to work for you. You know, if I'm taking an antibiotic for a sore throat and it doesn't work, I don't tell myself, "Well, this medicine didn't work, so I guess I'm going to have to learn to live with this and never take medicine again." I go back to the doctor and tell him to try something else and I keep trying until we find something that works.

So take a deep breath. Promise yourself to take things slowly, easily, and one step at a time. Most importantly, if you need medical help, *please* ask for it—it's only a phone call away.

Fear = False Evidence Appearing Real

"I'm just scared. I'm scared to raise [my children] alone, I'm scared to [take over my husband's business], and I'm scared for me emotionally. Things happened so fast and I was not left with any time to grieve. Shocked, overwhelmed, scared, stressed, sleep

deprived, poor diet—the list goes on and on."

"Everyone keeps saying things will get easier with time but I am not worried about the future right now, I am having a hard enough time making it through a day at a time. I am really scared."

"I feel like I've been knocked back to the start of the 'race' through no fault of my own."

"Typically, how long does it take to recover? Sometimes I think I am 'there' and then something triggers my emotions and I feel like I am back at square one."

"I thought I was making progress then I attended a memorial service for a very good friend. Suddenly I am feeling overwhelmed and afraid again and it's been [years] since my husband died."

Fear—of the future, of "starting from scratch," of being alone—is really simply fear of just one thing and it is the scariest thing on the planet: THE UNKNOWN.

I firmly believe that fear of the unknown is, without a doubt, the greatest fear of them all.

Sure, we've all been afraid before. Think back to your first day of high school (which terrified me), your first day on a new job (*any* new job), even the fear that you felt on your wedding day (come on, admit it—you were nervous). However, these and many other typical "life fears" were those that we were able to face and conquer because they were a lot more "tangible" than what you are facing right now: an unknown and uncertain future and certainly a life that you did not ask for or expect.

Do things "get easier with time" as our widowed friend was told? No… and yes!

How many times have you heard the well-worn cliché: "Time heals all wounds"?

How many people have said this to you since the loss of your husband? And upon hearing it, how many times have you wanted to scream out loud:

"When?"

When is time going to heal what are possibly the deepest wounds that you have ever had to endure, the deeply embedded wounds of grief. *When* does the pain go away? *When* do you quit being afraid? *When* oh *when* does time indeed "heal all wounds"?

I have news for you, both bad and good. First, the "bad news": TIME *ALONE* CANNOT, DOES NOT, AND WILL NOT "HEAL ALL WOUNDS."

Don't get discouraged. Remember, I said that there was bad news and good news as well.

When surgeons perform surgery, do they make an incision, conduct an operation and then simply walk away at the conclusion of surgery, saying, "Time will heal this wound"? Of course not—that scenario sounds ridiculous, doesn't it? We know that surgeons take great care to close the incision with a number of different tools. They dress the incision carefully and they check on the healing process regularly. Eventually, with proper tending, care, and time…the wound does heal, usually leaving some kind of a scar.

Now let's look at your grief and the fear-conquering process like a surgical incision. Are you truly waiting for "time to heal" or to make things easier? Are you waking up every day thinking, "Well, time has passed and everyone is telling me that time makes things easier and heals all wounds, but I don't feel 'healed' and I'm still scared. What's the *matter* with me?"

In fact, if you are simply waiting for time to heal the wounds and make the fear go away, the only thing that you are going to accomplish is a whole bunch of waiting. Just because the wound you've sustained isn't a physical wound does *not* mean that it's not a wound all the same—and time *alone* cannot be the only factor in helping the healing and fear-conquering processes of your grief. In other words, and just like a surgeon: YOU NEED TOOLS TOO!

You need to get your hands on every single grief-recovery tool that you can, which brings us to the "good news" part. There are many tools available to you that can help to educate you, comfort you, and *empower* you and the greatest weapons against fear are education and empowerment! Instead of sitting around, feeling as though you have no control over your healing journey, go get the tools that are out there that will help you take control of your healing journey and ultimately help you in conquering your fears.

What tools have you gathered to help you on your healing journey? Have you used tools of any kind—books, magazine articles, audio aids, teleseminars, coaching, counseling—tools that will get you moving past fear and toward healing? If your answer is no, then you are that patient lying on the operating table with a wide-open wound that time *alone* is not capable of healing.

Commit to surrounding yourself with the tools that you need to create the healing that time does eventually bring. Get busy beating your fears! Get your questions answered, see your feelings addressed, and start caring properly for your grief, that horrible "wound" that you have sustained. You've made a great start with this book—now go out and get more tools. Go to bookstores (online or in-person), research "grief helper" books that are going to best assist you, and then *read them*! Go to your local library and find out what they have on hand in the way of grief assistance. Lastly, and as always, if you feel that you need professional help, *get professional help.* There is absolutely no shame in it and it can be a powerful *tool* in helping you heal.

When you have the right tools in your arsenal and when you tend to and take care of that wound that will eventually turn into a "life scar," *then* time will help that wound—and *you*—heal.

A "PERFECT" MARRIAGE—AN IMPERFECT REALITY

> *"I have such feelings of guilt because [my husband and I] had not been very close for the years [prior to his death]. He wasn't much of a talker and I just quit trying. We didn't argue; there was just 'indifference.' We were married [very] young and we were considered the 'perfect' couple. Nobody would have ever guessed how we had drifted apart."*

> *"My husband and I were [on the verge of] getting a divorce. We really were not getting along very well for a lot of reasons, including his cheating on me more than once. He suffered a massive heart attack and died. Is it weird that I feel so much grief and sadness?"*

Regardless of the state of your marriage at the time of your husband's death, it is neither "weird" nor "stupid" to grieve the loss. Whatever the circumstances at that point in time, this man was still your husband. You built a life with him and you have lost him *and* that life. There is no shame or guilt to be had in mourning these losses.

You are reading letters from widows in combination with my musings and memories. All of us have gone on about how wonderful our husbands were: how we lost "best friends," "soul mates," "better halves," and so forth. Conversely, you are left with the certain knowledge that your marriage wasn't "perfect."

Guess what? *Nobody's* marriage either was or is "perfect."

Granted, we may not have had to deal with a marriage that was on the verge of divorce when our husbands died, but rest assured that *every single marriage* out there has encountered *some* kind of challenge or difficulty at some point in time. Why? Because at the heart of a marriage are two human beings—two *imperfect* human beings. Many people on the "outside" look at married couples and think "Oh, look how perfect they are," and don't have the remotest idea what is going on behind the "perfect" doors of the "perfect" couple's "perfect" house with the "perfect" front yard and the "perfect" children.

Are you getting the idea?

Your marriage wasn't perfect. My marriage wasn't perfect. *Nobody's* marriage was or is perfect. The fact that you were in a time of difficulty or may have been on the "verge of divorce" is not important right now. You are completely entitled to mourn, grieve, and go through the identical healing journey as any other widow and don't let anyone convince you otherwise—not even you.

> *"My husband died while he was with another woman. I had no idea he was involved with someone else until [I was informed about his death]. I'm embarrassed that people are finding out about this and I'm angry because I have no one to yell at or confront. Most of all, I feel stupid and like a hypocrite for grieving over someone who doesn't deserve it because he was cheating on me."*

"My husband was killed and I got [the] call from [his] mistress. I am devastated and deceived. I knew our marriage wasn't perfect but I honestly thought that we had overcome all the hurdles and our life would be great."

You have already learned that absolutely no marriage is "perfect." However and without a doubt, this is one of the more tragic and isolating situations surrounding widowhood. Not only have you suffered the loss of a spouse, but you have also suffered a loss of trust and what many consider to be the ultimate in betrayal. While widows grieve and mourn the loss of a love, you are mourning that and so much more.

You are most certainly not a "hypocrite" or "stupid" for grieving the death of your husband. It's not a question of *his* "deserve level"; it's a question of *your* "deserve level." You have every right to mourn your husband's passing. Furthermore, what on earth do *you* have to be embarrassed about? *You* didn't do anything wrong! If anything, you should be eliciting even more sympathy. I'm also curious as to how people are "finding out about this," since it is certainly nobody's business but your own.

Regardless, you owe no one any explanations, and you have my permission to walk away from anyone who starts asking questions or otherwise puts you into an awkward or embarrassing situation by asking questions that are well and truly none of their business. In other words, just because someone asks a question does not mean that you have to answer it (and I'd like to meet the person who is either insensitive enough or brainless enough to start questioning a widow about her late husband's unfortunate "extracurricular" activities).

Anger and betrayal that cannot ever truly be confronted is certainly an impossibly maddening situation. You have every right to want answers to your questions; the first of which is most likely, "Why?" However, you also know that you are not going to be able to confront your husband on this horribly hurtful issue. It is therefore up to you to learn how to deal with the completely justifiable anger that you are experiencing and eventually get to a place of peace in your heart. The following suggestions may be helpful to you:

Be Smart, Be Sure, Be Safe!

1. Do *not* face, meet with, or otherwise engage in confrontation with the "other woman" under any circumstances. Despite what you may have seen on television or in the movies, there is no advantage to be gained by starting a bitter war of words with someone who does not deserve your time or your very limited energy. She does not get to play any kind of role in your life. Relegate her to where she belongs—to a sad and eventually inconsequential part of history. She deserves no more attention than that.

2. Start journaling. Writing the letter to me was an excellent start, continuing to get your feelings onto paper can only help. You can be as sad or as angry or as bitter as you want and believe it or not, you will feel better for "getting it out."

3. Reach out and connect with other widows. You don't have to go into any particulars or specifics surrounding your husband's death. Just the fact that you are a widow is enough to warrant the support and love that you will receive. You will find wonderful resources to meet other widows in the back of the book.

4. Recognize that yours too is a "Pancake Tragedy" situation and, as such, you are *entitled* (hold onto that word) to grieve the betrayal as a separate and distinct loss.

5. Consider seeking counseling or therapy to deal with this particularly difficult situation.

6. If anyone has tried or is trying to confront you, harass or intimidate you, or otherwise make your life difficult as a result of your husband's death, seek legal counsel immediately. If you feel threatened or as though your life or welfare is in imminent danger, *do not hesitate to contact your local law enforcement agency.*

The "Married Widow"

"Technically, I am not yet a widow, but [due to a lengthy terminal illness situation] I am in preparation for life after loss, which is full of grieving if for no other reason than the loss of the life we once knew. I am caught in the middle; unable to truly grieve and yet I am also unable to go forward with my life. I am also mentally, physically, and emotionally exhausted. I am a professionally active woman who normally loves life and has sought continuous growth of life and spirit. I have read your entire newsletter collection [on the website] and although I am crying, you have helped me feel better than any other resource I have found. I understand your husband was ill for two years prior to his death. Please help me through this."

"My husband was diagnosed with [a terminal illness several years ago]. I am thankful that I still have him and yet I believe I have been grieving for several years. How did you handle your husband's deterioration?"

I can state unequivocally that you *have* been grieving for the entire duration of your husband's illness. For us, the grieving process began the moment we were given that ghastly diagnosis and that process continued daily because from that moment forward, we knew that Mike would never again be as good as he was "today."

Is there anything worse than watching your loved one "die by inches"? To see what long-term illness does little by little, to stand by and be completely helpless to do anything to stop it is truly hell on earth. I well remember whenever Mike would try to twist the lid off of a jar or tear a candy bar wrapper open, I would rush to do it for him, just so he wouldn't have to experience the pain of not being able to do it for himself. So for us, the grieving process starts long before the actual death because the day we received those respective diagnoses was the day that we "lost" our husbands as we knew them, and the transition from husband-wife to patient-nurse began. This transition alone requires a mourning period in and of itself—another unwelcome surprise of the grieving process.

I handled Mike's deterioration the same way that most would in the same situation—the very best way that I knew how. We had our "good days" and we also admittedly had our "bad days." We each did our best to understand what the other was going through, for as we know, the patient is the primary victim of the illness; however, every single person living in the household and the household itself is affected as well. Sometimes we fell short of expectations because we were human beings dealing with a horrendous situation but we never quit trying and we never quit loving one another.

Yours is an incredibly difficult position in which to be, a sort of "limbo" if you will. Do the very best that you can to take care of yourself health-wise and do *not* be shy about asking for help. Early in our own processes, I mistakenly felt that asking for help was akin to being weak, a failure or incapable of taking care of my family; a mistake that it took me a full year (plus a few loving but very firm threats from several family members) to rectify. When you receive offers from people to stay with your husband while you get some badly needed rest or to take a couple of hours away from the house or hospital, accept the offer!

I wish you as much peace as is possible as you continue on this journey and when the time comes and you feel ready, you know that help and support is close at hand.

> *"I am forty-three years old and am losing my husband to leukemia. He is in palliative care now and I am slowly accepting the fact that I will soon be alone. It is encouraging to know that there are others that have [gotten] through this and have come out the other side ok."*

Please accept my wishes for peace to you and your family as you move through this period of your journey with your husband. As have many thousands of women who are members of Widows Wear Stilettos, I too have been exactly where you are right now—at that moment in time when prayers for healing turn to prayers of peace for all of you and most especially for your husband.

IT's A "WRAP"...STILETTO-STYLE!

OK ladies, pencils and highlighters down. How many questions did you highlight? How many answers apply to you? I'll bet you highlighted more than one question, answer, or general areas to which you directly related. Just by seeing that you are not the only person dealing with the plethora of emotions surrounding your healing journey, you are hopefully left feeling a little less alone, a lot more empowered, and certainly better equipped to deal with *all* of the emotions with which you may be presented.

chapter three

WHAT'S APPROPRIATE
OR "IS IT OK TO...?"

"WHEN IS IT PROPER TO...?"

"What is appropriate...?"

"Is it OK to...?"

If I had a dime for every time I received a letter starting with those very words—well, let's just say I would rattle a lot.

Widows everywhere are very concerned with the "what's and when's" of widowhood, so much so that we refer to questions such as these as "Widow Etiquette."

From wedding rings to "Hubby Things" to "Dating or Waiting," everyone wants to know the "What's and When-May-I's" of widowhood. Please note that in and amongst all of the questions and answers, there is an important lesson running through the entire chapter. Let's see if you can figure out what that lesson is.

GETTING THROUGH THE "GOING THROUGH"

"My husband passed away suddenly. [His grown] children live out of state and I don't know how or when to disburse his things. I've been trying to consolidate his things because I know I'll have to move. However, I feel so 'stuck' with having to hold onto clothing, etc., because his children live out of town and haven't gotten around to going through his things. If I'm not able to disburse his items before I move, I'll have to put things in storage, which I don't want to do because it will cost extra money. Please note that we all have a wonderful family relationship. Any thoughts or advice on this?"

In your situation, what should ideally happen is a fair and equitable distribution of the responsibility. It's fabulous that you have a "wonderful family relationship" with everyone; however, if that's the case, the practical and financial burden of the "go through" should not fall squarely and solely on your shoulders. Aside from which, how are you supposed to decide who gets what on your own? Why are you expected to pay for it all? Additionally, you should not have to delay this process because of the children and the fact that they haven't "gotten around" to going through their father's things.

There are essentially two choices here. The children can come to your town and assist you with the process and take (or ship) things home or they can help you pay to ship things to them. Be sure that you have first gone through everything by yourself and have kept the item(s) that are rightfully yours. You'll want to do this on your own in order to avoid potential conflict or argument. Give them a time frame, a deadline, and their options, but the option that is *not* "on the menu" is sticking you with the cost and/or the entire decision-making responsibility.

You should not have to bear the brunt of all of this by yourself; nor should you have to incur additional expense to either store the items for whenever the children are "ready" to go through them or *really* incur additional expense in shipping (and thanks to rising fuel costs, those expenses aren't going to go down).

"Do I throw out all of 'our' stuff [pictures, furniture, old clothes, jewelry, knickknacks] and anything that reminds me of him? Is that the only way to 'move on'?"

This question is one of the foremost reasons that I always teach not to make *any* decisions concerning what to keep and what to dispose of shortly after a loss. Will there be items that you dispose of? Quite likely. But get rid of everything that belonged to the two of you in the interest of "moving on"? Absolutely *not!*

You *can* move forward from the loss of your husband into a new life while continuing to honor and treasure your life with him. Throwing away the things that belonged to your late husband or to you as a couple will not wipe out the life that you shared with him; it won't help you "move on"; and in time, you will come to regret having taken such a drastic measure.

There will come a time where you will pack up clothes for donation but by all means keep a few pieces that have sentimental meaning for you or your children. Pictures can be stored to be revisited when you feel ready to do so. Jewelry that you do not wish to wear can also be put away for your heirs. And don't feel shy about having subtle reminders of your husband about the house. For example, in the curio of our house there is an adorable statue of a horse wearing a police officer's cap, a saddle blanket with a police badge, and holding a pair of handcuffs in its mouth. This is only one of our understated and continually comforting nods to Mike's memory.

I always excitedly encourage anyone who is ready to take their "baby steps" into a new life but at the same time, I will continue to teach what has become one of my mantras:

YOU CAN HONOR YOUR PAST.
YOU CAN TREASURE YOUR PAST.
YOU CAN LOVE YOUR PAST.
YOU DO NOT HAVE TO *LIVE* IN YOUR PAST.

"I am finally going through my husband's things and I thought I was holding up okay, but then one day I just started crying and I couldn't stop. What makes me feel even worse is that I was starting to feel relieved that I was almost finished with going through everything. I feel like I've had a complete setback and like it's the day after his funeral. What happened? I was doing so well. And is it okay that I'm having this feeling of being relieved?"

I receive so very many letters that use the words, "setback," "backsliding," and "failure to progress" (that last one sounds like an unfavorable report card), all because a widow cried as she was going through her husband's things. Why would you feel that this is a setback? Because you cry at the memory of your late husband? Does that *really* qualify as a "setback"? Let's think this one through.

As you continue on your healing journey, and especially during your "going through" processes, those rough days are going to come and you *will* miss your husband. Why wouldn't you? This is the man with whom you built a family and a life, and yes, even if it was just the two of you, you were a family unit together. Does the passage of time temper these teary occurrences? Absolutely. But does it mean that you are having a "setback" when you cry or otherwise feel melancholy? That's an out-loud NO!

In the years since my husband's passing, much has happened in our household. I've watched my daughter celebrate her Bat Mitzvah, graduate from middle school, and attend her high school formal dances and proms. I taught her to drive (and came through it while remaining on speaking terms with her), helped her to open her first checking account, celebrated when she got her very first job, and witnessed her graduation from high school. I watched her win a national cheerleading championship and subsequently become a college cheerleader (her goal since she was eight years old), and I now watch her determinedly and successfully pursue the career that she has dreamed of all of her life while she continues to grow into adulthood. We've celebrated holidays, football game victories, birthdays, the day her college application was accepted—you name it, we've celebrated it. That's just the kind of household we have.

Guess what? I've cried virtually every time because her daddy wasn't here to see it. But did I ever once feel as though I was having a "setback"? Absolutely *not*.

A "setback" or "backsliding" means that you are indeed right back where you started, negating any and all progress that you've made. Pay attention carefully. Even if you lost your husband last week—*you have moved forward!* You are progressing; you are healing; you are s-l-o-w-l-y learning about this new life into which you are growing. As long as you continue to take those steps forward, a "setback" is not possible.

Many of you have heard me teach this: you must give yourself *permission* in all aspects of your healing journey—permission to cry, permission to be angry, permission to be "in charge" of your own healing, and so forth. In this instance, you must give yourself *permission* to remember your husband, even if it means remembering him with tears, all the while knowing that you are *not* having a setback. I assure you that if they aren't already, your tears will eventually be through the smiles of some pretty wonderful memories if you give yourself *permission* to acknowledge that this is normal, it is going to happen, and that it is perfectly fine for it to happen.

And if all else fails and you still feel like you are suffering a "setback," I want you to copy the following and paste it up on your bathroom mirror or refrigerator where you can't help but see it every day:

A SETBACK LETS YOU TAKE A *STEP* BACK TO LET YOU *SET* UP FOR A *COMEBACK*!

This philosophy works for quarterbacks, it works for presidents of corporations, and it can work for you too. Please don't minimize or trivialize the progress that you've made by unilaterally deciding that tears-equals-setback or "backsliding." Hold on to the certain promise that it *does* get better.

The "go through" process can be a sad and wistful process and unfortunately, not a lot of widows are prepared for that fact. I want to reassure you that it's perfectly fine to be sad. It is also perfectly normal to feel relieved that the "go through" part of the healing journey is almost behind you. As we just discussed, it's very much like feeling the relief that comes at the end of an illness. We certainly don't wish for any of our loved ones to be gone but we do long for the *suffering* to come to an end. There's a huge difference.

The same principle applies here—it is an extremely difficult process to go through your husband's belongings, make decisions, and in essence, end the chapter that was your life with him. Feeling relieved that this process is almost behind you is so very normal because in a fashion, a part of your suffering comes to an end as well. You are going to continue to have those days or those moments in time where you feel like "one step forward, two steps back," and that's normal too.

Please don't feel like you're having a "setback" or that you're otherwise going backward in your recovery processes. Each step forward that you take is enormous and you need a chance to accept and embrace the enormity of what has happened and the recovery that you are making.

> *"My daughter's mother-in-law recently died unexpectedly. Her [father-in-law] began seeing another woman [almost immediately] after the death. The concern is that the widower has so far refused to discuss parting with any of [his late wife's] belongings. There is a legitimate concern that some of these things may 'disappear' or jewelry may be dismantled to make items for his new love. How should [the children] approach their father to ask that they be allowed to go through and choose some special things that [belonged to] their mother."*

This is indeed a very sticky problem, but not at all unusual. For many, facing the pain of grief and being alone is far more difficult than simply filling the void with another romantic interest soon after the loss of a spouse. I have long taught that getting romantically and/or physically involved immediately after a spouse's death is not a healthy decision and that appears to be what is happening here. Worse, the children are suffering as a result, both from the practical standpoint of the disposition of their mother's belongings and the emotional standpoint of having to accept their father with another woman so soon after their mother's death.

The reality is that Dad can't have it all ways. I would certainly understand if he were not ready to dispose of or otherwise disburse his wife's belongings at this point, yet he is involved romantically with a woman whose motives are suspect to the family. If Dad is ready to be involved with another woman, then he is also ready to allow his children access to that which is rightfully theirs. He cannot have it both ways—it's either too soon or it isn't. On the other hand, approaching Dad in an adversarial or attacking manner (especially if the attack is in any way aimed toward his new lady friend) is not going to help things either; rather, it will simply serve to throw everyone on the defensive.

I would suggest that all concerned parties (and better they should be children, grandchildren, or siblings rather than in-laws) sit down together with Dad quietly, calmly, and rationally; a united front needs to be presented. Acknowledge the pain that they know Dad to have endured and that they understand that he is certainly entitled to find love again. Explain that while they are pleased to see him moving forward (whether they are or not), part of moving forward includes the "go through" process and that there are items of Mom's that they want and deserve to have. They need to *gently* point out that if he is able to move forward romantically, he can also move forward practically by allowing his children, grandchildren, etc., access to that which their (grand)mother wanted them to have.

In this situation, you don't get to be "over it and movin' on" in one sense (romantically), yet refuse to move forward practically by declining to discuss allowing family members access to Mom's belongings because it's "too soon." It's too soon or it isn't too soon but it can't be both. Make it clear that no one wants to take everything that belonged to Mom, just select items. It would also be reasonable to inquire as to what kind of financially protective measures Dad is taking in regard to his financial future and the new woman in his life, and this is for Dad's protection.

Holidays and Celebrations

> *"I am feeling the pain of preparing for our first Christmas without my husband. I am trying to go through the motions for our kids, but deep down I wish it were over with. I feel lost and I miss that whole 'Christmas spirit' feeling. So does my son. He does not have to say anything; I look in his eyes and the whole story is there."*

> *"My husband's favorite time of the year was Christmas and I just don't know how to handle the holidays and other events, especially where the children are concerned."*

Along the healing journey, holidays loom large before us and not necessarily in a happy way. Once a time of celebration and anticipation, holidays—*any* holidays—can quickly turn into dark clouds on a widow's horizon.

We lost Mike six days before Christmas and right in the middle of Hanukkah. In addition to the logistical challenges that we faced—a funeral during Christmas week, people trying to travel to California while most of the country was buried under six feet of snow, and so forth—there was also the matter of facing the holidays all by ourselves. Remember too that Kendall was only eleven years old, and despite how we may be feeling as widows, if you are also a mother, you realize that children are still entitled to be children. Like it or not, this includes holiday observances.

We have since gotten very good at tuning in to how we feel and what we feel like doing, or *don't* feel like doing, in observance of any holidays that occur during our year. Over the years, all of the holidays have taken on a different sort of "complexion" if you will, but they are nonetheless now a happy, peaceful, and yes, even joyous time for us. With time, and more importantly, with understanding and patience with yourself, this particular time of year will again be a time of peace and joy in your home and in your heart.

"I'm struggling as are so many other women. I lost my husband [a very short time ago and] the shock and grief has been over-whelming. With the holidays approaching, I'm leaning toward just going light on decorating, although I'm not sure I have the strength to go through the process of a tree and looking at ornaments that we collected. Some have told me not to run from this but I'm just feeling mentally and physically exhausted. Is that what I'm doing? Running? We have always made a big deal of the holidays but [it] is not the same right now. Plus, I'm trying to do what I need for me, not what everyone else thinks I should be doing."

Are you "running"? Absolutely not. What you are doing is *grieving*!

We are talking about a very short time since the loss of your husband and despite what those who surround us may think, we know that grief does not resolve in an overnight, "OK, that's over with" fashion. Certainly the holidays amplify the loss of our loved one and particularly in households where holidays were celebrated in a big way. Let's add in the fact that these are the very first holidays that you are facing without your husband and this makes for a very difficult time. Running? I don't think so.

What pleased me the most about your letter is that you are resolute in listening to *you* and how *you* want to handle things. Your observation that, "I'm trying to do what I need for me, not what everyone else thinks I should be doing" demonstrates great strength and conviction and you need to be proud of yourself for that. Continue to listen to that "little voice" inside; it will never steer you wrong, particularly during this challenging time.

"What is your opinion of going away for the holidays? My friends and family don't think it's 'appropriate,' but I have the opportunity to take a [vacation away from home], and I'd really like to do it. What do you think?"

What is inappropriate about your taking a vacation during the holidays? Not only is it just fine, it is a recommendation that I have previously made countless times. Many find it just too painful to stay in their homes at this time of year, surrounded by memories of a life that once was. Others simply want to begin creating new memories or do something different. Let me ask you a question that I ask every single time someone approaches me with an issue that begins with, "Everyone thinks I should/shouldn't…": How many of these disapproving folks are *widows* facing the holidays without their spouse?

I'm guessing none and I'm generally correct in this guess.

Wherever your destination and whatever your reasons, I again encourage you to listen to *you*. If you feel like going away for the holidays, you should not only do so, you should have a wonderful and peaceful time.

> *"I recently lost the love of my life. We have always sent out an annual Christmas letter to family and friends and many of our friends live some distance away and do not know of his death. Should I just send cards this year and add a few handwritten notes to those that need to be informed?"*

Our family was just like yours and many other families in that we also sent a photo card and an annual letter letting everyone know of the goings-on in our home during the previous year. I stopped those letters once my husband became ill, which was two years prior to his death. Since he died so close to Christmas, we actually didn't send cards that year. We resumed the card/letter tradition three years after Mike's death and that timing worked well for us. For others, the timing may be sooner or later still. There are no hard and fast rules here; this is about what makes you comfortable and what you feel is appropriate.

You have a great idea to send cards this year and include a short, handwritten note to those people who may be unaware of your husband's passing. In addition to those handwritten notes, you might send a letter, but rather than the usual holiday letter stuff, use the letter as an opportunity to thank everyone for their love, support, and assistance during your time of mourning and wish everyone a happy holiday and peaceful New Year. You can keep it lower-key for now (believe me, people will understand) and then reevaluate your feelings next year as to whether you want to resume your newsletter.

> *"I recently became a widow. I had only been married [less than a year and] we did not even get a chance to celebrate our first year anniversary. I still have the [top layer of our wedding] cake and people say I should throw it away. I feel like I should do something. If you could give me any ideas, I would appreciate it."*

I'm absolutely stunned that anyone would tell you to throw away the top layer of your wedding cake, which I find hardly a supportive or sensitive suggestion. What would that accomplish? Do people honestly believe that by throwing the cake away, you'll somehow feel better, or "forget" the day? Unbelievable. However, it really makes no difference as to what other people—including me—are telling you. How do *you* feel about the top layer of your cake? Do *you* want to throw it away? My guess is no.

There is nothing wrong with commemorating your wedding anniversary, especially under your particular set of circumstances. Your time together as a married couple was far too short and you have every right to honor and remember your husband and your time with him, both before and after your marriage.

Do you have a close family member or best friend with whom you might enjoy sharing the cake? Why not get together with just one or two people that are most supportive to enjoy the cake with a glass of champagne or sparkling apple cider. Yes, it will be wistful and yes, tears will likely be shed, but you will also find yourself enjoying the warmth of your memories as well. Most of all, you will be doing what *you* want to do, rather than what other people (likely none of whom are widowed) are telling you to do.

"In our home, birthdays were considered 'national holidays' and some of our friends are asking if I intend on planning a 'memorial' celebration of his life [on his birthday]. While I would like to do this, I'm not sure what to do, especially because I just finished with the funeral. Have you any advice for me?"

We are also a "birthdays take an entire month to observe" household, so I understand exactly what you're saying, and I had to giggle. I'm so happy to know we're not alone in our crazy and seemingly endless celebrating.

However, as with the previous letter, I'm always a little skeptical when I see letters that include the words "my family wants me to" or "my friends say I should," or words to that effect. When it comes to your husband's birthday, let's again leave the friends out of this and let me ask you, what do *you* want to do? What if you prefer to observe his birthday quietly and all by yourself, rather than have a "memorial celebration" of his life? You just finished having a "memorial celebration of his life." It's called a funeral.

If *you* feel like having a small dinner gathering or barbeque featuring some of your husband's favorite foods and drinks, that would be lovely, but remember, you are still trying to recover and people tend to forget that part. Don't feel like you have to have a "memorial celebration" with pictures and speeches and the like—you need to continue with the process of healing and the beginnings of moving forward.

Make sure that the control and the decision making stays with you and I would encourage you to ask yourself what it is that you *really* want to do and then follow your heart.

"Everyone always talks about missing their husband during the holidays. With me, it's Valentine's Day. That was our 'big deal' holiday and it's so hard to be without him on that day. Do you have any ideas on how to celebrate Valentine's Day if you don't have a husband or special someone in your life?"

It seems like we just got done putting away turkey leftovers and gift wrap and have managed to get the last of the pine needles vacuumed out of the carpeting or the candle wax cleaned out of the menorahs, being grateful all the while that we managed to survive the holidays and now we're staring at yet *another* difficult time. There's yet *another* holiday to get through without a husband: Valentine's Day. And if it's at all possible, this holiday is even more difficult to get through.

You're constantly surrounded by the "Day of Hearts and Flowers," usually starting the day after Christmas and it is *everywhere*! Valentine's Day is in grocery stores, in the lingerie department of your favorite store; heck, there are even Valentine decorations and gift suggestions at the local do-it-yourself monster-size home stores (although I have never thought in terms of a power saw as a Valentine's Day gift, but that's just me).

In our house, Valentine's Day was (and still is) an absolutely huge holiday. We decorated, we shopped, we loved surprising one another, and we celebrated both as a couple and as a family. It is definitely another one of those times where you likely feel your husband's absence acutely.

Here are a few of my tried-and-true favorite Valentine's Day ideas that will help put a smile on your face and bring peace to your heart:

You Deserve A Fabulous Valentine's Day

1. Invite a few friends over for a potluck dinner or a Decadent Dessert gathering at your home (yes, even including your married girlfriends—they can get out of the house on a night other than the fourteenth). Decorate your house and your table for the occasion and include festive drinks, such as champagne with a splash of Chambord (raspberry liqueur), Cosmopolitans, Shirley Temples with lots of maraschino cherries, or hot chocolate with pink marshmallows. I also included touches like large crystal brandy snifters filled with red licorice whips, Hershey's kisses, and of course, candy message hearts. Send everyone home with a heart-shaped key chain, a small heart-shaped picture frame, or a few foil-wrapped chocolate hearts in a decorative cellophane bag tied with ribbon as a memento of the evening.

2. Slumber parties aren't just for kids anymore. Have an old-fashioned slumber party—get into your flannel "jammies" with the feet in them and take turns playing with makeup or making fun of some of the articles in your favorite magazines. Have dance contests with music from whatever era brings back wonderful memories for you. Give one another at-home facials (you can get quality facial products at the drugstore without spending a ton of money). Take ridiculous pictures and make one another promise *never* to show them to anyone else, and no posting on the Internet either! Your "Girls Night In" might also feature a couple of romantic comedy DVDs. My favorites include *Love Actually, Pretty Woman, The Holiday, How to Marry a Millionaire,* and *Shirley Valentine.* Don't forget the popcorn, soda, and chocolate goodies.

3. Treat yourself! I'll never quit saying this: You *deserve* to be pampered and treated like the awesome woman that you are and if this means that for the time being, you have to do it yourself, then do it yourself! Visit a department store cosmetic counter or have an at-home beauty consultant come in and try a makeover—something completely different and just-for-fun—and remember, you can generally do this absolutely free of charge.

4. Book a mini-massage or a single spa treatment of some kind (these also need not be expensive). You don't have to go to the Spa Du Jour for an all-day extravaganza (which *can* be expensive). Do a little research. Better still, consult with your girlfriends and see if they have any recommendations.

5. When was the last time you took an actual bubble bath instead of just ten minutes in the shower before dashing off to work or to run the kids somewhere? Pour yourself a cool glass of your favorite beverage or cocktail, light an aromatherapy candle (Glade Apple-Cinnamon is the *best*!), add some bath salts, and jump in. No interruptions allowed!

6. Make yourself dinner. Not something out of a paper bag from Burger Barn or out of the freezer and into the microwave, but a real-deal Valentine's dinner. On one Valentine's Day a few years ago, not only was I alone, I had also managed to break two toes on my foot and was on crutches with my foot in a boot (and not the cute stiletto kind). How's *that* for a double-downer? Not to be dissuaded from treating myself, I bought a wonderful filet mignon to prepare at home, along with béarnaise

sauce, creamed spinach, garlic potatoes, berries with cream for dessert, and a fabulous champagne to go with it all. It was slow going with the crutches and the not-so-cute boot, but I made myself a beautiful dinner and enjoyed it tremendously. Just paying attention to myself in this very simple manner helped diminish the pain (well, except for my foot).

7. We always feel better when we are in service to others. Think about this: All of the shelters and soup kitchens have lots of volunteers and help during Thanksgiving and Christmas, but what about the rest of the year? These places still serve people in need and people in need is a year-round reality. Why not take a platter or two of Valentine's cookies or brownies down to a shelter, a soup kitchen, or to the children's wing of a hospital (with prior permission of course). Valentine's Day is all about love and that can also include love for our fellow man.

8. Lastly, don't be "afraid" of the day. It's OK to remember your beloved with tears and with smiles! If it's not too painful for you, go ahead and reread old love letters and cards or look back through photographs. Take a picnic to a favorite place that you shared (only a native Californian would suggest a picnic in February) and enjoy your memories all by yourself. This may sound very solitary or even downright depressing, but you will be surprised at how peaceful you will feel when you allow yourself to remember, rather than working overtime trying to forget that which is unavoidably unforgettable.

GENERALLY SPEAKING...

> *"I'm really worried about what will people think when I get rid of [my husband's] things. I think that it's time because it's been [just over a year] since his death, but other people that have volunteered to help me have told me that it's too soon."*

We are far enough along in the book for you to have gotten a pretty good idea about how I feel concerning other people's opinions, observations, and insights as to your healing journey and the decisions that you make along the way. However, I can't resist asking the obvious again: How many of these "other people" are the widow, living your life, inside of your house, and traveling on your healing journey? More to the point, where do these people find the nerve to venture any opinions whatsoever concerning when, why, or how you dispose of or distribute your husband's belongings?

This is one of the reasons that you may wish to keep the "go through" process private. While it might certainly help to have additional sets of hands helping you, the fact remains that once you let others in, you are subject to their opinions as well and those opinions will not be limited to simply when you decide to go through your husband's things. Those opinions can extend to what you decide to keep, throw away, donate, or pass along as heirloom. I can also promise you that at least one person will ask you, "Can I *please* have this?" making for an incredibly awkward moment.

Like you, I had many offers from family and close friends to help me go through things and I turned down every single offer that I received. I had to make this particularly painful part of the healing journey on my own and I needed to keep that part of our life private. Not only did I want to take my time during the go-through process (which others may tend to "rush" on your behalf), I did not want to worry about making anyone uncomfortable due to any one or all of the emotions that I knew I would experience— from mournful sobbing to hysterical laughter and right back to sobbing again. I wanted to take the time to reminisce, ponder, cry, laugh, be quiet, be angry; be everything that I knew I was going to be and that need was best served alone.

Is there such a thing as getting rid of things or making any kind of decisions too soon? Yes, and that time would be immediately after the death, which is too soon to make any major decisions about almost anything. That said, the fact remains that this too is an *opinion* and in any case, it's not the situation here. Your timing as to the decision to go through your husband's things is not only time-appropriate, the decision remains yours alone. No one, not even your children, have any business dictating to you otherwise.

> *"How can widows diplomatically tell people if they do not prefer the prefix 'Ms.' before their name? I have received cards or wedding invitations or condolence cards with the prefix 'Ms.' and I've even heard of widows receiving mail addressed to 'Ms.' with their maiden name. When I have brought it up, I usually get a look [that says], 'You're not over him yet?' I notice on your website that you are referred to as 'Ms.' [and] I realize that some widows may prefer to be addressed as 'Ms.,' however, it hurts me. Could this keep happening until or unless I remarry?"*

What if you choose not to remarry? Does this mean that you should keep on having your feelings hurt? That doesn't sound like much of a solution.

If something is hurting you, you have the right to *politely* put a stop to it. Keep in mind that while most people are not intentionally setting out to hurt you, at the same time, they may not know proper etiquette either. Most people either don't realize or don't remember that the prefix "Ms." was originally designed and intended as a way to address a woman if you didn't know her marital status.

I long ago learned that people don't know *what* to do with widows in general and this is a perfect example. And I have honestly *never* heard of anyone reverting to using a widow's maiden name—even many divorced women still use and go by their married names. I would definitely and loudly take issue with anyone who used a widow's maiden name. I didn't understand why it happened in the movie, *Private Benjamin,* and I don't understand why it happens now.

The word "diplomatic" is important and you are wise to use that approach. A gentle correction is fine—just let people know that you prefer to be addressed as "Mrs." rather than "Ms." Now, if people look at you like you're not "over him yet" as you say, then let them look! What do you care? These are your feelings we're talking about and you have every right to them. As you have learned, most people don't know what to do or say when there has been a death and it's much easier for *them* if you are "over it."

I receive designation as both "Ms." and "Mrs." and as long as they get my name right, the "title" makes no difference to me at all. However, those are *my* feelings, not yours. If you don't like being referred to as "Ms.", then by all means, let people know and absolutely feel free to remind them that a husband's death does not "erase" a marriage and relegate anyone to her maiden name.

"I was married for [many] years and was a 'Mrs.' Now I don't know if I am 'The Widow' or 'Ms.' or 'Mrs.'"

As stated before, "Ms." and "Mrs." are both appropriate designations; it is really your personal preference. However, while you are technically a widow until or unless you remarry, "The Widow" is not an appropriate title or designation, if for no other reason than we are not living in the 1800s. Remember, being a widow *shapes* who you are; it does not *define* who you are. "Widow" is a martial status designation, used mostly when filling out governmental forms and should not be used as a "title." In other words, while I treasure my last name, I would never want to be referred to as "The Widow Fleet."

"Is it appropriate to invite the ex-wife to your husband's memorial mass? She was married to [him] for [over twenty] years. I was married to [him] for [almost thirty] years."

I admire and applaud your sensitivity in asking this question. It is a very kind gesture on your part to acknowledge your husband's life prior to your time with him. I believe that if it is in your heart to do so, it is absolutely appropriate to include your husband's ex-wife at the memorial mass. She spent over twenty years as his wife and as such, she no doubt mourns his passing in her own way. It would be not only appropriate, but also a great kindness to invite her.

However, as I continually teach, you must also be true to you and operate within your comfort levels. *You* are the widow. If theirs was a bitter or acrimonious divorce, if you feel as though she would make a scene or otherwise create an unbearably uncomfortable situation for you or for your family, then the obvious answer would be not to include her. Only you can make that determination and you should feel free to do so.

> *"Should I move my husband's pictures and awards out of the living room? I feel bad about other people seeing [the awards], but at the same time, I feel that I am doing my husband wrong. What should I do?"*

The only person who knows when the time is right to move pictures and awards is *you*. If you haven't already done so, that means it's not time to do so…yet. That day will come and the way you will know that it's the right time is you will wake up one day and you will know. I know that may sound dumb, but that's exactly how it happens. For example, one morning, I walked into my living room and I just knew that it was time to take my husband's pictures and awards and put them away. It happened just like that. I left everything in its place until *I* felt that the time had come to do otherwise.

Please don't worry about other people feeling bad upon coming over and seeing these things on display and please don't let anyone tell you what to do in this regard. This is about you and your healing processes. Many are the times that I encourage and remind widows to seize and retain ownership of their healing journey and this is one of those times. Remember, when it comes to matters such as this, it is all about you and *your* feelings.

"I was asking [my widowed friend] if there was a [different] term for 'mother-in-law' after your husband dies and she didn't know."

Your friend's mother-in-law is still her mother-in-law until or unless she chooses to remarry. No divorce took place, so all "in-law" terminology remains the correct terminology.

"IT'S MY RING AND I'LL DO WHAT I WANT...MAYBE"

"How long is it 'proper' to wear your wedding ring after your husband dies? Friends and family comment that I should stop wearing mine because it's been over two years since my husband's death and that I should be 'over everything' by now."

"What hurts me is when people mention that since my husband died, we are no longer married and that I shouldn't wear my rings. Are these people right in what they are saying?"

"What is appropriate in regard to wearing a wedding ring after a spouse dies? I feel it is ok to wear my wedding ring, and would feel lost without it. I just want to know if there is some sort of protocol for this."

"My husband and I were married after years of dating. [Almost immediately] after our wedding, he was taken away from me [in an accident]. We loved being married even though it was for only [a very short time]. I am wondering if it is okay to [continue to] wear my wedding ring? I wasn't sure if that is something I can do now."

"My wedding ring and engagement ring are beautiful and I like to wear them. Recently I was told it is in bad taste to continue wearing the rings after your husband has died. What do you think?"

Let me ask you this: Out of all of the friends and family who are telling you that you should quit wearing your rings because you should be "over it" or because "You're not married anymore" or because *they* think it's in "bad taste," how many of them are also the widow and have endured the suffering, the pain, and the loss in the same way that you have?

I'm guessing the answer is just you. That means that *no one else* is qualified to dictate when you should be "over it." End of discussion.

Despite any observations, pronouncements, or judgments that may come from those around you, there is no "proper" or "improper" time to take off your rings. This most personal decision will and must be *yours*. Should you decide to continue to wear your rings, be it for ten minutes or twenty years after your husband's death, the decision to do so is certainly and most emphatically *not* in "bad taste."

I have written extensively regarding people who fancy themselves as what I have termed to be the all-knowing experts on the subject entitled, "You and Your Pain." Whether intentional or otherwise, these people are capable of causing widows plenty of headache and heartache. Just by virtue of the fact that you are questioning the propriety of wearing your rings means that these people have collectively caused you to doubt your own judgment, rather than support you in your decision-making process.

Some widows remove their wedding rings right away, while others never remove them. As I did with every single aspect of my healing journey, I also took "baby steps" regarding my rings. Almost one year into my own healing journey, I moved my rings to my right hand. Even though I was moving forward with life in a healthy and timely fashion, wearing the rings on my right hand continued to comfort me. I wore my rings for about three years after Mike's passing, and yes, I continued to wear them on my right hand even after I started dating again. I removed the rings only when *I* was ready to do so and not one second before.

A dear and longtime member of Widows Wear Stilettos shared a wonderful wedding ring idea with me. She took her rings and her late husband's ring to a jeweler and had the rings re-designed and turned into one piece of jewelry. She wears this lovely combination of past and present with pride, with love, and without having to endure the unsolicited opinions of others.

When it comes to your wedding rings, there are only two factors that you may need to consider:

1) If your engagement and/or wedding rings were heirlooms from your husband's family, you should make the offer to return the rings to his family. Chances are excellent that they will refuse the return of the jewelry out of respect to you and what you have been through; however, I believe it to be appropriate to at least make the gesture.

2) The presence of your rings on your *right* hand should not be an issue. Many women (myself included) wear beautiful jewelry on their right ring finger. However, should you eventually resume dating or enter into a new relationship, the presence of your rings on your *left* hand may become an issue. A new man may think that you have been unable to bid goodbye to the past and are unable or unwilling to move forward from your husband's death. Sensitivity is required on the part of both of you here—just as he will need to be sensitive to your feelings behind your wearing your rings, you must be sensitive to his feelings as well.

You must also remember that as we discussed earlier, many people want you to be "over" your husband's death because it's easier for *them* if you are "over it." However, these are *your* feelings that we're talking about here. So, other than the two considerations that I just outlined, if wearing your rings brings you pleasure, consolation, happiness, or whatever it is that you seek as you progress on your healing journey (and it is *your* healing journey), you go right ahead and wear your rings.

"Dating Game" or "Waiting Game"?

"When is it acceptable to start dating again?"

"I'm getting a lot of opinions on how long I should wait to start going out on dates. I'm not even ready yet, but what if I'm ready and it's not the 'appropriate' time yet?"

"Some people are telling me to wait at least [until] a year has passed [since the loss] and other people are telling me to wait even longer. What happens if I don't want to wait a year or five years to start dating again?"

"I'm so tired of people who don't know what they're talking about [because they are not widowed] telling me how long I 'have to' wait to start going out [with men], but then I think that maybe they are right. What is the normal amount of time to wait [to begin dating again]?"

Questions such as these warm my heart. While a time of hope and anticipation, the prospect of dating can also be a very difficult and scary moment in time for a widow and by considering reentry into the "World of Dating," you are actually taking a huge step forward on your healing journey. This is definitely "cause for applause" and congratulations.

Then I see the words, "People are telling me" or "What is 'normal'?" and I get cranky all over again.

I made a very conscious decision to wait for at least a year before I would even entertain the idea of dating again. I made that decision based upon a lot of factors, not the least of which were my daughter, my business, my health, my father's death occurring so quickly after losing Mike, and the fact that I wanted to invite companionship into my life for the right reasons, not as some half-baked and vain attempt to fill the extremely large void in my life that Mike had left behind. Plus, the simple fact is that *no one* knows me and my personality as well as I do and I knew that I would need at least one year of recovery time. In reality, my first date was about a year and a half after Mike's death—this is the particular timing that worked for me, thereby making it the "appropriate" timing to resume dating.

However, even after all these years and after becoming an expert in the field of loss recovery, I would *still* never deign to tell anyone when it is "appropriate" to begin dating after the loss of a spouse. Now, does that mean that I applaud the widow who has gotten herself embroiled in a relationship within a few short weeks after her husband's death? No, but not for the reasons that you may think. It has nothing to do with the whole "What will people say/think" mindset with which so many of us seem to be burdened, and everything to do with the healing journey that every widow must take and the processes that she may be trying to avoid by re-involving herself too soon.

So now that we know that there is no such thing as a carved-in-stone "appropriate" time to begin dating again, what *does* happen if you *don't* choose to wait "a year or five years" until you resume dating?

NOTHING!

You do not lose your birthday, your credit cards do not get cancelled, the Boogie Man does not come swooping down upon you, and the earth will not open up and swallow you whole. The only thing that happens by going against your own best judgment and waiting that one year or five years or however long you wait is that you have chosen to postpone that which your heart is telling you it's all right to do. Now you have effectively kissed years of your life goodbye and those are years that you cannot get back.

Furthermore, how exactly are "people" who are telling you to wait for "x" amount of years going to be directly affected by your decision to date again or not? They will not be affected whatsoever. They are not impacted by your dating decisions in any way. No one is driving home after work thinking, "I wonder if that Susie is dating again? How dare she!" The fact is that our lives are important to us and most people are not spending a great deal of time wondering what we're doing.

If your decision to resume dating is ultimately greeted by raised eyebrows, unsolicited opinions, or anything other than encouragement and support, then it's time to find some other people to get yourself around, preferably compassionate, supportive Energy Givers!

I honestly believe that the late, great Ricky Nelson said it best when he said, "You can't please everyone, so you've got to please yourself."

It's A "Wrap"...Stiletto-Style!

Well? Have you guessed it yet? Did you catch the lesson-thread running through the entire chapter and the one common denominator that virtually every answer contains, whether direct or implied?

The undercurrent that ran through this chapter and was at the basis of every single answer to virtually every single question is: Your journey belongs to no one but YOU and whatever you think is "appropriate" for you IS APPROPRIATE!

As long as you are fulfilling your duties as a parent and your obligations as an employee (if applicable), and you are not coping in a destructive manner, *you* are the one who gets to decide what is and is not appropriate as you continue along on your healing journey. Sometimes we all need to be reminded of the little voice inside of each one of us—and with many widows, sometimes that voice goes on vacation, particularly if there are enough people around us trying to drown out that little voice.

Once again, this is about you taking charge of your journey and having the courage of whatever convictions you may have. Whether it is deciding if you should keep your husband's favorite chair or deciding that this is the week that you are going to go on your very first date, the decision is *yours*—and that automatically makes it appropriate.

chapter four

FINANCES, LEGALITY, AND "WORKING" YOUR WAY THROUGH

THE FINANCIAL TRANSITIONS AND VARIOUS LEGALITIES SURROUNDING widowhood are possibly the least popular subjects on which I teach, often boring and rife with the potential for complications. Besides, who likes to deal with all that paperwork? Believe me, I don't like teaching it any more than you like learning about it.

However, (and ironically), these lessons are also the most important aspects of widowhood as a smooth financial and legal transition contributes directly not only to your eventual financial security, but to your mental and emotional security as well.

Also contained in this very important chapter are questions and answers concerning a return to the workplace. Whether you are returning after a bereavement leave of absence or you are making a return to the workplace after being away for an extended period of time, you will have many questions concerning the how's and when's of your reentry into the world of "nine-to-five with an hour for lunch," an assortment of which you will likely find answered right here.

Sadly, I also receive a great many letters having to do with breakdowns within families that all come back to one potentially painful and ugly subject—the division of money and property. As uncomfortable as this subject can be, it also cannot be ignored, as the disintegration of families over money is a far-too-common occurrence among thousands of families. Once a loss has occurred, many behave as though it is a free-for-all feeding frenzy, or what I call the "What's In It For Me?" Syndrome. It's disgusting, it's reprehensible, and it continues to happen way too often.

It is time to tackle one of the most difficult, uncomfortable, and incredibly vital subjects that you will encounter along your widowhood journey. Take notes and remember that if you need to consult an expert in any one or all of the following areas, do so *immediately*!

Getting It Together and Keeping It That Way

"Do you have a checklist of what I need to do to take care of everything that needs to be handled after my husband's death?"

"I'm so scattered right now and if that's not bad enough, everyone [banks, accountants, credit card companies] want something different, they want something that I don't have or can't find, or they just want something else. Help!"

"I wish all this legal stuff could wait, but I know that it can't. But I don't want to deal with it now. If I had some idea where to start or how to put everything in order, it would help so much."

"My husband always took care of all of the financial stuff and now he's not here to ask. I know there are all kinds of changes I have to make but I don't even know where to start."

These are indeed among the most common requests that I receive. My first book, *Widows Wear Stilettos*, contains checklists, organizational suggestions, and lists of recommended items to have on hand to keep you organized as you take care of the financial and practical affairs associated with your husband's death and transitioning your assets accordingly.

Nothing of a financial nature is going to happen without issuance of your husband's death certificate. Your funeral or hospice director can and should be taking care of this for you. The time parameters within which death certificates are issued differ literally from county to county in every state. Keep yourself organized and be sure to follow up accordingly. If you're told that it takes thirty days to obtain death certificates and you haven't received them within the allotted time, call the responsible person on the thirty-first day.

"Where does one find financial assistance and help with children?"

Various government programs are available in all fifty of the United States, as well as in other countries. The best place to start in the United States is with the Social Security Administration who can guide you to the agency (or agencies) that will be relevant to the aid that you seek. You can also go to your city and state's websites or the front pages of your telephone book, which contain a comprehensive list of all governmental agencies at the city, county, state, and federal levels. Depending on the state in which you reside, financial assistance for you and/or for your children may be found at any one or several levels of government.

> *"Do you know if it's normal for Social Security to give you the runaround after the passing of a child's father? We are going through that now since the baby's father was ill for several years [before his recent death]. He was turned down three times for disability from Social Security and now they're delaying [survivor benefits] and saying [that], 'There are complications.'"*

Your husband's disability and seeking Social Security disability benefits prior to his death have nothing whatsoever to do with your husband's subsequent death and your filing for survivor benefits, both for yourself and on behalf of your children. These are two separate and distinct issues. If Social Security is "delaying due to complications," they need to come forth and list specifically what those alleged complications are, so that if you are in a position to help resolve those issues, you can do so. They also need to advise you of the time parameters within which they anticipate these complications to be resolved. Whatever the situation, it doesn't just get to go on and on with no resolution in sight. Furthermore, you may also be entitled to the Social Security one-time lump-sum death benefit and if you do qualify, this benefit should be immediately forthcoming.

If you feel that you have been unfairly denied benefits, Social Security has their own appeals process. Review their appeals process prior to retaining counsel to ensure that you even need a lawyer. Consult your telephone book or search online for "Legal Aid" or "Lawyers Referral Services" and get referrals to attorneys that specialize in Social Security law. Many attorneys will hold an initial consultation with you free of charge.

> *"My husband died [earlier this year] and we were married for fifty years. When he died, I lost all of his military retirement pay. Is there any group of military widows that are fighting to change this situation?"*

The military can be a tricky road to navigate. Sadly, and too often, survivors simply accept the word "no" at face value without gathering all of the facts and more importantly, without fighting back.

Contact Legal Aid, your local Lawyer Referral Service, the Internet, or the telephone book and consult with an attorney who specializes in this area of the law. Find out what rights you have as the survivor of a military retiree. Next, go on to the Internet and do some research to find out if there are any organizations ("grassroots" or otherwise) that are working to change the policies concerning surviving spouses. A great place to start is with the American Widow Project. If they don't have the answer, they will be able to direct you accordingly. Another excellent resource and advocate for widows and widowers of military personnel are the Paralyzed Veterans of America, who can help you determine to what benefits you may be entitled and will do so absolutely free of charge. Contact information for these groups is listed in the back of this book.

And *always* write to your congressperson and your senator—that's why we put them into office! Bring this situation to their attention; jump up and down and make some noise. Remember, you are not the only person in this situation and yours is a plight that can and should attract significant attention.

> *"[Our] father was only sixty years old when he passed. Now that he is gone, concerns are turning to our mother, who through all of this has maintained strength for all of us. Dad was getting a Veterans Administration check every month, which is what they existed on. Is there any financial assistance available to our mother until she can get on her feet?"*

You don't mention if Mom is still receiving benefits. Regardless, she still needs to see what benefits are available to her through the Veterans Administration. She also needs to visit the Social Security Administration as soon as possible to apply for survivor benefits. These benefits will be determined based on her present income and other factors. She may also be entitled to the one-time death benefit payout. Granted, it is a nominal amount; however, as I'm fond of saying, it all spends. Instructions on how to contact both the Social Security Administration and the Department of Veterans Affairs are listed in the back of this book.

> *"[I am in] a terrible situation because of [my husband's] death [regarding] medical insurance. Since we owned our own business, we had coverage through that, but COBRA [the Consolidated Omnibus Budget Reconciliation Act of 1985, which is the right to continuation of insurance benefits after employment has terminated] has long since passed. I took on private insurance, but [the premium] increases got so huge that it was impossible to keep. If something were to happen to me, I do not know what I would do. How do you manage?"*

I manage just like everyone else in the United States has to manage. I pay an exorbitant premium every single month (which irritates me to no end) and as is also the case with everyone else, that premium has been steadily increasing yearly.

That said, as we all know, being without medical insurance of any kind is akin to playing Russian roulette with your health and your financial well-being. It really takes only one illness to wipe you out financially, which actually happened to us after my husband's death—and we *had* medical insurance. Do your research and check out as many different plans as possible and in your research, find out what kind of state assistance is offered where you live. Somewhere, someone has a plan that they can tailor to your needs. For example, if you are in good general health, you may opt for an insurance plan that has a higher deductible. You may also wish to consult with an insurance broker, who can do a lot of this legwork for you and present the best possible option(s) to you.

> *"My husband died [from] a massive heart attack. We had no insurance and I still owe the hospital [tens of thousands of dollars]. I heard that [according to my state's law] I do not have to pay the rest of this bill because it is in his name. Is this correct?"*

If the bills do not have your name on them, you may not necessarily be liable for the debt incurred. However, as with all other financial and legal matters, laws as to financial liability (or liabilities) after spousal death differ greatly from state to state as well as from country to country. You will need to consult with an attorney who specializes in estate matters in order to determine your responsibility (if any) for these bills.

> *"My recently widowed friend discovered that her husband had taken out a second [trust deed on the house] and [also] had several hundred thousand dollars in credit card debt that she did not know about. Is she liable for any part of this debt [since it was incurred without her knowledge]?"*

As previously stated, laws as to financial liabilities vary widely and your friend should consult with an attorney who specializes in estate matters. However, if the credit cards did not have her name on them, she may not necessarily be liable for the debt incurred. As to the second trust deed, the same question applies: Was the loan also in her name or in her husband's name alone? Depending on the laws where you live, a loan cannot be secured in the name of someone who doesn't sign the appropriate documents. Again, an attorney specializing in estate and/or real estate matters would be able to shed more light on this and should be consulted promptly.

EVERYONE IS AN "EXPERT"—NOT!

> *"Since my husband's death, I have many people giving me all kinds of financial advice. I want to let things go for awhile to just try and adjust to my situation without worrying about all of the financial stuff but people won't leave me alone about the money that I've received and what I should be doing with it."*
>
> *"My husband had a life insurance policy through his [employer]. Since I [received] the money, my parents keep telling me that I*

> *need to give it to them to invest for me because they think I'm too young to know what to do. I haven't given [the money] to them yet and I don't know if I should."*

Isn't it funny how everyone on the planet becomes a "financial expert" when it comes to *your* money? As tempting as it sounds, while you should not act impulsively or hastily when it comes to finances, "letting things go" is not necessarily helpful either. If the greatest fear is the fear of the unknown, then the largest source of stress comes from and is caused by indecision.

As parents, we do sometimes tend to imagine ourselves to be experts on absolutely every subject from the American Stock Exchange to the Zero Cost Collar and everything in between. Now, add in that as parents, there is no worse pain than seeing your child suffering in any way. Throw in the fact that as parents, we also want to rush in and "fix everything" for our children, no matter their age or life experience. Then factor in that right now, you are exhausted, grieving, and likely not thinking clearly. Add it all up and in this case, you could have a recipe for catastrophe.

The reality is that simply because we are parents, we are not automatically or necessarily financial authorities. Once in a while, we *don't* "always know best." More importantly, if you are old enough to get married, have children, build a life with someone, and then go through the horrendous life experience of widowhood, then you are also old enough to take command of your financial well-being.

Regardless of the amount of money or assets with which you have been left, you *must* consult with your accountant (or whomever does your taxes) and a *certified* financial planner or advisor. Please do not take this vitally important advice from your parents or your best buddy or Uncle Fred or Mutual Funds 'R Us or from anyone who fancies themselves a financial whiz. You will need actual experts who can help you determine what is best going to benefit you both in regard to your taxes as well as your future financial security.

> *"My husband died in an accident. He had planned ahead with life*
> *insurance and he has left a large sum of money in death benefits.*
> *You really seem like you know how to manage yourself. Can you*
> *help me? I am really confused and afraid."*

I humbly thank you for the compliment. However, the reason that I "know how to manage" myself as you so kindly put it is because I *always* make it a point to surround myself with the best people that I can find. For example, I've written books and articles and recorded a CD; I've coached hundreds of wonderful women like you on grief and loss recovery; and I have the privilege of speaking all over the country and appearing in the media. All of that is wonderful, but behind the scenes, I have an entire team of experts with whom I constantly consult, from whom I learn and without whom I would be totally lost. I have a brilliant literary agent and agency behind me; editors and a publisher who work their collective tails off; and top-notch media coaches and mentors, because my expertise does not lie in those areas.

Similarly, for all matters financial and legal, I have a fabulous accountant, a super attorney, and a trustworthy *certified* financial planner. You need to find the same kind of experts that can help you wisely plan for the present and for the future, regardless of the sum of money involved. As stated earlier, now is not the time to take advice from *anyone* other than those who specialize in the very complex area(s) of financial planning.

> *"My husband recently passed away. He left money to our children*
> *through a life insurance policy, but since they are [minors], the*
> *insurance company is not releasing the money. How do I go about*
> *getting help?"*

Depending upon where you live, if your children are under legal age, they generally cannot receive benefits directly, but the benefits can be held in a trust for them by a trustee, who is usually the parent. If you are experiencing any difficulty with an insurance company, you should consult your state's insurance commissioner, who will be able to assist you. Alternatively, you might consider consulting an attorney who specializes in this area of the law. You'll also want to make sure that you have any paperwork that the insurance company will need, such as your husband's death certificate, your marriage certificate, the children's birth certificates, all Social Security numbers (including yours), and banking information.

What Can Wait—and What Cannot

> *"I am so overwhelmed right now. It seems like everything [finan-cial/legal] has to be done at the same time and I don't even know where to begin."*

> *"How long can I wait before acting on my husband's will?"*

> *"Is there any harm in waiting to sell [our house, my husband's car, etc.]?"*

The financial transitioning and decision making is certainly one of the most daunting and overwhelming parts of the healing journey. I'm about to make it just a little bit easier:

CAROLE'S
"WHAT ABSOLUTELY CANNOT WAIT" LIST

Every attempt should be made to complete the following within the first thirty to sixty days after your spouse's death:

1. Anything that has to do with the generation of immediate income to your household (once death certificates have been received). This includes filing for any governmental benefits to which you may be entitled (i.e., Social Security, Veterans Administration, etc.); life insurance benefits; survivor's pensions or adjustments to an existing pension and continuity of medical insurance benefits (if applicable).

2. Appropriate disposition and disbursement of assets and items as set forth in a will. If the will must first go through a probate process, steps should be taken to begin that process with your attorney.

3. Enacting of all credit life insurance policies held on credit cards, mortgages, automobile loans, etc. You don't want to "overpay" on anything where insurance proceeds should be applied instead.

CAROLE'S
"WHAT CAN WAIT FOR A WHILE" LIST

Everything else!

While it certainly feels like everything needs to be done at the same time, what actually matters immediately is that you are able to continue taking care of yourself, your children, and your household. As soon as you are in receipt of the death certificate and other pertinent paperwork, you need to act as quickly as possible in assuring that bills can continue to be paid in a timely fashion and that bequests set forth in a will are promptly handled (as long as the latter does not create any undue hardship to you). The last thing that you need to be worried about is how the mortgage is going to get paid next month so the sooner you accomplish these things, the more richly deserved peace of mind you'll have.

Other than that, absolutely everything else can wait for a bit. If you can financially manage your home and your husband's car, there is absolutely no rush to dispose of either. In fact, unless you feel otherwise, there are no rules anywhere that say that you *ever* have to get rid of your home or your husband's car, if that's not what you want to do.

> *"People say 'Don't make any big changes for a year,' but the 'big changes' have already been rolling out. [The amount of money that I have] could get frittered away on maintaining [an unaffordable situation] for a year or I could use it to expedite a change. My ability to navigate this is really questionable, but if I wait a year, the money will be spent on [a home which is] not affordable for me."*

Speaking generally, I'm one of those "one year people" as well. I believe that major decisions (sale of property or any other major financial decisions) are best left until you are in a place of more sound emotional stability. I cannot even count the number of letters from women who sold their homes immediately after their husbands' death because it was too difficult to stay and then lived to regret that decision both financially and emotionally. Decisions such as these can impact your financial security for the rest of your life.

However, if you are in a financial situation where absent a second income, maintaining your home or any other assets would pose financial difficulty or peril, I believe that any waiting period or time frame is superseded; your fiscal well-being and security is paramount. Before making any decisions, you will of course want to consult with appropriate experts in the real estate market where you live, as well as with your accountant and financial advisor.

RETURNING TO WORK (AFTER THE FUNERAL/"BEREAVEMENT LEAVE")

> *"I am going back to work tomorrow after two weeks off [after my husband's death and funeral]. I know that I have to get back to my normal life but I am scared of losing my cool. Nobody will understand what I am going through."*
>
> *"I have to go back to work as I have used up all of my time off that I had coming to me. How am I supposed to go back to work and be 'professional' when I feel like part of me died along with my husband?"*

The return to a "normal life" takes time, certainly longer than the usual corporate-mandated three days or two weeks or whatever time off you were permitted to take. While you must physically return to work, your return to a "normal life" doesn't happen all of a sudden simply because you went back to work on Monday morning.

Your coworkers and superiors will likely understand that you will not be your usual dynamic self. Do the best you can as this calls for taking your time with you. If you need help with projects, if you're not working up to par quite yet, or if you're having difficulty concentrating, ask for help. I'll bet that your coworkers would be all too happy to pitch in and help you out.

Even though you have made the return to work, remember that you still need to be patient with yourself. Chances are excellent that you will be surrounded by a great deal of compassion and support.

> *"I took time off [after the funeral] and have gone back to work.*
> *Everyone keeps looking at me with pity and I feel like they tiptoe*
> *around me and feel sorry for me. It makes me very uncomfortable,*
> *like I'm not the same person anymore."*

You must remember that as a society, we do not know how to deal with death and moreover, society isn't really interested in learning how to deal with it either. People don't know how to act around you because they are uncomfortable and afraid—afraid of saying the wrong thing, afraid of doing the wrong thing, afraid that you'll spontaneously combust; the list goes on and on.

To their credit, they are looking at you with pity because they feel terrible for you. They don't want to make demands on you because they don't know exactly how much you are capable of handling right now. It's perfectly OK to welcome their sympathy because you deserve it. However, if you feel like they are "tiptoeing" around you, as unfair as this may be, it is going to be up to you to put them at ease.

Ask these nervous coworkers out for lunch or to coffee and don't be afraid to talk about your late husband. You don't have to go into great details or disclose your deepest emotions, but you can certainly talk about the experience of the loss. Go ahead and talk about other things too: what's going on in the office, in the world, the latest celebrity gossip. Show them that you *are* still you.

Above all else, remember that honesty is still the best policy. If you're having a rough time, it's OK to say so. If people seem uncomfortable, look them in the eye, smile, and say, "I can tell you're worried about me, but I'm hanging in there. Thank you for being so worried about me," because at the heart of it, these people really do care.

> *"I try to go about my normal workday, but there are times when*
> *I feel the emotions [of the loss] creeping up during the workday. I*
> *know it's not professional but I don't know how to stop it."*

This is a very common problem among widows who have to return to the workplace after the bereavement period is over. Even though the "leave" is over, the bereavement certainly has not ended; in fact, it's likely just begun.

At the time of Mike's death, I was self-employed, meaning that while I didn't have a specific bereavement period set by an employer or company, any entrepreneur knows that if you're not working, you're also not making any money (in other words, and contrary to popular myth, no, you do not get to "take off" as long as you wish).

I am a big believer in "compartmentalizing" grief, which is a part of returning to the necessities of life (work being chief among those necessities); while at the same time, allowing yourself time, space, and permission to continue the mourning process. So many widows think that once they return to work that somehow the grief process ends with the first day back. Nothing could be further from the truth.

In the first weeks and months following Mike's death, I used to make a daily "deal" with myself. I'd tell myself, "You can't feel bad right now because you have to …," and that blank would be filled in with whatever work or other activities were taking place at that moment in time. However, I also made a deal with myself that I got to feel totally lousy at a certain time that night and I kept that "appointment" with myself. By compartmentalizing my life and my grief into distinct time frames, I was able to accomplish the tasks at hand—knowing that the time would come later on that was reserved just for me and the tumult of emotions with which I was dealing.

Does learning how to compartmentalize happen overnight? Absolutely not. Does it mean that you will never feel bad in the course of your day? Of course not. Yet, the knowledge that you have set time aside for the very necessary purpose of grieving, mourning, and missing your late husband will make the necessity of getting through your workday much easier.

People are always asking me how it is possible to be happy and positive after everything I've been through, which remember, is the identical experience to yours. It's directly attributable to having given myself permission every single day to take the time to feel just as bad as I wanted, and by doing that, I was able to eventually heal and move forward.

Setting time aside for yourself on a daily basis, even if it's only a few minutes, will throughout the day allow you to tell yourself, "I'm not feeling good this minute, but I'm going to put this aside until later and then I can feel however I want." And as crazy as this may sound, you will actually start to look forward to that time spent alone with your grief because you have created time for and allowed yourself the freedom to grieve.

"I think about working a [full day] and it just makes me tired to think about it."

Let's ask some honest questions. Does it make you tired to think about returning to work because you aren't getting proper rest right now? Maybe it's because you are completely overwhelmed with the tasks involved during and after the loss of a spouse, which is certainly reasonable. Or are you simply afraid of going back and being around your work colleagues? Maybe it is a combination of all three, plus a few that I haven't listed.

Determine why it is that you are tired at the thought of going back to working a full day, whatever that full day entails. Next, sit down with your immediate supervisor and see what alternatives might be available to you. Many employers are only too happy to work with you as you ease back into a daily work routine. Perhaps you can telecommute from home (which is becoming more and more popular with the advent and advancement of our computer technology) or possibly return to work on a part-time or "reduced-hours" basis.

Don't be afraid to bring up this situation and how you are feeling to your employer. Hopefully you will be met with compassion, understanding, and a possible "game plan" as to how you might return to your professional life in a manner that will benefit all concerned.

RETURNING TO WORK (AFTER EXTENDED ABSENCE FROM THE WORKPLACE)

"It's been three months [since my husband's death] and because of finances, I have to try to reenter the workforce after being 'out' for [over twenty years]. Where do I start?"

"[My husband] was the major contributor to our finances and my wages were [a fraction] of our total income. Is there some sort of program that I can do to get myself retrained?"

"I am so scared. I haven't worked since I started having children [I have three] and there [have] been a lot of changes in technology. I'm not a computer whiz and I'm afraid I can't compete."

Returning to work after an extended absence lasting anywhere from several months to many years can indeed be an intimidating prospect. Competition in the workplace has increased; many salaries and/or benefits have decreased and technologically, it is indeed a "whole new world."

Begin by sitting down and making a list of any and all skills that you possess. Leave out nothing. Thanks to the fact that the majority of the population has at-home computers, many, if not most of us have rudimentary typing skills at the very least, which is a great start. If you need to improve your typing skills, there are at-home courses and software to go with your at-home computer to help you do just that. You also want to consider your occupation prior to leaving the workplace. Is it something to which you might want to return? If so, will your current experience or education still suffice or will there be "boning up" to do?

If you have never been in the workplace, do not despair—there is plenty of assistance available for you. Start by checking with your local Employment Development Department or the state agency that administers unemployment benefits, state disability benefits, and so forth. These agencies have all sorts of job resources, job availability notices, vocational training, and career counseling to help you reenter the workforce.

Don't forget to check out your local community colleges, which are not only fantastic places to either learn new skills or improve your existing skills, but they have job resources and vocational training opportunities as well. Every learning institution also has a career center of some kind. You can also obtain training, degrees, and certifications for many different careers at online schools, private trade or technical schools, many of which offer financial assistance as well as job placement assistance once you have completed your education.[3]

Please do not let your lack of technological ability discourage you or otherwise become a deterrent in your return to the workplace or pursuit of a new career. Anyone who knows me will happily (and laughingly) tell you that my technological prowess consists mostly of operating liquid eyeliner. In other words, *you can do it*!

> *"How do I handle it when someone who is interviewing me asks why I've been away from the workplace for so long? Is it proper to tell them that I'm coming back because I'm widowed?"*

One of the most common mistakes made in an interview situation by just about everyone is over-disclosure. I always encourage honesty, i.e., "I chose to stay at home and raise a family" or "I worked out of my home." However, you need only answer what is asked of you. No interviewer is going to come out directly and ask any questions concerning your marital status, as it is illegal to ask such a question. You are not required to disclose your marital status in the course of an interview and you are certainly not required or otherwise obligated in any way to disclose the fact that you are returning to the workplace as a widow (or any details associated with that fact).

---

3 A word of caution: While there are many excellent online, trade, and technical schools, there are also the "fly-by-nights" out there who will take thousands of dollars from you in exchange for a degree that isn't worth the paper on which it's printed. Do your research carefully and thoroughly by checking for accreditation or certification with government agencies, as well as with the Better Business Bureau.

After you land the job, your marital status will undoubtedly come up in conversation because your new work colleagues will want to get to know you, not to mention the fact that you will be disclosing your marital status on tax forms and paperwork associated with company benefits. Here again, however, you are not obligated to go into great details concerning your widowhood, and as a new employee, you will want to be very careful about how much personal information to share and with whom you share it.

> *"I went out and got a job. I don't know if this is too early or if it will be good for me to be out of the house all day. What do you think?"*

I think it's a wonderful idea and I applaud your making this very brave move forward on your healing journey. I can't imagine why it *wouldn't* be good for you to be "out of the house all day," since a change of scenery—even for a few hours a day—can do wonders for your widow-tude, your outlook, and your confidence level. You are going to meet new people, gain new experiences, and begin broadening your horizons. I think that you are a fabulous example to widows everywhere and I'm proud of you.

MONEY, THE FAMILY TREE, AND THE BREAKING BRANCHES

> *"My biggest problem is my in-laws [because] they don't give me respect as their son's widow. The day my husband died, his mom asked me for his [vehicle]. [A few days] later, she asked me to give her a line of credit against my house (which I didn't do). Before my husband died they weren't very interested in our lives but since he passed, they act like they care so much."*

It's a sad fact that when a death occurs, sometimes families splinter. They can go a little "squirrely." And when it comes to matters of money or property, it can get downright divisive. I've never understood this, but it does happen nonetheless. Furthermore, I do not at all understand any family member unilaterally deciding that they are entitled to any property or monetary gains or lines of credit under any circumstances, particularly when there is a widow and/or children involved.

Lack of moral decency or integrity notwithstanding, and regardless of familial relationship to your husband, *no one* has any business coming in and appropriating anything. Even if your husband had all of those items outlined in a will to be divided at a later time, unless it is stated otherwise, *you* are the one in charge and *you* are the one who disburses property to the appropriate parties as either set forth in a will or to whomever you feel should receive the property.

It is clearly taking advantage of you to behave in the manner that your in-laws have behaved, especially at a time of such vulnerability; and if you need the assistance of an attorney to reclaim what is or should be rightfully yours, by all means, retain an attorney.

"When I married my husband, my stepdaughter decided she wanted to live with us on a permanent basis. I opened my heart and my home to her, and felt that we got along well even though I stepped into her life [during] her teenage years. My husband also had an adult son [and when] his son was married, once again I welcomed him and his new bride into my heart. [They have] two children whom I considered to be my grandchildren and who[m] I adore. My husband then passed away and I guess what really surprises me is that all [the children] want is money. Should I just move forward with my life and put this in the past?"

"[My late husband] had three grown children and they were not happy that [my husband] divorced their mother [many years ago] and later married [me]. The real problem is that the will left everything to me. [It was written several years prior to my husband's illness] and was not written under duress. I am [now] being blamed. [The children] feel that they have the right to come into our home and take whatever they want. I have repeatedly

told them that there are many things that I am willing to give to them. I don't feel I am being unreasonable in my offers of items that belong to their father; however, I am unwilling to open the front door and let them [take whatever they want]. One of the [children] continually asks how much money I got and what my financial situation is. As far as I am concerned and under these circumstances, my financial situation is none of [their] business. I would like to know what to say or how to approach this sticky situation without alienating them further."

We've already learned and it is a pathetically sad fact that at the time of a death, many families go completely sideways. It is indeed a pitiful situation and you can now see just how common these situations are.

Let's start with the financial aspects. Whether the circumstances are pleasant or not is of absolutely no consequence. The bottom line is that your financial situation is none of anyone's business. Period. As long as your husband did not make a provision in a will that you are somehow shielding (and I'm confident that this is most certainly not the case), you owe no one any explanations or accountings as to your financial state of affairs.

As to actual items of value (either real or sentimental), it is your decision to disburse among the children as you decide. For example, items such as photographs in which they appear that involve their father prior to your coming into his life; their school photos that their father may have had; mementos of when their father and mother were married, etc., can and should go to them. And guess what? When *you* decide to start going through things, then and only then will they receive anything. You are not obligated to "open your front door" to anyone! This is an extremely personal part of the healing journey and one that you (and all widows out there) have every right to keep to yourself.

I also want you to remember that these are *adults* (at least chronologically) with whom you are dealing. "Alienating them further" is not an issue, because they are already alienated, a choice that *they* made. Whether or not you start handing over property or writing checks, they are not going to become a loving, supportive part of your life. You will not win any popularity contests with such people.

I do understand that this may sound very cold and it's a desperately difficult concept to embrace. Nevertheless, you have been through quite enough without having people like this causing you additional pain.

> *"I was twenty-three years old with a [young child] when my husband passed away. Right away, my in-laws started making the arrangements for the funeral. When they found out that I was entitled to insurance, they got really greedy. Ever since my husband's passing, all I hear about is money. When I try to tell people what my in-laws did to me, they tell me to let them be, that they're just grieving. What about me and my grief?"*

I know that when you're a very young widow, it can be difficult to stand up to relatives and in-laws and friends (well-meaning or otherwise), but you're going to have to do it. You will need to find your voice, take charge (regardless of how young or old you are), and let everyone know in no uncertain terms that *you* are the boss. You are an adult, the widow of your husband, and the mother of your child. Your in-laws are not in charge unless *you* give the control to them. If things start or continue to take an ugly turn, don't try to handle this situation by yourself. Enlist the advice of an attorney who specializes in estate matters to help you.

WHAT'S THE (LEGAL) DEAL?

> *"Six months [after my husband's death], my in-laws changed [my husband's] tombstone, removing any mention of me. I am moving [out of state] and would like to disinter my husband and move him [as well]. What are my rights?"*

I would first take issue with the cemetery or mortuary for allowing such a change without notifying you. As to your rights to move and/or transport remains (especially out of state), this is a highly sensitive matter and one that requires the input and/or assistance of an attorney who specializes in estate matters. Don't forget to mention the change of tombstone without your knowledge or consent and be prepared to give the attorney the name, address, and telephone number of the cemetery or mortuary that allowed this situation to take place.

> *"[An in-law] cremated and buried my husband while I was out of town [for another family bereavement]. What can I do about what [the in-law] did to me and my [children]?"*

I'm very unclear as to your in-law's rights to do what they did. However, in addition to your in-law and as stated above, I would also definitely take issue with the cemetery or mortuary for allowing a cremation to take place without notifying you at the very least. Start by asking what proof was requested by the cemetery or mortuary demonstrating that the in-law had any authority whatsoever to grant permission for cremation, or make decisions on behalf of your late husband. As to your rights, this too is a highly sensitive matter and one that requires the input and/or assistance of an attorney specializing in estate matters. Remember to mention the cremation without your knowledge or consent because you were out of town and as stated earlier, be sure to have the name, address, and telephone number of the cemetery or mortuary at the ready for your attorney.

I know that practical matters can be both overwhelming and time consuming but you cannot wait on this. You need to know exactly what your rights are and what legal recourses are available to you. Should you decide to proceed with a lawsuit, there are strict time limitations as to when you can do so, and when that time has lapsed, it has lapsed. There is no such thing as "do overs" or "Oh, I forgot" when it comes to the law, not even for bereavement reasons.

Regardless of what the law(s) are where you live, these sorts of actions are absolutely unconscionable and you have every right to be angry, disgusted, and hurt.

> *"I have never seen a situation like mine. I'm actually in a fight*
> *for money with my husband's mistress. She says that he told her he*
> *wanted her to have [a certain sum of money] and that she has the*
> *same right to it that I do. I don't think she has any rights at all and*
> *think that any money should go to me and to our children. Have*
> *you ever heard of this happening and what should I do?"*

Have I heard of this happening? Sadly, yes I have. As you have already learned, I have received quite a few letters that are similar in nature, where the tragedy of losing one's husband is compounded by the emotional tumult of betrayal.

Let's take just a moment and remove the obvious emotionally disturbing upheaval out of the situation and look at this from a strictly legal point of view. Is there any written provision *anywhere* for this woman (such as in a will or a life insurance policy)? If not, she is going to have a very difficult time making any claims on your husband's estate and that's just from a legal standpoint. If there is nothing in writing anywhere and she still attempts to make a claim, imagine her having to face you in a legal setting, be it before a judge or an arbitrator, in order to see this claim to fruition. I doubt seriously that she would triumph in such a setting.

What she is doing is not unlike what so many attempt to do—take advantage of a woman who has just lost her husband and is in a state of shock, exhaustion, and vulnerability. She is counting on being able to (a) upset you with the revelation that a mistress exists, and (b) either intimidate you into giving her money to which she believes she is entitled or bank on your shock, exhaustion, and vulnerability in the hopes that you will give her money to make her "go away."

Obviously, if she produces legitimate written proof that financial provision was made for her, you will need to speak with an attorney in order to determine if her claims are legally justifiable or if you can or should contest the claim(s). Regardless of what kind of proof does or does not exist, if this woman is aggressive, if she is harassing you and your family, or if she continues to try to make claims that cannot be substantiated, you must enlist the assistance of an attorney and if necessary, local law enforcement authorities.

"My husband was killed [in an automobile accident] and we have a [young child]. I feel like I am being rushed to address [the accident] and the money and other things that I am just not ready to deal with right now. Am I being selfish for not wanting to do this right now? What should I do? How do I handle this?"

I know that finances and legalities are the very last things that you want to be thinking about right now. Nonetheless, and as addressed earlier, finances and legalities are two of the few things that you do need to address as soon as possible. As you have now learned, just about everything else in the world can wait but I do recommend that anything that has to do with the generation of income and security to the widowed household be accomplished as soon as possible.

If you have not already done so, you need to file claims with Social Security, both as a widow and on behalf of your child. You may be entitled to collecting two sums per month—one addressed to you and one on behalf of your child. The sums of money will be based on several factors, including your own income and any other income such as survivor's pension, etc. Please do not wait on this. You may also want to consult with an attorney specializing in personal injury and wrongful death to seek damages against the other parties involved. Again, there are very strict time limits as to filing personal injury claims and those time limits depend on where you live.

I know that all of this is undoubtedly making your head spin and believe me, I understand. As you know, I lost Mike right before Christmas; however, on December twenty-sixth, I was on the phone setting things in motion. It doesn't all have to be done in one day but it does have to be done, and when it comes to filing claims or potential lawsuits of *any* kind, there is always a "ticking clock" of sorts.

The only things you need to concentrate on right now are:

1. Filing the claims with Social Security on behalf of you and your child; and

2. Consulting with an attorney regarding the accident situation surrounding your husband's death.

That's it. That's all you have to worry about right this minute. If people come around asking about wills and so forth (that's the "What's in It for Me" crowd referred to earlier), you do *not* have to worry about that right now.

TAKING CARE OF BUSINESS—YOUR OWN

> *"My husband didn't have any life insurance when he died and it was a real struggle to make ends meet. I don't want my children to have to go through the same thing when I die but I can't afford a big fancy life insurance [policy]. How can I protect my kids so they don't have to ever worry?"*

We too were left in a horrible financial challenge because of a lack of adequate preparedness on our part. I learned from that error and have since seen to it that my family is well protected. Moreover, it has become sort of a "second mission" of mine to make sure that all widows everywhere are educated as to how to best protect their loved ones.

One of the biggest myths out there is that a "big fancy insurance policy" costs hundreds and hundreds of dollars and is financially prohibitive. We tend to get the word "insurance" stuck in our heads and automatically equate the cost of life insurance to that of automobile insurance, homeowner insurance, and medical insurance. The surprising fact is that life insurance is the least expensive kind of insurance to carry and the one type of insurance that *everyone* is going to need at some point in time.

Sacrificing a trip to your favorite fast-food hangout or coffee house five times a *month* can easily pay for a substantial life insurance policy, so that your family will never have to struggle in the ways that we did and that you have. Remember too that the younger you are, the less expensive life insurance will be for you.

Think about this: We have automobile insurance because we *might* have a car accident. We carry homeowners insurance because something *might* happen to our house or the property inside. Yet the one thing that is a *sure* thing—the fact that the time will come when we will no longer be here—is the one thing for which we choose to forego protection. Have you seen commercials or heard people talk about life insurance in terms of, "being prepared for the 'unexpected'"? At what point did death become "unexpected"? While the date may be unexpected, the *eventuality* of death is not. Instead of thinking about "being prepared for the unexpected," we need to instead think about "being prepared for the *inevitable*."

Start by consulting with the insurance company with whom you insure your automobile, and/or your house. Your agent will analyze your living situation and lifestyle and help you determine exactly how much coverage you need. In other words, an unmarried twenty-seven-year-old who rents an apartment and has no dependents does not require the same kind of coverage as the single mother with children who already are or will be going to college.

Get more than one quote and be absolutely *sure* that you are dealing with a reputable, well-established company. You don't want to pay premiums to a shady organization that either doesn't promptly pay out to your loved ones or may not even be in business when the time comes to make a claim. If you have any doubts about the company that is trying to get your business, you can always check them out with your state's Department of Insurance and the Better Business Bureau.

You have already experienced what can happen when you are not adequately prepared financially prior to a loss. Don't do the same thing to the people you love. Learn from your previous experience, be smart, and be *prepared*!

> *"What happens if you die and you don't have a will? My husband had one, but I don't have one. I'm wondering if I really need to worry about it."*

If you die without having executed a valid will, you will have died intestate. This means that the state in which you live decides how your assets and property will be divided and disbursed. Do you really want the state to make those determinations? I doubt it. What if your husband had died without having a will in place—think about what might have happened to you and the assets that you and he shared. You might have had no say in how those assets were divided.

Obviously, no one likes to discuss wills, because that involves planning for...well, not being here anymore and that's an uncomfortable and unpleasant thought. However, I feel that it is downright irresponsible not to have at least a basic will in place, so that you are the one who decides who gets what and when. Wills don't have to be long, complicated affairs and depending on where you live, even a handwritten will may be sufficient (check the laws of the state in which you reside). There are also simple "form" wills available at office supply stores as well as many websites that give free guidance.

One more thing—keep absolutely *everything* in one place: your will, insurance polices, and a typewritten sheet of instructions. I have all important papers, account numbers, telephone numbers, bank and insurance company names in one place and at least two people know where that information is kept. There is nothing worse than having to go on a scavenger hunt for important papers, or worse yet, knowing that somewhere a policy or account exists and you don't know where to find it.

Don't force people who are in mourning to play "hide and seek." Keep everything together and be sure to update the information when and if it's needed.

> *"Everything [credit cards, bank accounts] was in my husband's name. Now that he's gone, even though the bank accounts got switched over [to my name], I have no credit."*

"I'm thirty-seven years old and very embarrassed. I feel stupid for not having credit and things in my own name. I don't know what to do or even where to start and I can't imagine what people are going to think."

First of all, please don't be embarrassed or ashamed. Although it doesn't happen as often in this day and age as it did in our mothers' and grandmothers' respective eras, there are those women who do not have their own financial means, credit cards, or bank accounts. There is no shame to be had in that but it is also now time for you to establish your financial independence and standing.

If you held a credit card jointly with your husband, contact that creditor and request that the account be switched into your name alone. They may ask for proof of your husband's death and in most cases, a photocopy of the death certificate will be sufficient. Depending on the company (as company policies do vary), the card will either be reissued in your name alone or the account will be closed and reopened in your name solely with any remaining balances transferred to the new account.

Next, go down to the local bank branch where you do your regular banking and see what kind of credit card offers they might have for you. Explain your situation and that you are looking to establish credit in your own name. If your bank cannot accommodate you (because many banks do require a credit history), go online and investigate credit card companies that specialize in helping people establish credit for the first time.

Once you are granted a credit card, you will likely be started out with a small line of credit (anywhere from two hundred dollars to a thousand dollars), so that the bank or company can see how you handle credit. Use the card and pay it off every month for at least six months. Once they see that you handle credit responsibly, they may give you a credit increase. To establish a well-rounded credit history, I suggest starting out with one major credit card (considered worldwide to be Visa, MasterCard, American Express, and Discover); one department store credit card; and one gasoline credit card.

Once you have established a good credit history, you will be able to secure loans for things such as cars, homes, education, and so forth.

While you should absolutely not be ashamed or "feel stupid" that you don't have anything in your name, you now understand just how important it is to have control over your own finances. Establish and protect your credit history and if you should remarry, *always* keep at least one credit card and one bank account in your name *alone*.

It's A "Wrap"...Stiletto-Style!

Whew! I know that was a lot of information to absorb but there is little that is more important in this book than your financial well-being in all respects. Please also be reminded: Don't forget to get help if you need it (much of which is free, and *all* of which is crucial).

One last thing: There was once a time when the man of the house took care of everything, a time when most women not only had no idea where the checkbook was, but they weren't even allowed to have accounts in their own names. The same held true for credit cards and any other sort of financial holdings or assets.

That time period was the early 1960s, the 1950s, and all eras prior. Welcome to the Twenty-First Century.

Times indeed have changed folks. No longer can you afford to be blissfully unaware. This is about being responsible. Widows are perfect "poster children" for the slogan, "Be Prepared" and if you are not prepared, you had better get that way *fast*. Go back over the tips on how to organize your own financial situation(s) so that your loved ones will not have to be in a position of uncertainty or worse, a financial or legal fight. They deserve the same peace of mind that you do—make sure that you provide it to them.

chapter five

THE QUESTIONS, QUANDARIES, DOS, DON'TS, AND DUMBFOUNDING OF DATING

WOULD IT SURPRISE YOU TO LEARN THAT I SPEND JUST AS MUCH TIME talking about dating and love post-loss as I do talking about actual loss?

It surely did surprise me.

It wasn't even just the volume of letters that I have received (and continue to receive) from widows of all ages on the subject of dating; from the media to the "woman on the street," virtually everyone wants to know how we widows deal with every single aspect of, as one journalist delicately said to me, "the dating thing."

Answer: Any way we want to. But let's back up for a few minutes.

There is no question that dating is a lightning-rod subject with widows everywhere, fraught with anxiety that you yourself may have experienced. Why?

1) First, there can be an inordinate amount of pressure put on the widow when it comes to dating. You may be goaded into dating before you are ready to do so or conversely, you may be expected

to be a bereaved widow forever, relegated to wearing an imaginary black veil and never even thinking about dating again as long as you live (the latter expectation generally originating from children and other relatives).

2) Next, there are the emotions that you are no doubt trying to reconcile concerning the dating processes—feelings that range from guilt to doubt to fear and everything in between (and we're going to work on all of those things right now).

3) There are also and quite naturally the normal everyday questions surrounding dating that every single unattached gal out there has, i.e., when, where, and how do you meet quality people and of course all of the "Why isn't he…" questions ("Why isn't he calling me / answering my texts / answering my emails / professing eternal love" and so on).

Before we go any further, let me first congratulate you for even reading this part of the book. If you're reading this chapter, it means that on some level, you are at least ready to entertain the possibility of dating again. That's a huge step forward in your recovery and unfortunately, not enough people recognize this as one of the "big moments" that it is. You need to be very proud of yourself, if only for simply reading this chapter.

While you're patting yourself on the back, I know that there are zillions of questions racing about in your mind and I would be willing to bet that you'll find most (if not all) of those questions right here. So sit back, grab the Ben & Jerry's, and take your first steps back into Dating Land.

How Do You Know When You're Ready to Date?

"It's been five years since my husband died. I'm really tired of being alone but I'm not sure if I'm ready to be going out on dates. How did you know when you were ready [to date again]?"

"I would love to start dating again but it scares me and I simply have no idea how to do it. [We] were married for [many] happy years so it's been a long time since I've done anything like that. I took a first step last month and went [on a vacation] on my own and loved it. I think I'm ready for the 'big plunge' back into dating."

"It's been eleven months for me [since the death of my husband] and the idea of dating has some appeal, yet the actual event scares me to death."

"I took a chance recently and attempted to connect for a few lunches with a male friend I've known a while. His aggressiveness put me back in the cave. I guess I'm not ready yet."

"Part of me hates [being] alone, but the other part is scared to try dating again."

How can you tell if or when you're ready to date again? I'm so glad you asked!

Welcome to:

Carole's "Surefire No-Doubt-About-It Ways To Tell That You're Ready To Date Again" List

(Well, as "surefire" as one can be anyway!)
Review the following carefully, several times if necessary:

You Have Reclaimed You

Immediately following your husband's death, at the height of grief or during what may very well be the worst time in your life is not the time to jump headlong back into dating. It is most certainly not the time to introduce a new person into your life and into your heart. Prior to the resumption of dating, you must first recover from the death of your husband and as you know, you cannot accomplish that in "hurry-up" fashion. You must take the time and patience with you to both sufficiently recover from the trauma that you have experienced and begin to get to know yourself.

You Realize That You Are "Not Guilty"!

When you have been functioning in life as one-half of a couple, you become "conditioned" to thinking of yourself in those terms. All of sudden, you are no longer one-half of "Mr. and Mrs. The-Two-Of-You," yet your emotional being is still in the "one-half of a couple" mindset. When you find yourself attracted to someone or you make a decision to resume dating, you may feel guilty, as if you are "cheating" on your late spouse or your children or his family or your country or all of the above! While guilt is a perfectly normal emotion to encounter during the healing process, it can nonetheless hold you back from the resumption of dating.

Realizing and accepting that there is no reason to feel guilty about dating or seeking companionship is a necessary step toward the knowledge that you are ready to reenter the world of dating.

The Absence of Anger

It is absolutely normal to feel angry at whatever circumstances took your husband from you; after all, you're a good person and you did not deserve this. Sadly, however, many choose to stay "in the angry" or "in the bitter" to the point that they are unable to move forward with their lives. These same people may take this anger out on their children, their friends, their work colleagues and yes, prospective dates as well.

The resolution of your anger is an important step toward readying yourself for dating again. When you have made peace with the circumstances that took your husband's life and you have begun to move forward from that loss into your new life, you are truly ready to begin exploring the world of dating again.

The Ability to Leave the "Ghost of Husband Past" in the Past

We tend to have "selective amnesia" when it comes to our late husbands, remembering only the good—the good times that we had with them and the good memories that we'll have always. That's fine, but don't hold up your husband's memory as a "yardstick" against which you are measuring prospective dates. They will not be able to compete. It's unfair to start sentences with, "Joe always used to...." or "Sam would have never...", because absolutely nobody "always" did this or "never" did that. Everyone deserves to be judged on their own merits and should not be compared to anyone in your past. By all means, honor, keep, and treasure the wonderful memories that you have; however, you need to be able to put the Ghost of Husband Past in its proper place in order to enjoy someone new.

Are You Happy Being on Your Own?

Are you content within yourself on your own, without the necessity of the presence of another person? Being happy by yourself means a contentment to be in your home by yourself (with or without children) and having a life that is your own and is fulfilling in its own right. Do you have your own career, your own hobbies, your own pursuits, your own set of friends with whom you play sports, dine, or hang out? When you are content with yourself and by yourself, you are genuinely ready to begin the dating process again, because you are not simply "filling the void" that your last partner left behind. You are instead opening your heart and your mind to the possibility of a new relationship.

Can You Go Out Alone and Have Fun?

The "companion" element to being happy on your own is the ability to go out alone and enjoy yourself. Have you been out for a meal by yourself? How about a movie or a comedy club? As a society, we are accustomed to either traveling in packs or with a spouse/significant other. However, you must be happy and content with your own company, both within your four walls as well as in the "outside world." This contentment will enable you to make wise decisions in your dating choices and when you do meet that "someone special," it will be for all of the right reasons.

Are You "Emotionally Available"?

Your emotional availability will have everything to do with (a) the amount of time that you have spent recovering from the death of your husband, and (b) your willingness to make yourself emotionally available. Years ago, I once dated a man who had not recovered from a break up in high school—thirty years earlier! This gentleman made a conscious decision not to make himself emotionally available to anyone else because of one prior bad experience that took place decades earlier.

Examine yourself carefully and ask yourself if you are truly ready for the dating experience. Are you are capable of making yourself emotionally available to another? If you don't feel quite ready yet, back up and take more time for you, it's OK (but please don't take thirty years).

Are You Allowing "Analysis Paralysis" to Stop You?
There are several factors that may be capable of holding you back from the resumption of dating. Otherwise known as "Analysis Paralysis," these factors may include fear—the fear of experiencing another loss, the fear of intimacy and vulnerability, or the fear of being hurt again. It could be the "last ten pounds" that you think you need to lose (funny how it's always ten pounds). Once you have isolated, identified, addressed, and moved forward from whatever it is that you feel might be preventing you from dating again, you will then be able to jump enthusiastically into the dating world in a positive way.

(P.S. No one cares about the "last ten pounds"!)

When You're Ready, You Really Will Know!
I have a wonderful analogy that I've used since I was a teenager. The whole process of reentering the dating world after any kind of loss—be it death, divorce, or breakup—is like "testing" a bruise to see if it still hurts. Have you ever had a really terrible bruise? What's the first thing that you do? You're always pushing on it, aren't you? Sometimes it looks like the bruise is all cleared up, yet when you push on the spot, it still hurts.

By the same token, there is a "bruise" of sorts on your heart as you recover from the loss of your husband. As with a physical bruise, push on that spot in your heart periodically. If it's still too painful, quit pushing, and don't let anyone else push either! Just like with a bruise, eventually, that tender spot in your heart does heal, and so will you. As with everything else on your healing journey, you will know when the time is right if you listen to and trust in yourself.

What if You're "Supposed" to be Ready to Date and You're Not?

"[My husband died several months ago]. My family seems to think that my late husband would be okay with me 'moving on' and meeting other men. I do not want to meet other men romantically right now."

"I am moving forward [in the dating process], I do see that, but I also see [that] I have a long way to go."

"So many people say 'Oh, you're so young, you'll remarry,' that I should start dating and 'move on.' I know I'm young, but I'm just not ready yet."

"It's been a year and I should feel fine, but I still feel so lonely."

"I'm so sick of people trying to fix me up on blind dates because they think it's time for me to be dating. One of my work friends even threatened to put my picture on [a well-known online dating site]. Sometimes I think, 'Why can't people just leave me alone?' and other times I think that something is wrong with me. It's only been nine months [since the death], which doesn't feel like very long. So is there something wrong with me?"

It's lovely that people are able to know what your late husband would want for you; however, this is not about what your late husband would want or what anyone else wants for that matter. It's about what *you* want to do with *your* life, the emphasis here is on *you* and *your*, since we sometimes tend to lose sight of exactly whose life it is.

Moreover, I certainly don't blame any one of you for being sick of people who clearly choose not to listen to you when you tell them that you are not ready to begin dating again. Reread the "bruise" analogy; if you don't feel ready to begin dating again, it simply means that it's not time yet! You may need a little (or a lot) more time, which is perfectly okay. Whatever the case, always, *always* listen to that little voice inside of you; it will never steer you wrong. If something doesn't feel right to you, it's not right. Don't force yourself to resume dating based upon other people's opinions of what you "should" be doing at any point on your healing journey and *please* don't feel guilty for not wanting to plan a future with someone when you are still recovering from your immediate past.

You say that after a year, you "should" feel fine. We learned in Chapter Three (What's Appropriate or "Is It OK To...") that the only "should" with which you need be concerned is that you *should* be listening to that little voice inside of you. That's it. There is no statute of limitations on grief.

While I would be very concerned if it were five or ten years after your husband's death and you were still in the first throes of grief (and I do work with women who have that issue), let me switch up your thinking a little bit. Instead of thinking that, "It's been a year, I 'should' be fine by now," how about, "It's *only* been a year and I'm going to give myself a break. Look how far I've come!"

P.S. Anyone who is threatening to put a profile of you on any online dating site without your direct knowledge, consent, and compliance is not only completely insensitive and morally out of line, there could be legal ramifications involved. Mention the words, "invasion of privacy," "identity theft," "potential criminal trespass," or "lawsuit" and I'll wager that you won't have issues with that person again.

"I'm 'Cheating' on My Husband" (Part 1)

> *"I went out with friends last Saturday. I had a good time, but I still had the feeling that I was cheating on my husband."*

> *"I was [fixed up with a friend of a mutual friend]. I knew I was not ready [and] I was honest with this [man]. He tried so hard to please me [but I felt that] I was cheating on my husband. That hit me hard."*

"A very attractive man recently asked me out and I went out with him. It was great to feel 'alive' again, but it was a bit strange, like the feeling of, 'Is this okay? Am I cheating?'"

Are you "cheating" because you went out on a date? Absolutely positively not! You are *not* cheating!

Regardless of our widely varied religious denominations or the specific words used in our respective wedding ceremonies, the phrase that we need to remember is something to the effect of, "Till death do us part." Both you and your husband upheld that vow. Therefore, dating after a spousal death should not and cannot *ever* be construed as cheating.

Your husband is no longer here and while that is a tragedy, you are also entitled to move forward with your life. My constant reminder to widows everywhere is that YOU'RE STILL HERE; a phrase that you have read numerous times at this point. Your being here gives you one very basic and important entitlement—the right to a life filled with abundance, and as you know, this abundance includes companionship if you so choose.

Many people do not realize or recognize the heart's infinite capacity to love. Consequently, becoming involved with another on any level has *nothing* to do with the love that you have for your late husband. That love was then, is now, and will always be a part of you and this is a fact that will never change. The lesson here is that loving another does not in *any way* diminish or dishonor the love that you have for your late husband.

You are continuing forward with your life, a life that can and should include companionship and love if you choose it. The fact that you feel ready to begin dating again is actually a cause for congratulations. You have come a very long way on your healing journey and to be able to open your heart and your mind to the possibilities of companionship and new love is a wonderful accomplishment. You need to recognize and be proud of yourself for that.

"My husband and I were happy for [many] years [until his long-term illness]. I got to hold him and tell him I loved [him while he was] on his deathbed. I met a man [shortly after the death] and started a relationship [and] people say it was too soon. [Now] my husband's family doesn't want anything to do with me because they say [that] if I loved him, I would not [have] met another man so soon [after the death]. I [now] feel like I am cheating on my husband, and I loved him so much."

The things people say and judgments they can cast are truly two of my favorite subjects. Believe it or not, there will come a day when you will laugh about the absolute insensitivity of people; it's just amazing, isn't it? Trust me when I tell you, I've truly heard it all.

The bottom line here is that *no one* has a clue as to what you've been through and what you're currently going through, making them ill-equipped to tell you anything. More importantly, and I repeat this constantly, this is *your* healing journey. *You* are in charge. *You* are the boss. No one else gets to tell you when or how to be "over it" or when to resume dating or in general, how to lead your life, and it *is* your life.

Let's get something straight immediately and I repeat: You were *not* and you are *not* cheating on your husband and, frankly, it doesn't matter if you started seeing someone the day after he died. You were a loving and caring wife for a great many years. How many can say that these days? Furthermore, has anyone (in his family or otherwise) bothered to acknowledge your role as a loving, long-term caregiver during his illness and the wonderful wife you were for your entire adult life? Likely, the answer is no. People are generally quicker to criticize than to commend, a sad fact, but a fact nonetheless. You have my sincere admiration.

Is shortly after a spouse's death a little soon to resume dating or enter into a relationship? Yes it is, but not because of the reasons you outlined and despite what you may believe or what other people think. It's a bit soon because you need time to recover from the experience that was the death of your spouse.

You need to get to know this wonderful woman called "You." You need and are entitled to time on your own.

Please hear my heart on this—as I said earlier, it has *nothing* to do with the love that you have for your late husband, which you must realize will never end. You are going forward into a new life. My only concern and what I would ask any widow who entered into a relationship very soon after the death of a spouse is, are you inviting another into your life for the *right* reasons, rather than to fill a void (which, by the way, is a completely normal reaction)?

Whatever the case, we need to rid you of the guilt and the toxic input of people who have no business judging you. You have *nothing* to feel guilty about. Let's quit starting sentences with "People say…" and, instead, begin your sentences (and your thought processes) with, "I have done the very best that I can under some horribly challenging circumstances. I am stronger than most people on the planet. I have the peace of knowing that I am a woman of character, strength, and integrity." How about that!

Who's Going to Want Me Now?

> *"It's almost impossible to get a date once people hear that you're a widow."*
>
> *"Sometimes I think it would have been easier if I was divorced instead of widowed. At least that way, people wouldn't look at me funny."*

When it comes to returning to the dating arena, I won't argue the point that in some cases, being divorced might be easier than being widowed. Though it's a sad point to make, the reality is that divorce has become commonplace and simply does not carry the same stigma that it did in years past. Add in the fact that though there are millions of us out there, a widow is sometimes viewed as anything from someone to be pitied and coddled, to someone that should be avoided at all costs (after all, we may well be contagious).

I too have been the victim of men who are less than, shall we say, *enlightened* when it came to the discovery of my widowed status. I've had men lean away from me and a man even *physically backed away from me* when I told him that I was a widow. That hurts a lot and I know that it can discourage you from even wanting to try to date again. However, I have to once again remind you that when it comes to your widowhood, it's a minority of men who behave like idiots or insensitive dolts or treat you like you are the Ghost of Christmas Yet to Come. Many more men out there will look at you with admiration for having had a marriage that lasted forever (because remember: it did) and for being the woman of strength that you are.

> *"Should I even be thinking of dating again? I feel like 'damaged goods.'"*

"Damaged goods"? *Seriously?* You're not a dented can of tomatoes that got dropped in the pasta sauce section of the grocery store so let's get rid of *that* widow-tude right now. You're a woman who has endured one of the greatest trials of her life. How on *earth* does that qualify you or any other widow as "damaged"? If you are looking for a couple of analogies, how about "strong as an oak tree" or "tough as nails"? Try *those* comparisons on for size.

Why does it seem so difficult to meet men as a widow? That's an easy question to answer. Regardless of age, we have far more life experience than most and we are not willing to simply settle for just anyone. We have lived a life that has included burying a spouse. We have grieved and recovered. We have had challenges and we have had to rebuild our lives. Many of us have raised children on our own. We have made mistakes and we have recovered from those mistakes. Most importantly, we have lived to tell the story. In other words, we're just not willing to compromise *who* we are and what we want at this point in our lives. I certainly didn't and there's nothing wrong with that.

There are plenty of wonderful men out there who are not going to use your marital status as a reason to avoid you, and remember, somewhere out there is one absolutely *awesome* man who is looking for you just as hard and as passionately as you are looking for him. Don't give up—he really is out there.

> *"The dating 'deal breaker' is [when dates] ask my marital status.*
> *When I [tell them that I am a] widow, they ask how my husband*
> *died. If I tell the truth, they ask how and why. [They then ask to*
> *hear] the 'gory details,' ending any chances of me having a good*
> *time. If I don't [give details], it only makes them more curious. If*
> *I ever do date again, what do I say [to dates]?"*

This is the double whammy with which many widows have to deal—the circumstances surrounding a husband's death, compounded by the apparent insensitivity of the people who insist on details.

In my substantial dating experience since my husband's death and without exception, *everyone* has inquired as to the circumstances surrounding my husband's death. I would tell them that he had Lou Gehrig's Disease (because not many people are familiar with the term "ALS") and the usual response was, "I'm so sorry." I then said, "Thank you," and that's it. I moved on. I would not go into any further details until or unless a friendship was to have ensued. Why? Because I am neither compelled nor obligated to reveal that much of myself that early in the dating process, and besides, the "details" are nobody's business. The few times that I was pressed for details, such as "How old was he when he died?" or "How long was he sick?" I would very politely decline to answer, saying something like, "I'd rather talk about the present than the past," and then turn the conversation right back over to my date. It worked every time.

Paraphrasing the iconic Abigail "Dear Abby" Van Buren, my mother long ago taught me that, "Just because someone asks a question does not mean that you have to answer it." These are exceptionally wise words. Consequently, you are not obligated to provide any particulars surrounding your husband's death until the time comes that you feel ready to do so. If someone continues to push you for details or makes you feel in any way uncomfortable, please feel free to say, "I choose not to discuss the details," and then seriously reconsider ever going out with them again. If your deferring creates "curiosity," then that is *their* problem. It is *not* your obligation to satisfy anyone's morbid (and rude) curiosity; rather, it is your companion's responsibility to get a clue, get some sensitivity, and move on from the subject. This is not appropriate first date conversation.

Foremost, I don't want to see you give up on dating or seeking companionship. Giving up won't ever get you what you seek and what you deserve and what you deserve is someone who is kind, sensitive, and worthy of you.

P.S. Just so you won't feel entirely alone, I actually had one guy years ago ask me, "Were you still able to have sex with him [my late husband] when he was sick?" Suffice it to say, I did not go out with him again.

How Do You Meet People?

> *"Since my husband's death, I have been dating, going out for coffee, etc. I had one relationship with a man for a year, who lied to me and cheated on me. Are there any decent men out there, where do you find them, and do you think that it is possible to find love again?"*

We have all been cheated on, lied to, taken advantage of, and otherwise treated shabbily and unfairly by those who lack integrity, honesty, character, scruples, moral decency, gainful employment, or good hygiene. Should we learn from our past experiences in order to avoid repeating history? Definitely. Should we take our past out on our future? Absolutely not. To make the unilateral decision that, *"all* men lie and *all* men cheat" unfairly condemns an entire species because of the actions of a few.

Do you believe that most people are inherently good, decent, loyal, loving and are looking for someone exactly like you just as ardently as you are looking for them? As hard as it may be and while you shouldn't trust in a blindly haphazard fashion, you must nonetheless have the ability to trust the new person or people whom you introduce into your life, rather than judge them on the misdeeds and wrongdoings of the last person in your life. Although I'm sorry to hear that you met someone who didn't turn out to be such a winner in the character and integrity department, I'm pleased to hear that you are dating and open to the possibility of a relationship. Many encounter difficulty with being this open, especially after an experience such as yours.

After my husband's death, I too was involved in a long-term relationship with a man. On the surface, he appeared to be everything for which I had been searching—"surface" being the operative word. For numerous reasons, things did not turn out as well as one hopes when beginning a relationship. Since ending the relationship many years ago and prior to meeting and subsequently committing to the man with whom I am in love, I have dated an interesting assortment—men who became good friends, as well as some who could only be coined as charter members of the Liar and Loser Brigade. However, I refused to let the past relationship that didn't work or those members of the Liar and Loser Brigade dictate my future actions or determine my destiny or destroy my belief in the goodness and decency of people in general and men specifically.

By continuing to believe in the inherent good in people, reminding myself that someone out there was searching for me just as hard I was searching for him, and by refusing to give up (even though I was tempted several times to do so), I was subsequently blessed with a man who is truly a dream come true. So I absolutely and obviously believe that there are wonderful men out there and that we cannot and must not judge all men by the few idiots who may cross our paths.

I stubbornly and resolutely believe in love. While the love that I have for Mike will never die and that love will now and forever occupy a precious corner of my heart that will always be his alone, I do also live by example the message that I teach: I'm still *here*, I'm *alive*, and I'm *entitled* to live the life that I now live, a life with love in it. So then, dear friend, are you.

Where to meet men? They're all over the place! They're at work, they're at the gym, they're at church or synagogue, and they definitely turn up when and where you're not looking...my beloved certainly did. Also, don't eliminate online dating as a possibility; as you read on, you will learn that there are many advantages to using reputable online dating services to meet eligible men.

Do you remember when you first began dating as a teenager? Dating didn't just become challenging—it's *always* been that way. It's just that at this point in our lives and after what we have been through, we have a lot less patience for all of the garbage. Don't let Mr. Liar-Cheater-Loser-Man decide your destiny for you; he is simply *not* worth it.

By the way, have you stopped to look at how far you've come since you were widowed? Look at what you have overcome to get to this point in your life. You need to celebrate your wanting and willingness to get "out and amongst 'em." You *know* that there is a wonderful life out there and it's great that you want to be a part of it. *Don't give up!*

> *"When it comes to meeting men, what do I do? I do not go to church, so that is out [and I] hate bars! My friends are all associated with work and [there's] no one there. I tried online [dating which] is how I met the man [who hurt me], so that is clearly out for me. I am just so lonely and so tired of trying. I know in my heart [that my husband] would want me to go on with my life, but how?"*

You're giving up because of one man? Really? *One* man hurt you and behaved like a jackass and so you're throwing in the towel? Sorry, Girlfriend, not acceptable. I first want you to go back and reread the previous question and answer section and hopefully that will help you with a change of heart. If that doesn't help, and to also reassure you that I understand too well how you feel, read on for one of many stories from:

CAROLE'S DATING DISASTER DIARY
(OR, "TALES FROM THE GYPPED")

I once had a date with a gentleman whom I had met through a well-known and widely advertised online dating website. Since I was always honest in my online profile, I foolishly assumed that everyone else would be honest as well and that this person's information and photograph were accurate. I took my time, exchanged a number of emails with him and two weeks later, we had a pleasant telephone conversation. He asked me to dinner and I agreed to meet him at a restaurant later that week.

Literally beginning the following morning, I was sorry that I had ever said yes to a date with this guy. During our conversation the evening before, I had made a comment about often working late into the night and he apparently thought it would be hilarious to call me up at *7:00 a.m.* the next morning. When I let him know in no uncertain terms that I did not find this at all funny (having had only three hours sleep as I had been up most of the previous night with my sick daughter), he said that he would call me later, which he did—*hourly*. Why wasn't I available to take his calls? Because, in addition to staying up all night with the sick child, I was also undergoing an MRI examination at the hospital that same day.

As Saturday night neared, I was feeling more and more apprehensive about this person. Not especially relishing the thought of wasting time, energy, and makeup to go on a date with him, but feeling like I had to do the "right thing," I decided to keep the date and showed up at the restaurant where he was waiting for me outside. I immediately knew that I had made a tremendous error in judgment. He bore very little resemblance to the picture he had posted online (although he may have resembled the picture at one time twenty-five or thirty years ago), and although I consider myself an affectionate person, the manner in which he tried to greet me can only be described as far too space-invasive and extremely inappropriate for a first-time meeting.

The evening passed unbearably slowly, with him sitting way too closely, trying to feed me his dessert (a little smarmy for a first date), and continually berating me for not returning any of the hourly telephone calls. When I finally told him that I had been undergoing an MRI (of the brain no less), his reply was—wait for it—

"Oh."

Not "Oh, is everything OK?" or "Oh, I'm so sorry" or "Oh, I can't believe I woke you up at an ungodly hour and thereafter pursued you in a manner befitting garden-variety stalkers who drive windowless vans." Just "Oh."

As the end of the evening drew to its merciful close after almost three hours of this torture, I discovered that he'd saved his very best "bomb-shell" for last. He told me that he had "told a little story" on his profile (which is code for "I outright lied") and informed me that his age was not in the early-fifties range as previously stated, but was in fact dangerously teetering on the cusp of *seventy*. This revelation was followed by a list of excuses for the lies, such as, "I don't like women in my age group; they don't get pedicures."

Yep. That's right. Lack of pedicures was his deal breaker. I am not kidding.

I was *livid*. Lying is not only totally unacceptable, but if someone is lying about something as silly as their age, what *else* are they lying about? I can absolutely guarantee you that if someone is lying about their age, there are more lies awaiting you just around the corner.

He then asked me when he could call me again and when I calmly replied, "Never," he was baffled. I told him that I didn't date liars, to which he replied, "But I didn't lie!"

Um...what?

I returned home mumbling and grumbling and blaming my late husband yet *again* for another horrendous date and *this* one was the last straw. I announced to Kendall that I was never going to utilize online dating ever again, along with the popular, "All men are jerks, jackasses, idiots, liars, mouth-breathing bottom-feeders..." diatribe that I hear from so many of you.

The poor girl listened to this nonsensical tirade for about a half-hour before she said, "If you quit trying to meet someone, if you quit dating, and if you blame all online dating on this guy, he's won. Why should you spend the rest of your life alone because of this guy or because of a few losers?"

You can't argue with solid logic. So, as they say, I went "back to the drawing board."

I wish I could tell you that my "Dating Disaster Diary" and "Tales from the Gypped" ended with this now-hilarious story. Unfortunately, it doesn't end there. After this nightmare date, a full year and a half passed before I met my beloved and in the interim, there were certainly a few more dating disasters. But the important thing is that thanks to some very wise words from a very astute young lady, *I didn't give up!*

I know that it's discouraging and disheartening when you get dropped on your head, lied to, disappointed, cheated on, or treated in a fashion other than what all of you deserve and you all deserve to be treated like royalty. However, giving up on dating gets you nowhere. Giving up means that you have resigned yourself to a life that you *did not choose.* Giving up means that you are letting other people (losers) or circumstances beyond your control (death) decide your destiny, which is completely unacceptable. Instead of giving up, get *back* up! You did it after you lost your husband and you can do it again now.

> *"I have been widowed for five years. Lately I am feeling bored with my friends and our activities. I like to dress nice[ly], wear makeup, and do 'girlie' things. I would also like a male companion for friendship. How can I get out of the rut I am in of 'same old same old' situation?"*

What a great widow-tude. It's wonderful that you still "turn it out" by dressing well, wearing makeup, etc., and, combined with your active life, it means that you are fully embracing your return to life after the loss of your precious husband. It is also wonderful that you have a circle of friends with whom to participate in activities. Why do you think you're bored with your friends? Are *they* the ones in a rut from which they don't want to break free? Have you tried suggesting new or different activities to them and been met with resistance? Try suggesting things like a new restaurant; a "mystery" dinner or weekend; hosting a "Girls Night In," complete with specialty drinks (which don't necessarily have to be alcoholic), fun and easy appetizers, and perhaps a video or two. Or get a theatre group together and go see a play (something like, *Menopause, The Musical,* which is uproarious fun) and then out to dinner afterwards. How about a Sunday champagne brunch? There's so much out there to explore.

As far as male companionship goes, and as you can see, I continually coach that you do actually have to *leave the house* to meet people. You have to be willing to make the effort. Read on to learn how to do just that.

AND *WHERE* DO YOU MEET PEOPLE?

> *"My second husband died so this is my 'second time around' [as a widow]. I am again at the point where I am ready to begin dating but where do you look for dates?"*

> *"My husband died very suddenly and needless to say it was shocking for me and my young [children]. I have devoted myself to them, as they are my life, and yet at the same time I feel that I would like to start dating again. Where would be the best place to start looking again? Are there any websites that you could guide me to where I might find men who themselves were widowed?"*

> *"I signed up for two online dating services and put in my description [that] I am looking for a 'real relationship.' I received no responses."*

*"I'm interested in trying online dating, but it scares me a little bit.
Have you tried it and what do you think of it?"*

I am so glad that you feel ready to begin dating again. As you have read, many in our situation feel that they are either cheating on their late husbands or have an, "I 'caught my limit,' it's all over for me now" widow-tude and are somehow not entitled to companionship or love once again. Nothing could be further from the truth and I'm happy to see that you realize that fact.

However, as you know, it is very difficult to find others in our particular situation. Rather than limit yourself to dating widowers only (which can also have its drawbacks), I would encourage you to keep an open mind and date men who are also single or divorced as well.

As you read earlier, men really *are* everywhere, and as you have also learned, online dating is a resource not to be discounted. There are many online dating websites that you can investigate and there are sites for literally every interest, religion, hobby, and preference that you can imagine.

One "Site" Does Not Fit All

In selecting a dating website, here are some tips that you will want to keep in mind:

1. Make sure that the site has a solid, dependable customer service department, one that you can reach both by telephone and email.

2. Review the sites' membership policies carefully, as well as what the membership costs include. Different sites charge for different features and there is a wide price variance between sites. Also keep in mind that some of the best dating sites do not have fancy advertisements on television or in magazines, advertising which is being paid for in part by your membership dollars. Do your homework carefully.

3. Make *absolutely sure* that the site's emailing communication methods are "double blind." In other words, all emailing with other members takes place *through the site* and protects all of your personal information.

4. Also make absolutely sure that the site has a one-click method of blocking communication from people with whom you don't wish to communicate.

If you've tried online dating and received few or no responses, it's time to revisit your profile to make sure that you are putting your best foot forward. Creating an online profile that attracts others is simple. Here are a few suggestions:

PROFILE PERFECTION

1. The first paragraph should contain a little bit about you: your interests, likes, what you are looking for in a person and in a relationship. Please note that *any* mention of finances (either what you earn or the earning potential you're looking for in a partner) is not appropriate in a profile. In fact, until you become a couple, financial discussions and disclosures are simply inappropriate.

2. Next, *gently* outline the things in which you are not interested. This helps cut down on hearing from people that you wouldn't consider dating, i.e., someone who only wants a casual relationship if you don't; someone who is too far away geographically for your preferences; someone who wants to have children if you don't want to and vice-versa, etc. For example, I do not like motorcycles at all and expressed that in my profile by saying, "If your idea of fun is jumping onto a motorcycle for a Sunday afternoon ride, I'll be waiting to meet you afterward for cocktails," which sounds much nicer and more inviting than, "I hate motorcycles, they scare the cootie out of me, I want nothing to do with them, and if you think you're going to get me onto the back of one, you need your head examined." My profile also stated that I "prefer sunsets to sunrises," which again, is much nicer than saying, "I hate mornings and talking to me before noon is tantamount to stepping into a hornets' nest." You get the general idea.

3. You must be honest in absolutely every single aspect of your profile—yes, *every* single aspect. That includes your age, height, body type, employment, and marital status. Many people think, "I'll tell a little white lie (or a great big huge lie) for now and when they meet me in person, it won't matter because I will have already dazzled them and won them over with my winsome personality and rapier wit." Sorry people, this is not acceptable behavior. Remember the lesson you just learned: Lying = Deal breaker. *It goes for girls too!*

4. Beware the "overshare." As women, especially when we're nervous, we tend to talk, sometimes too much. Too much talking can lead to too much sharing. Do not include your "widow details" in your profile (i.e., when or how you lost your husband; how much you miss being married, etc.); it will be seen as code for "Not Ready to be Dating." Virtually every site on which I've done research has a pre-fab area to indicate marital status. Indicate that you are a widow in this area only. No further explanations are necessary at that point.

5. The same holds true for any past dating fiascos, debacles, or your own Dating Diary Disasters and Tales from the Gypped. These can make for interesting and funny stories once you are on a date (and it's also fun to hear what the guys have been through), but you don't want to appear embittered in a profile. Upbeat and positive is the name of the game.

6. There is absolutely nothing wrong with looking for or wanting a "real relationship"; I did too. However, if that is exactly what you are saying in your profile (along with things like "marriage-minded" or "looking to settle down"), it can be interpreted as, "I'm going to be asking you how many children you want on our first date." As it is with stating your likes and dislikes in the profile, success is again going to be in how you present your dating preferences as well. I too was interested in only those who were looking for a potential relationship and expressed that as follows: "If you are a player, serial dater, 'big talker,'⁴ emotionally unavailable, 'scared' of the potential of a relationship, don't know what you want, or you are looking for a strictly 'intimate encounter' or 'cyber' situation, I respect your choices but we are not a match."

In this fashion, I was able to convey exactly what I was looking for, without leaving a potential date feeling as though he was going

---

4   Big Talker: Defined as someone who tells you that they are looking for a relationship in order to secure "booty call privileges" or otherwise falsely lure you into believing that they are looking for their "one and only."

to be held hostage at an engagement ring store after knowing him for only three days.

7. Realizing that we are a visual society, you *must* post a picture with your profile if you expect any responses (and I *never* responded to someone who did not have a picture posted or worse, someone who posted a picture but "blanked" or "pixeled out" his face). Post a recent picture; a photograph that has been taken within the last year is usually sufficient unless you've made a dramatic change to your appearance in *any* respect.

8. Be smart about the picture(s) that you are posting by asking yourself about the kind of message that you want to send. Many sites do not allow anything that they deem inappropriate (be aware that the standards and practices of appropriateness vary greatly among sites); however, it's still wise to remember that posting pictures that are too revealing send a message that is entirely wrong. Posting pictures that are fun, a little bit flirty, and show you off in a flattering way is great and you will receive sincere compliments. However, posting pictures of you in lingerie or pictures that are especially revealing or provocative will send messages that you do not want to be sending. Instead of sincere compliments, you will be receiving sincere propositions. Also included here would be taking pictures of yourself in the bathroom or bedroom mirror. All of us have at least one friend—hand them the camera, pose, and smile.

9. Don't post any group photos. It's frustrating to someone who doesn't know you to have to try and figure out which person is you.

10. *Under no circumstances should you ever include any identifying features in your profile.* This includes your full name, your work or home addresses (not even street names), phone numbers, personal email addresses, even the license plate number on your car. Keep yourself protected at all times by being smart.

Always remember that as with my previous Dating Diary Disaster story, you can do all of the right things, you can proceed in just the right way, and still wind up with a complete lemon. However, don't choose to be like our sweet friend who tried it once, got stuck with a lemon of her own, and wants to give up. Keep trying!

Dating has never been easy and it's not necessarily fun absolutely one hundred percent of the time, but if you remember that most people (yes, including men!) are good people and you don't give up, the next letter that you write to me might be about your wonderful dating success story. Now that's a letter that I can't wait to receive.

PROCEED WITH CAUTION

You're sitting at a bar in a restaurant waiting to be called for your table. A very good looking man comes up to you, shakes your hand, and says, "I know you don't know me, but let's get out of here, get in my car, and go someplace else." Would you go? What if the same gentleman said, "I'm on my way out right now, but could you just give me your full name, address, and telephone number so we can hook up later on?" Would you give that information to him?

These may sound like ridiculous scenarios, but you would be shocked at the number of women who would laugh at these scenarios yet readily give out their personal information over the Internet. Internet dating can be a lot of fun and who knows where it can take you. However, you absolutely must exercise good sense and prudence when it comes to Internet dating or any kind of dating come to that. The Internet tends to give people a feeling of security because of the "anonymity factor" and the fact that you are browsing while sitting in the comfort and safety of your home. However, you must remember that at the outset, you are initially communicating with strangers.

So above all else, let's keep you safe:

1. If someone's very first email to you is asking to meet you that same day or night, the answer is no. This is not up for negotiation. The first email is supposed to be an introduction and remember, you don't know them! If this is someone in whom you might be interested, let them know that you don't just meet up after an introductory email, but that you would like to get to know them better via email. If they aren't happy with this answer, you have just discovered the reason for the "Block This Member" button.

2. If someone is pushing you to reveal your personal information too quickly, it needs to be a huge warning sign to you. For example, I received emails more than once that essentially said, "I don't like to type so just give me your phone number." Guess what? It's the twenty-first century. Learn to use a keyboard. To my mind, it's too bad if someone doesn't like to type, but the answer was still and always no. I have never been so desperate for companionship that I would compromise my personal safety. If someone continues to pressure you, or gets aggressive in any way, they get blocked. Anyone who is truly "quality" will proceed at your comfort level and be happy to do so. I always proceeded in very gradual stages—I first communicated via website email, then moved to personal email, and then gave my phone number. This progression usually took about two to three weeks. Yes, it takes longer, but we're talking about safety here; is that something you want to rush or otherwise compromise?

3. When reading someone's profile, always be wary of phraseology such as, "Seeking discreet relationship" or "Looking for a special arrangement." Phrases such as these suggest that Super Slime is looking for "fun on the side" and in the case of the

latter statement, may also be looking for someone to foot his bills as well.

4. I REPEAT: Never ever include personal information in your profile or when emailing at the outset. No last names, telephone numbers, email addresses, street addresses, etc. Take your time to get to know someone very well before you start exchanging personal information.

5. ALWAYS meet for the first few times in a public place and keep your car and your cell phone with you at all times.

6. Have FUN! You've earned it!

"WHAT WILL 'THE WORLD' THINK?"

"I met a man [and] things have been really good. When this man came into my life, things changed. He's a wonderful human being who lets me cry on his shoulder when I need to. We talk about my husband without there being any resentment. But sometimes I feel guilty for going on and trying to have a life. I worry sometimes about what other people say. I think I just need reassurance that I'm not doing anything wrong."

"Everyone has something to say about the new man in my life and not all of it is good. They don't have a problem with him [but] they have a problem seeing me with someone else. My husband was a great guy, but he's not here anymore. Does that mean that I'm supposed to live the rest of my life alone?"

"I never thought I could fall in love with anyone after my husband, but I did. What shocks me is that no one seems very happy for me and all they want to talk about is my husband."

> *"I can't believe how many other people don't approve of my dating again [since my husband's death]. I waited [a long time] before I started going out again and everyone makes me feel like it's only been ten minutes [since the death]. And none of these people have ever lost their husband or wife. What right do they have to tell me what to do?"*

There is one word that I keep seeing over and over in these letters and hundreds more like them: "They."

We certainly are worried about the "they" in our lives, aren't we? Our minds are filled with worry and wonder over "they," what "they" will say, what "they" will think, how "they" will react, "they" will never accept anyone else, "they" don't approve…ENOUGH ALREADY!

I said it earlier and it definitely bears repeating: *No one* has any business or any right dictating to you how you should or should not be leading your life, least of all anyone who has not gone through the heartbreak of losing their spouse.

Our first friend asked for "reassurance" that she was not "doing anything wrong." Well, here it is and it comes from someone who has been there and has earned every right and authority in saying the following: YOU ARE DOING NOTHING WRONG!

Now as you well know, I don't advocate getting involved too soon after your husband's death. However, you'll also recall that this has nothing to do with it being "too soon" or "their" timetable. This is about *you*, the time that you need to recover and your general well-being. That said, it well and truly *does not matter* how long or how short of a time has passed since you lost your husband, even if it were only "ten minutes" as another one of our friends commented, and no, you are most certainly *not* supposed to "live the rest of your life alone."

Even though it has been many years since my husband's death, and despite the fact that it was one of his biggest worries and wishes that I find love again and continue to live my life, I am quite confident that there are people out there with whom I was or am currently acquainted that would not necessarily "approve" of my being in love again or the dating process that led up to being in love again. "They" would prefer to have me live the rest of my days as "The Widow Fleet," shrouded in black and bemoaning a life that came to an end many years ago. I also discovered long ago that living life according to an opinion poll will get you absolutely nowhere, except possibly living in a place called Miserableville.

People who are real and true *friends* (and that includes relatives) will want and pray for your healed heart and ultimate happiness. A *friend* in the true sense of the word will rejoice right along with you for moving forward into your new life. *Friends* realize that—here come those words again:

YOU CAN HONOR YOUR PAST.
YOU CAN TREASURE YOUR PAST.
YOU CAN LOVE YOUR PAST.
YOU DO NOT HAVE TO *LIVE* IN YOUR PAST.

And it might be up to you to help others in your social circle realize that fact.

However, if all "they" want to talk about is your late husband (and I've been there too), talk about him for a few minutes and then gently guide the conversation in another direction. If these are people that cannot or will not get behind your moving forward with life, or worst of all, feel that it is their place and their right to cast judgment or unsolicited opinion on your choice(s): FIND NEW FRIENDS!

By now, you have likely discovered that my three favorite words to constantly use in and with the widowed community have always been *"you're still here,"* because you *are* still here! There *is* a life out there and it is a good life—even a great life—and you have every right in the world to explore all that life has to offer you, including love and companionship. "They" can live their lives however they so desire, as can you.

The next time "they" offer an unwelcome opinion or judgment, look them straight in their collective eyes and ask, "What has your widowhood journey been like for *you?*" Trust me, it works.

"What Will the Children Think?"

> *"I'm contemplating dating but I don't want the complications of dating again and I don't want to worry about my [child] and what another man in my life might mean to her. But I am too young to think of never being in love again. Do you have any advice on dating and what that might mean for our [young children]?"*
>
> *"I still have children at home. I don't know if I should start dating because of my kids. I'm worried what will they think, but I also don't want to be alone for the rest of my life either."*
>
> *"My daughter would probably be ok with [my dating] but the boys, absolutely not. I feel like there is no hope and that is just downright depressing."*

I'm glad that you acknowledge that you should not have to think in terms of a life without companionship and yes, even love. As you've seen, many in our situation feel that they are either cheating on their late husbands or are somehow not entitled to love once again. Nothing could be further from the truth and I'm happy that you realize that fact.

The complexities of dating as a widow aren't much different than those complexities were before we got married. True, there are some less-evolved men who will look at you peculiarly when you tell them that you are widowed; however and happily, I remind you that they are in the minority. The response that you will generally receive will be one of admiration at your courage to go forward in a positive way after such a horrific experience.

The first piece of advice that I always give concerning dating and your children is that regardless of your child's age, do *not* introduce every single person with whom you spend time to your child and that *includes* adult children as well. Until or unless the relationship becomes serious (or at the very least, exclusive), no child needs to meet every single man with whom you spend time. Of course it's perfectly acceptable to date more than one man at a time and I certainly advocate letting your children know that you are dating; however, children do not need to meet a rotating roster of men.

Using myself as an example and as I have already shared, I did a significant amount of dating in the years since my husband's passing. With all of the dating that I have done in those years, in fact, my daughter (who is now an adult) has met only *two* men in person—the ex-boyfriend with whom I broke up years ago and the man to whom I am committed now.

Our children, particularly very young children, will take their cues from Mom. You will raise them to understand that Daddy was a wonderful man who loved them very much and you will help create, honor, and preserve memories of Daddy for them. However, you will also help them to understand that going forward with life includes companionship and love and the best way to teach is by setting a healthy example.

I also want to remind you again that loving another does not in any way diminish the love that you have for your late husband. It's important to once more recognize that the heart has an infinite capacity to love, there are no "love quotas" or limits on love and you are entitled to make that return to the abundant life we're talking about—one that includes love, laughter, and happiness. Just as you had to learn this very important lesson, you must in turn teach this lesson to your children as well.

> *"I lost my husband after a short [illness]. He was my world and I was his rock. We have grown children that are very dear to me. Our youngest is having a hard time with me going out with our best friend [because our] friend is a man and she looks at it as if I am dating. But we are friends and have been for [many] years. Am I wrong to keep this friendship going?"*

I believe that sometimes it's easier having younger children than older children when one has lost her husband. While younger children readily take their cues from us, older children sometimes forget that we were here first and that we are "all grown up" too. In other words, *we* are the parent.

What may be happening here is quite common. Your children are "transposing" their grief onto you, not realizing that losing a spouse is quite different than losing a parent. As you know, I lost both my husband and my father in very close proximity to one another and I can absolutely attest to the fact that while both kinds of grief are overwhelming, they are also completely different in complexion and loss perspective.

Secondly, your children may see your getting involved with another man as "disloyalty" to their father and his memory. Just as the thousands of widows with whom I work eventually realize, what children also need to understand is that while you will always love their father, you also have a right to a life that includes companionship, platonic or otherwise.

If you had told me that you were beginning a romantic relationship very soon after your husband's death, I would be more cautionary in my advice; in other words, the heart has to heal first before introducing new love into it. However, that's not the case here. Some would have you believe that a close-knit, yet platonic relationship between a man and a woman is impossible (reference the brilliant movie, *When Harry Met Sally...*), and this view may also be held by your children. I happen to strongly disagree. One of my best friends on the entire planet is a man. He has been one of my best friends for many years. He has stood by me through thick, thin, and everything in between. However, it is now, it has always been, and it will always be a *friendship*, and nothing more.

If hanging out with your friend brings you solace or support or, dare I say it, fun, then you go right ahead. Guess what else? No one, and I mean *no one*, gets to impose their idea of what your grief should or should not be or what it should entail. Get a little stubborn here; your children may be adults, but you know what? So is Mom and she is entitled to a life of her own. In other words, as my late daddy would say in his very Oklahoman way, "The tail does not wag the dog."

> *"My husband passed away and I [began] dating someone. I felt that we were going slowly and being respectful of the children and their feelings. However my in-laws began commenting negatively*

about the relationship and now the children feel disloyal to their dad. It is tearing our family apart. [One of the children] says that I am still married to my husband. Any advice?"

"My grown daughter tells me that I shouldn't marry again. She doesn't understand that I don't want to be an 'old grandma' sitting in a rocking chair for the rest of my life. My husband and I were very active, always going out to eat, dance, etc. I don't think that my [children] will ever accept any other man. They adored their father so much."

I don't think that my late husband had a bigger fan on the planet than Kendall. It didn't matter if he was driving a police car, sitting on top of a horse, or confined to a wheelchair unable to speak. Daddy was her idol. No one stood taller in her eyes and to this very day (and in her own words), he is her hero and he always will be.

But Kendall also understood at an unusually young age that not only was it OK for me to date and fall in love again, it was the right and healthy thing to do. She also knew that her daddy worried constantly about me "going out and finding love again" (those were his exact words) and that I was too young to think of my entire lifetime in terms of being all alone.

After what you now know to be a significant amount of dating over quite a number of years, I was blessed enough to meet and subsequently fall in love with a wonderful man. He brings an incredible amount of happiness into our home and into our lives. I'm ever thankful (not to mention incredibly lucky) for his presence. He and Kendall have a great relationship; however, she has never once viewed him as either a "threat" to her daddy's memory or as a "replacement" for her daddy nor has he once tried to behave as such. She is happy for me in my own right and understands that my loving another man who is also a "father figure" to her is in no way or measure, any "disloyalty" (real or imagined) to her daddy or to his memory, a memory that both of us treasure now and always.

Many (if not most) children tend to see their parents as, well, parents.

That's fine of course, but what they may occasionally lose sight of is that: Parents are *people* too.

In other words, as you have learned, you have a *right* to a life that includes companionship. Naturally, your children adored their father, and that will never change nor should it. However, they need to realize that just as a widow's heart has the capacity to love again, they too can also open their hearts to new possibilities as well without feeling any kind of betrayal or disloyalty to their father or to his memory. Simply put, this does not have to be an "either-or, choosing one or the other" proposition.

This is a conversation that you will need to have with your children when the time is right for you. The reality is that if they do not approve of you dating or possibly marrying once again, that is a problem for *them*, not for you. We do not require the approval of *anyone* in order to lead our lives in positive, constructive ways and that includes loving another human being and being loved in return.

I will say it yet again—the words in the wedding ceremony are, "Till death do us part," if not those exact words, then words to that effect. This means that once your spouse passes away, *you are no longer legally married*. Furthermore, these words don't just pertain to the legal aspects of marriage. I am not a theologian; however, to the best of my knowledge and no matter the faith, the words in most wedding ceremonies are still by and large the same: "Till death do us part." Even religions where one marries for "all time and eternity" permit the widowed to remarry for their time spent on earth. And all religions, whatever the form, teach, choose, and encourage LIFE.

Therefore, there is nothing wrong with your dating, seeking companionship, and falling in love subsequent to your husband's death. You have done all of the right things as a wife and you are now doing all of the right things in moving forward after your husband's death. You don't dictate how your [adult] children lead their lives and conversely, they don't get to dictate how you live yours.

"I've been romantically involved with a man [for several months] who lost his wife around the same time [that I lost my husband several years ago], but who is also left caring for young children (mine are young adults). He is still struggling and is worried about his children's well-being (including their coping with him dating me). I want very much to stick with the relationship, understanding that he can't 'give his all.' I think people can cautiously move forward in a new relationship while healing, and this man is definitely worth the trouble. Because of the kids, I'm rarely at his house and I don't spend the night with him at all. Any thoughts or tips?"

I think that your insight and approach to your situation is very wise. You have both certainly been widowed long enough that entering into a new relationship is appropriate. We also know that the only healing journey that we can control is our own and perhaps your new man is not quite as far along in the healing processes as you are.

The fact that your man has young children certainly must be factored into the relationship equation. You don't mention the ages of his children, but in an age-appropriate manner, his children can be helped to understand that Mom is no longer here, that moving forward with life is absolutely normal, and that love and companionship are a part of the moving forward process. However, it's going to be up to Dad to have that conversation with his children, and without you in the room.

I must reiterate that your open-but-cautious approach to this situation is to be commended and I believe that you're taking all of the right steps here.

Dating and Discouraged

> *"The dating scene is a joke, especially since all of the men I have met so far are divorced. While I know that there are a lot of similarities with divorce, being widowed is a completely different 'animal.' I hate to go to church gatherings or single events. It is just easier to stay away."*

> *"I felt ready for a relationship, [but] all I have had are a string of first dates. I gave up and haven't dated for years."*

It sounds as though you have been open to dating and I'm very pleased to hear that. It also sounds like you've experienced much the same thing with dating that I have. It can indeed be discouraging at times and it can also be pretty hilarious; as you have read, I definitely have some hysterical "horror stories" to tell.

(I feel another book coming on. Stay tuned).

I want you to again remember back to when you first began dating. Dating didn't just become challenging since you became a widow, it's always been that way. Please don't give up though. While there are definitely members of the Liar and Loser Brigade out there, and there always will be, you have learned that there are also wonderful men out there as well.

The fact is that many of the single men that you meet will have been divorced and that's just fine. In fact, rare was the time that I dated a man who had never been married. While a divorcé might not *directly* relate to what you've been through, that doesn't mean that he's not a suitable candidate for dating. Look for someone with whom you share similar pursuits, interests, goals, ambitions, and with whom you can have some good old-fashioned *fun*.

As far as singles events go, I'm with you. I'd frankly rather have a root canal. I don't blame you at all for not wanting to attend singles events. When it comes to church gatherings, concentrate instead on the spiritual aspects or go to church events that aren't necessarily "singles" oriented. Meanwhile, do you have a girlfriend or two (including those of your friends who are married) that can get out for an evening periodically for a movie, dinner, or a cocktail? What about going out on your own? Have you tried going out by yourself? It might seem weird at first, but give it a try. It can be a lot of fun and also goes a long way to helping you move forward into a life of independence.

> *"So far the Lord has not brought anyone into my path. I could join something like [an online dating site] but there are lots of reasons not to: 1) I don't want to 'get ahead' of God; 2) I personally know there are some real slime balls on there, and I don't want to have to [deal with it]; 3) I would like to have a little bit more [of a] romantic story to tell than, 'I met my husband on [a dating site]'; and, 4) It costs money. Do you have any help or counsel for this? Just knowing someone else has faced this would be encouraging."*

My goal here is to help you progress in the ways that I believe you want to move. We are not here on earth to lead a life of emotional or spiritual poverty. We are meant to live a life of abundance. Those who have had a happy and successful marriage as you have are quite likely to marry again, should they choose to do so. What I'm hearing is that you'd like companionship but that you're a little scared of what's "out there." You know what? That's OK! The first step in conquering fear is identifying it. We've done that, what next?

Have you actually tried online dating yet? Don't discount online dating unless you have given it a real chance. Remember that the one huge advantage to online dating is that *you* maintain the control. You decide with whom you communicate and how or if you even want to communicate with them at all. You didn't mention your religious affiliation, but just about all faiths have online dating sites. However, if you prefer, there are also many sites that are not religiously affiliated.

Let's quickly examine your reasons for not wanting to venture out and some of my observations and suggestions:

1) "I don't want to 'get ahead' of God."

I have a wonderful little sign that hangs in my private office that I've had for many years. It reads, "Reach up as far as you can, and God will reach down the rest of the way." In other words and to my way of thinking, God *always* holds up his end of the bargain but you have to do *your* part as well. Like it or not, that includes putting yourself "out there." Scary? A little bit but I promise you, eligible men who are worthy of your time and effort will not simply line up at your front door. You *have* to make the effort. As great as God is, He is not going to "put" people in your path until you actually *get out onto the path.*

2) "I personally know there are some real slime balls on there, and I don't want to have to [deal with it]."

You'll get no argument with me in that regard because I've met and unfortunately spent time with a lot of those slime balls. As you can see, I have experienced my own personal and tremendous waste of time, energy, and makeup to be sure (and if you knew just how much makeup it takes to be me, you would understand why I get so irritated).

But I want you to think back to the days before the Internet, back to the days where we had to date the "old-fashioned way." There were slime balls around then too and dealing with them was a pain in the backside, wasn't it? Make no mistake, it is absolutely true, as was the world before the Internet came into our lives, the "idiot factor" on the Internet is also plentiful. However, you must keep in mind that as with the winning field goal kick in a football game, it only takes one. Just one wonderful man, and when you find that one, it makes the slime balls of the world a distant memory— believe me, I know.

3) "I would like to have a little bit more romantic story to tell than, 'I met my husband on [a dating site],'"

We all love a romantic story, but *how* you meet someone is

far less important than the fact that you actually *met* someone who is wonderful and worthy of your heart. It's rather like being more concerned with having a huge *wedding* versus having a great *marriage.* Which is more important: being with someone wonderful or the method(s) involved in meeting them?

4) "It costs money."

Take a little time and do the homework that I mentioned earlier. You'll find that not all online dating websites cost the same and different sites offer different perks. Since your faith is a very high priority in your life, you will definitely want to check out dating websites that are faith-based.

> *"It's been [several] years since my husband died. I've tried [Internet dating] websites, church, community groups, and professional groups. I'm not finding anyone available. I'm afraid it's me, I'm afraid it's everyone else ... I'm just afraid and discouraged. I just don't know what to do next."*

Somehow, we expect that because we've been happily and successfully married, the Dating World has somehow gotten easier or different. The facts remain that dating is still a challenge and that there are still some pretty rotten people out there.

However, it's also an absolute guarantee that you're not going to find the wonderful guys in the world if you quit trying! By all means continue to keep active in church activities and community groups; you might even think about visiting other churches' functions as well. Keep trying reputable Internet dating sites and use the previous suggestions and guidance to help maximize your Internet dating experience. Yes, you may run across lemons, jerks, idiots, and the dubious letter writers looking for money or citizenship, but that's what your delete button is for.

Also, have a double-look at the profile that you post and check it against the profile suggestions listed earlier. Is your profile well written? Are you including a recent picture (remember, that's absolutely vital if you want to receive quality responses)? Have a trusted friend look it over and make suggestions if necessary and it's OK to post on more than one dating site too.

Remember what I said earlier—it only takes *one* and when you find that one special someone, it is not only *so* worth all of the previous effort, but I also promise you that the jerks will be magically relegated to great storytelling at parties or anecdotes in books!

> *"I think I am ready to date. I gave [a gentleman whom I met] my telephone number [at his request] and told him to call me sometime. He said he would call me and he did not. I was so disappointed and felt rejected even though he was not misleading me in any way. Why am I feeling like this? I could curse my husband for making me go through this again. I never thought in a million years I would have to date again. Not only do I feel rejected, but everybody [I know] is either getting married (they are the same age as me) or happy with their boyfriends. What is your suggestion regarding my dating scenario and why I am letting this situation get to me?"*

> *"It's just my luck to meet a man who [also] lost his wife and after several dates, he simply stops calling. I am so tempted to email him and tell him [that] in the future, [he should] treat any woman he sees the way he would have wanted his late wife to have been treated if he died first. I do not understand how anyone can treat another person that way, especially someone who has experienced the pain [that we both] experienced. Any clues as to the 'why?'"*

If I could answer the eternal mystery as to why men act the way that they do, *especially* when they act like they are interested and pursue you like crazy and then evaporate into thin air, I think that I probably would rule the world. Seriously.

The fact is that before we married our husbands, there were millions of guys like this out there. Newsflash—They're *still* out there!

In my dating past, I certainly met more than my fair share of these jerks. I totally believed them (yes, "them," as in plural) when I received the extremely popular, "You're So Incredible; Where Have You Been All My Life?; I Think I'm In Love With You" speeches and was thereafter dropped on my head without another word and certainly without any reason as to why a disappearing act was in order. In other words, you are not alone in your experience.

As women, we have always and forever perceived this behavior as rejection, like his lack of follow-through (or at the very least, good manners) is *our* fault or that it's because of something that we've done or haven't done or can otherwise control.

Guess what? IT'S *NOT* YOU...IT REALLY *IS* HIM!

Think about this: Do you *really* want to be with someone who doesn't even have the courtesy to make a phone call? Do you *really* want to be with someone else who has been dating you for a while, gets your hopes up, and then simply falls off the face of the earth without so much as a phone call, an email, or even that idiotically wimpy, pathetic cliché, "It's not you; it's me"? Of course not.

You need someone who is going to be sensitive to you and to your situation; you've been through enough. And just so you don't feel completely alone—after every single lousy date that I've ever had (and there have obviously been a considerable number of lousy dates), I would inevitably look to the ceiling in my bedroom and say, "Fleet, how could you *do* this to me?" I say it laughingly now (and I'm sure he's someplace laughing right back at me), but many were the times when I too cursed Mike for catapulting me headlong back into the World of Dating.

I know it's horribly difficult to be surrounded by people who are getting married or happily-in-love with boyfriends or who otherwise seem like they have it all while you are left on your own, all by yourself. Instead of focusing on what's going on in other people's lives (which is easy to do), let's instead keep the focus on you. What about *your* life? What do *you* like to do? What are *your* interests? What are some things that you can do to get out, have fun, and begin to embrace your new life? Focus on you—you *deserve* the attention.

"I would like to start to date again, but have found that most men around my age are jerks. I expected that by this age, they would have more class than they do. Do you have any suggestions for me?"

Please know that being a jerk is not particular to any one age group. "Jerk-hood" is pretty much universal and knows no age, gender, or any other sort of boundaries. Remember what I said earlier? There are lots of fantastic men out there and one super-special gentleman is looking for you too. If you haven't found him yet, keep looking, otherwise, I can absolutely guarantee that you won't find him if you decide that "All the world is a jerk" and give up.

"Why do your girlfriends see you as 'competition' [since becoming widowed], as though I would think to lower myself [by chasing their boyfriends or husbands]. It hurts me terribly."

When I receive mail like this from Widows Wear Stilettos members who have already been through so much, I really just want to gather these other woefully insecure, misinformed, jealous, pathetic women, lock them into a room with me and explain the facts of life to them, and none too nicely.

Why *do* people think that because we're widowed, we are all of a sudden lurking in the shadows and hiding in the bushes and skulking about in dark alleys, ready and waiting to pounce on the "innocent and unsuspecting" husbands and boyfriends of other women? We can lump people like these in alongside the family members who want to know what the deceased left to them in his will and they ask this question at the funeral service. Exactly where do their brains go? I wish I could answer that question intelligently; however, the fact is that it is difficult to respond intelligently to that which is based in utter stupidity.

When my husband Mike was alive and like most married couples, we too had many "couple friends," with whom we would socialize. Whether it was dinners, parties, or other social get-togethers of any and all kinds, we were a collectively happy gathering of Mr. & Mrs. Two-by-Twos. Never in a million years did it dawn on me that once my "couple" status tragically (and certainly unwillingly) changed to "widowed," I would be viewed by some as a threat, a menacing, cold, and calculating *man-eater*.

I recall my first "man-eater" experience with the wife-half of one of our formerly friendly "couple friends" shortly after Mike's death. Though not one of my closest friends, this woman, a highly educated professional, was nonetheless cheerfully affable and genial prior to Mike's illness and concerned and supportive throughout Mike's illness.

Until the night that he closed his eyes for the last time.

Immediately after Mike's passing, this woman's demeanor toward me flipped 180 degrees. Once warm and welcoming, I remember being so confused at her cold, distant, barely civil acknowledgment when we would run into one another. Try explaining *that* to a young child who was also once greeted with hugs.

Bewildered, I asked another friend about this woman's behavior, to which she replied, "You don't know? She thinks you'll go after [her husband] now that Mike is gone."

I was stunned.

As with most "widow lessons" learned along my own healing journey, I quickly discovered that I was not the only one who was treated in this manner by female halves of former "couple friends." While I am sure that there are exceptions out there somewhere, not *one* of the thousands of widows with whom I have spoken, emailed, coached, or otherwise come into contact have *ever* gone after someone else's boyfriend, husband, or significant other; if for no other reason than it is a clear violation of the "Girl Code," not to mention the fact that most widows simply are not interested in those who are unavailable.

We all know that there are women out there who are incredibly insecure and will always see any other woman as "competition" in one respect or another; be it because of appearance, career, social status, financial status, or their new and unfortunate widowed marital status. Now, factor in that these women also believe you to be the "poor helpless widow" who men are going to feel sorry for and rush to "rescue," like any of us have to play the "widow card" to get male attention.

I am deeply sorry that I don't have a better answer for you, other than to say that I too have been in your position many times over, enough times to have warranted an entire chapter in a book. So have thousands of other widows just like you.

If you have had a "man-eater" experience, then you either have been or are being treated as though you are waiting around corners with a man-sized butterfly net, waiting to capture someone else's "prey" or "property." Please know that these pathetic little girls who now see you as "competition" are just that—little girls who are not worthy of you or the pleasure of your company. Rather than view you with respect as the model of strength that you are, they instead prefer to see you as some kind of threat. Go ahead and let them. Get away from them as fast as you can and get yourself ready to find other absolutely amazing girlfriends and "sisters of the heart" at Widows Wear Stilettos who will see you and love you for the fantastic person that you are.

IT'S A "WRAP"...STILETTO-STYLE!

So how are you feeling right now?
   a. Excited?
   b. Scared?
   c. Not ready at all for this madness and thinking that one of us is out of their minds for even discussing the subject?
   d. All of the above.

If you picked "All of the above," congratulations! That makes you a one hundred percent absolutely normal widow who is contemplating taking a leap of faith with a lot of courage.

Remember what you learned at the very beginning of the chapter—this most important step has to be taken in your way and in your time. Don't let anyone—*anyone*—rush you or otherwise pressure you into taking that step back into dating one *second* sooner than you are ready.

If you are at the other end of the spectrum, ready to date and finding nothing but closed doors and brick walls where you reasonably expected support and enthusiasm from those closest to you, quick quiz:

Q: Whose life is it?
A: I think you get the point.

One more thing—remember that the definition of courage isn't "not being afraid." True courage is being afraid and doing it anyway!

chapter six

LOVE IS ALL AROUND YOU...REALLY!

I KNOW WHAT YOU'RE THINKING RIGHT NOW. YOU'RE READING THAT CHAPTER title and thinking, *"Seriously?"*

I'll be honest with you. After losing Mike, the only thing that the thought of being in love again left me with was a slightly nauseated feeling, followed by extreme exhaustion and a strong desire to resume the fetal position while eating French fries, guzzling Coke, and watching reruns of *The Golden Girls*.[5]

Love? You must be kidding me. I mean, after all, Mike was the love of my life.

A life that was now over.

Shattered.

Finished.

Are you nodding along? Of course you are, because your husband was the love of your life too. Me? I knew my husband for almost fifteen years before I even married him. He was my buddy, my partner in crime, and yes, the love of my life for almost *half* of my life... and then he was gone.

---

5 *The Golden Girls*, 1985–1992; Touchstone Television, Witt/Thomas/Harris Productions

But let me ask you this: If your husband was the "love of your life" and he is now no longer here, does that mean that you *never* get to love again? *Ever?* Does it mean that you will not open your heart to the possibility that love can and will exist for you once again? Does it mean that you are not entitled to love and be loved in return again?

Now, if you have lost your husband recently, you are just setting out on your healing journey and for that reason, you are not yet ready to entertain such a concept as loving once again; it's way too soon. However, if it has been awhile since your husband's passing (and only *you* are capable of defining the word "awhile") and you:

Feel "stuck" in your grief;

Feel as though you want to move forward and that you're ready to move forward but you just can't seem to do so;

Feel as though you are cheating on your husband if you think in terms of loving again;

…then I have a very important message for you, a message that I want you to think about carefully.

It is absolutely true that Mike was the love of my life and a fantastic life it was indeed. However, the sad reality is that our fantastic life ended on December 19, 2000, at the very moment that Mike left us. With Mike's passing, the life that I shared with him also ended. It was sad, it was undeniably tragic, but it was also a fact.

There is no question that Mike was the "love of my life," until the life that we lived together as a couple and as a family came to an end. Though I didn't realize it at the time, and whether I liked it or not, my daughter and I, at that very moment, entered a new life.

Let me say that again: A NEW LIFE.

During his illness, Mike worried constantly that I would "jump into the grave" with him (once again, his exact words). He did not want me to live in fear, in sorrow, or in a state of grief for the rest of my days. I would venture to guess that your husband would not have wanted that for you either. Yes, your husband was the love of your life, until that life came to an end. Please know that your heart has a tremendous capacity to love and allowing new love into your life in no way disrespects your husband's memory or the love that you will *always* have for him.

In other words—say it with me:

YOU CAN HONOR YOUR PAST.
YOU CAN TREASURE YOUR PAST.
YOU CAN LOVE YOUR PAST.
YOU DO NOT HAVE TO *LIVE* IN YOUR PAST.

"BUT I'M AFRAID"

> *"My husband died suddenly of a heart attack and I've been a widow for [many years] now. My problem is that I'm feeling like it's not possible to have a normal relationship because of what happened. I feel so confused. My life was so wonderful with my late husband and we had very few problems. I feel like I'm going crazy. Could this all be from losing my husband when we were so young?"*

> *"I'm afraid of falling in love again—what if I lost him too?"*

> *"I am finding it very hard to open my heart to love again. It all seems so pointless to me at times. I had a life, we made a good team, and then it is over."*

You are perfectly justified in your fear of losing love once again and the age at which you lost your love really doesn't have anything to do with it. You lost your husband and the life that the two of you built was ripped away from you. Furthermore, we are all aware of the statistics that tell us that generally speaking, women outlive men. The reality is that if you commit yourself again, you have to face the possibility that you could wind up a widow once again, a scary prospect to be sure.

While I certainly share that fear with you, at the same time, I could not see myself letting fear stand in the way of any happiness to which I—and every single other woman out there—am absolutely entitled. Should you choose it, that happiness also includes love and I don't believe that fear deserves to be given the power over anyone's destiny of happiness.

With regard to widowhood, it is completely understandable to fear losing a love once again and winding up "back where you started" as it were. However, you must not and cannot let this fear stand in the way of your potential happiness. I personally cannot imagine missing out on the love and the life that I now know out of a fear of loss. Do I have that fear? Of course I do, every single day, but not to the point where I would rather insulate myself with a case of "Analysis Paralysis" than live this life.

Don't allow fears of a repeat of the widow experience paralyze you—that's a surrender of power and fear shouldn't be given that kind of power. Above all, remember what I said earlier, being courageous doesn't mean, "Don't be afraid." The real definition of courage is being afraid and going forward anyway.

"How Do I Know That It's Really Love?"

> "How do I know that it's love and I'm not just afraid [of being on my own]?"

> "I'm trying to figure out if I'm in love with this man and it's not as easy as you think."

> "I'm either in love or just really lonely. I can't tell which one though."

"I want to be in love with someone so much that I think I might be confusing wanting to be in love with actually being in love."

Okay, if I weren't already ruling the world because I had correctly answered the question of why men don't call when they say they will, I know this—if I had the answer to, "How do I know that it's really love?", I would definitely ascend that "rule the world" throne.

Unfortunately, there isn't a soul on the planet that can answer that question for you. The answer to this most important question has to come from within yourself but there are certainly several factors that you *must* consider before you decide or declare that you are in love with a new man. Let's briefly review those very important considerations:

1. *How much time has passed since the death of your husband?*
   If your husband's death was recent, the truth is that you have barely recovered from loss and adjusted to life on your own, let alone be in a position to get to know someone well enough to declare that you are in love. Meeting someone while recovering (in all respects) from your husband's death is *not* the time to introduce a new person into your life and into your heart. You *must* first recover from the death of your husband and you must be willing to take the *time* to do so. Even though it is certainly tempting to fill that immense void with a new person, the fact is that you must first be available in all respects, especially emotionally, and that kind of availability does not happen overnight.

2. *Am I happy on my own, in my own right?*
   As we discussed earlier, being happy on your own means feeling *contentment* to be by yourself and that you have a life that is your own and is fulfilling in and of itself, independent of children. Remember that children grow up and into lives of their own, and of course as parents, that is exactly what we want them to do. Therefore, if you are dependent on your children or *their* activities

to fill your days, keep you company, entertain you, or otherwise fill that void, that's not fair to any of you. Remember that this is a time of discovery; a time of learning all about you as a woman and that discovery takes time.

3. Do I go or have I gone out by myself and did I enjoy myself?

I continue to readily and happily admit that I *am* the clichéd "People Person." If it is difficult to go out alone as a woman, it is twice as difficult for the People Person, who wants little more than to be surrounded by a gaggle of her "sister-girlfriends." Yet I knew that the only way that I could truly move forward and eventually open my heart to another male presence in my life for all of the *right* reasons, was to make absolutely sure that I could go out and enjoy myself, *all by myself.* Once I learned that I was capable of enjoying my own company—be it at a comedy club, in a restaurant, or at a movie—I knew that I was ready to introduce romantic companionship into my life because I wasn't simply filling a void by doing so.

THE "INVISIBLE YARDSTICK" STRIKES AGAIN

"I've met someone new but I'm afraid that he doesn't 'measure up' to my [late] husband."

"My husband used to bring me flowers and presents for no reason and was very romantic. The man I'm seeing now is not the same way and it makes me miss my husband even more."

"I started seeing a man who [physically] resembles my husband. People say that I'm seeing him because he reminds me of [my husband] and maybe they're right."

"Whenever I go out with someone, I wind up thinking, '[My husband] wouldn't do that' or '[My husband] was so much funnier or smarter' or stuff like that. I know it's probably bad of

> *me to think that way and I know it's not very fair to the [man] to*
> *compare him [to my husband] but I can't help it."*

As you know, I am always quick to congratulate any widow who has made an attempt to return to the World of Dating—it's a huge step in a positive, "forward-thinking" direction; it's an incredibly courageous step to take; and I believe that it warrants a sincere "Go Girl!" from anyone and everyone surrounding her. On the other hand, there can be a bit of a difference between "head-ready" and "heart-ready."

When it comes to dating, sometimes our heads can get a little ahead of our hearts and that happens for any number of reasons. Perhaps there are people around you (aka, "they") who are telling you that you should be back "out there." Perhaps you're "testing the waters," or maybe you're just testing yourself.

As you saw in Chapter Five (The Questions, Quandaries, Dos, Don'ts, and Dumbfounding of Dating), I am often asked how one knows when they are ready to date. Interestingly, in the tens of thousands of letters that I have received, not *one* widow has ever asked me how they know when they are *not* ready to date. The questions above are good examples and clear indications of women who are not ready to date...not just yet.

All people everywhere have the unequivocal right to be judged on their own merits as a person and not to have to worry over being compared to anyone else. Think of it this way: How would *you* feel being compared to someone else, for *any* reason? I certainly wouldn't want people holding the "invisible yardstick" up against me to see how I measure up to anyone in their past and I'm sure that you feel the same way.

The reality is that no one is going to be exactly like your husband. If you are sitting there on a date while some poor guy is trying his very best to impress you and all you can think about are the qualities that he supposedly lacks or how "inferior" he is to your late husband, then that's just not fair to either one of you. Give yourself permission to take a step back from dating, acknowledge that you need more time to acclimate to your new life, and try again when you feel confident that you can enjoy someone for who he is, not for the person that you wish he could be.

It's A "Wrap"...Stiletto-Style!

Your husband absolutely was the love of your life and you will *always* love your husband. Always. However, this is a new life now, a new beginning. So in this new life, will you open your heart to the possibility of one day loving again and allowing yourself to be loved in return? Think about the possibilities.

Years ago, my rabbi gave me a beautiful poem which says, in part:

> ...And if you cannot give me away,
> at least let me live on your eyes and not on your mind.
> You can love me most
> by letting hands touch hands,
> by letting bodies touch bodies.
> Love doesn't die.
> People do.
> So, when all that's left of me
> Is love,
> Give me away. [6]

Choose now to love, remember, and honor the "love of your life" by continuing to move *forward* with your own life—your new life.

---

6 Excerpted from "When I Die" by Merritt Malloy.

chapter seven

THE INTRICACIES OF INTIMACY

"Sex makes everything more complicated.
Even not having it, because the not having it makes it
complicated."[7]

WITH KUDOS TO THE WRITER OF THIS MARVELOUSLY INSIGHTFUL PHRASE, when it comes to this most sensitive and simultaneously hot button issue, I believe that truer words have never been written.

We miss intimacy, except for when we *don't* miss it. We want intimacy because we miss the closeness and the sharing and let's face it, the just plain "it-feels-so-good" of it all, except when we *don't* want it because it's hard to imagine ourselves being intimate with anyone other than our husbands.

Yet intimacy is a necessary and fundamental part of the human condition, a need that never really goes away. Not with time, not with age, and certainly not because of widowhood.

---

7   From *The Holiday,* Sony Pictures, released 2007.

Never in a million years would I ever tell anyone, widowed or otherwise, when to engage in intimacy with a partner. To me, this is among the most intensely personal and private decisions that one can make. I also recognize that each one of us has very strong opinions concerning at what point intimacy should occur within a relationship. That said, this is one of the most common subjects on which I receive letters, which clearly means that intimacy, in any and all of its forms, is on the minds of millions of women, widowed and otherwise.

The *Real* "Fear Factor"

> *"I miss being close with a man, but I'm so afraid of what [a man] will think of me without clothes on. I'm [still young], but I've had two children and I'm not exactly a bikini model."*

Thanks in large part to the thousands of magazines, billboards, television shows, red-carpet critics, and beauty "experts" (self-declared and otherwise) that now flood our daily existence, body image has become an issue of utterly gigantic proportions,, creating an "ideal" that few of us have any hope of achieving. I have fantastic news for you—most bikini models aren't even bikini models and they will be the first ones to tell you so.

Supermodel Cindy Crawford, who is without a doubt, one of the most beautiful women in the world (inside and out), once famously said, "Even *I* don't look like Cindy Crawford in the morning. I don't want to have to be beautiful all the time. I want to be able to look cruddy in my weekend sweats, with a pimple on my face and pimple cream on top of the pimple. The expectation to always be beautiful bothers me."

When that precious moment arrives, the moment in time when you and a man who has earned the privilege of being with you take this very important step, he is not going to be standing there with a clipboard going over every single one of your flaws; and let's be honest, most of the flaws that we see are flaws that *we* see (if those flaws even exist at all). Men don't see those flaws and men aren't looking for flaws because, quite frankly, *men honestly do not care,* (and they will tell you so!).

A man cares about only one thing—the fact that he gets to be with a fantastic woman like you. He is not there to judge or criticize; he is there to be with *you.* So relax. The only thing that he will be thinking is, "I am so lucky to be with this woman." He will not be searching for stretch marks or misplaced dimples or otherwise ticking off a checklist of perceived imperfections that you imagine yourself to have. Besides, he's also thinking about his *own* imperfections. I mean, he's a human being too!

> *"My husband is the only man that I've ever been physically intimate with. I wouldn't even begin to know how to be with a stranger."*
>
> *"I have only ever been with my husband. What if I do [something] 'wrong'?"*

To my way of thinking, I would have to know someone pretty well before I made the very important decision to become intimate. Without getting preachy or otherwise standing on moral ceremony, and understanding that the decision to become intimate is possibly the most hugely personal decision that one can make, the easiest and most obvious reply here is that if he is a "stranger," you are not going to be physically intimate with him, are you? You are instead and hopefully taking your time getting to know somebody absolutely wonderful before taking such an important step.

As to doing something "wrong," be assured that there aren't many variations on this wonderfully delightful theme. In other words, with the exception of perhaps yelling out the wrong name at an inopportune moment, what on earth could you possibly do "wrong"?

It truly doesn't matter if you have slept with only your husband or if you have slept with more than one man in your lifetime; the fact remains that the first time with someone new is indeed the "first time." It is a time of delight and discovery, each of the other. There is no "right" or "wrong." There is only the two of you getting to know one another in a most loving way.

> *"I worry that if anyone ever does come along, and I get much older,*
> *[that] physical intimacy won't be the same. I rage at the waste."*

You're absolutely right—when you become older, physical intimacy isn't the same. In my most humble opinion, it actually gets *better* but only if you have the widow-tude that it can get better. I honestly don't know where people get it in their heads that physical intimacy (or the need for physical intimacy) diminishes or goes away altogether. It starts in your head, my friend. It all begins with you.

If you decide that physical intimacy won't be the same (which I can only imagine translates into, "as good as it was before"), then you are right. It is truly a self-fulfilling prophecy. As the saying goes: If you think you can, you can, and if you think you can't, you're right.

I don't ever want you to think of the years without a man in your life as "wasted" years. Remember, in order to have a fulfilling relationship with another, you must be content with yourself in your own right, as an individual. In no way would I ever consider the many years spent on my own as having been "wasted" years, but rather as time to have gotten to know myself, transition into a new life, and make the decision concerning intimacy for all of the *right* reasons.

All of that said, I do want you to think about this: You can't start to do something "sooner," but you have the power to change today and tomorrow right now! Make the choice to live the abundant life that you clearly want to live. You have the power and the strength within you to do it.

"I'm 'Cheating' on My Husband" (Part 2)

> *"I am involved with a man [and] he is willing to do (and has done)*
> *everything in order to be with me. I really do want to be with him*
> *but what do I do about the [cheating] guilt?"*

> *"How am I supposed to be intimate with someone when I feel like*
> *I'm having an affair? My husband has been gone for [years] but I*
> *can't seem to get over these feelings [of cheating]."*

"I go out on dates, but whenever someone even tries to kiss me good night, I just see my husband's face. If I can't even let someone kiss me, how am I supposed to do anything more than that?"

What is called for here is a quick reminder of the vows that every single one of us recited. In one form or another, regardless of whether we had a huge wedding or a "just the two of us" ceremony, and whatever our particular religious affiliation, every single one of us said, in one way or another: *"till death do us part."*

In short, dear friends, you upheld your end of the bargain. Death has parted you and your husband, therefore, there is *no cheating going on here.*

What I have actually found at the heart of questions such as these is a deeply held fallacy, a myth that has existed for far too long. Too many of you feel that by dating again or falling in love again or becoming intimate again, even though you are not really cheating per se, you feel as though you are either cheating on the life that you had with your husband or that you are diminishing or disrespecting his memory. Folks, this simply isn't the case.

You have already learned that:

YOU CAN HONOR YOUR PAST.
YOU CAN TREASURE YOUR PAST.
YOU CAN LOVE YOUR PAST.
YOU DO NOT HAVE TO *LIVE* IN YOUR PAST.

These words continue to hold true here, at possibly one of the most important times of your life. Remember what we discussed earlier—the love that you have for your late husband will never ever go away. Not ever. However, you are also not destined to remain in everlasting mourning, that is *not* why you are here. If you choose it, living a life of abundance includes companionship, love, and yes, physical intimacy, which is an important and beautiful expression of that love.

Remember that sometimes all we need is a sort of "permission." We need to hear that it's OK to be in love again and that expression of that love in a physical sense is not only normal, it's wonderful!

Read (and recite out loud if you have to) the following affirmation, every single day if necessary:

CAROLE'S
"I AM ABSOLUTELY NOT CHEATING" AFFIRMATION

I recognize that:

1. I will take great comfort and strength in the knowledge that I upheld my wedding vows until the very moment that my husband passed away.

2. Just by virtue of the fact that I am here, I am entitled to a life filled with happiness and abundance and that happiness and abundance can include the love of another man. I am not now nor will I ever be "cheating" on my late husband.

3. The heart has an infinite capacity to love and that loving another does not in any way diminish the love that I have now and always will have for my late husband.

4. In no way does my loving another dishonor the memory of my late husband or the life that we had together, regardless of how long that life lasted.

5. By moving forward in a positive way and allowing myself to love again, I not only embrace a new life full of possibilities, I also carry forward the legacies of love and laughter left to me.

THE "RULES"

"I don't believe in being physically involved unless you're married and when I say that, [both men and women] look at me like I'm crazy. But I can't help how I was raised and how I feel. I probably won't find anyone that feels like I do, but I am not going to quit feeling this way."

If men and women are looking at you like you're "crazy," let them look! Who cares? You are not living your life according to an opinion poll and certainly this particular and deeply personal area of your life is absolutely, positively, *nobody else's business!* Moreover, I would be extremely selective as to the people with whom I chose to discuss this extremely private area of your life.

I firmly believe that anyone who truly cares about you will care about the "whole you," including your particular set of values. You don't have to defend yourself by stating that you are "not going to quit feeling this way." This is who you are and this is how you conduct yourself. You need make no explanations, apologies or set up any defenses because of your particular set of beliefs.

If you think that you won't find anyone who feels as you do, then you won't find them. It's a guarantee. It's a fact that we gravitate toward what we focus on and if you have already decided that you're not going to meet someone with the same value system that you have, well, you're going to gravitate toward that focus and you've just pretty much decided your own fate.

Don't be so quick to assume that you won't meet anyone who feels the same way about physical involvement as you do. Whether it's a first marriage or a subsequent marriage, you will discover that more and more, people of all backgrounds and faiths are choosing to wait until marriage to become intimate, for any number of reasons. If you believe that intimacy should take place only within the confines of marriage, then you stick to your guns, without making apologies or excuses to *anyone.*

> *"I have certain 'expectations' before I will become intimate with anyone. Is that wrong?"*

My personal expectations prior to intimacy included the nonnegotiable understanding that ours would be an exclusive and monogamous relationship. While many might not agree with those expectations, does that make having those expectations "wrong"? Absolutely not. They were *my* expectations and the way that I have chosen to govern myself. In other words, it's what worked for me.

As with the previous letter, many women's expectations include the commitment of marriage prior to engaging in intimacy. Other women's expectations might include a hefty bank account balance and a foreign luxury car consisting of letters and numbers rather than an actual model name. Now these might not be *my* expectations but whatever my own personal opinions might be, I would never deign to dictate what your or anyone else's expectations of a partner should be.

Your expectations, whatever they are, are exactly those...*yours*, thus making those expectations right for *you*. Hopefully, you will meet someone who will respect and fulfill every expectation and hope that is in your heart.

> *"I haven't been with anyone [intimately] since my husband and we were married [many years ago]. Have the 'rules' [concerning sex] changed since then?"*

"Rules" are rather like the expectations that we just discussed. Everyone has their own set of "rules" or guidelines or "conscience-keepers" by which they abide. I'll start with the bottom line:

> The only governing body
> who governs your body
> is YOU!

You are the only person to whom you are accountable. I can offer my point of view; I can certainly share how I have conducted myself; and I'm happy to offer advice and my opinion, but as far as rules are concerned, those have to come from within you.

The only rule that I would absolutely beg you to follow is one very simple rule, a rule that will be included in any book that I author (except perhaps a cookbook).

BE SMART—BE SAFE!

If your choice is to be sexually active, you must use a condom. This is not a subject up for debate. Any man that refuses to respect this rule gets shown the door. If you are worried about spoiling the mood or are too embarrassed to discuss the health, safety, and well-being of the two of you, you are simply not yet ready for intimacy. If you are firmly established as a monogamous couple, but either one or both of you have had multiple partners or had unprotected sex prior to your committing to one another, for your own peace of mind, both of you must get tested for anything and everything for which the medical community offers a test.

"What do you think of the 'Five Date Rule'? And what if you're not ready [to become intimate] after only five dates?"

This question admittedly makes me smile, for it evokes fond memories of many years ago. Years ago, my friend Sharla and I would always wish one another luck upon embarking on yet *another* new dating adventure and constantly reminded one another, "Don't forget the 'Five Date Rule'!" I won't disclose exactly how many years ago these exchanges took place but I will say that at the time, shoulder pads, hairstyles, and nighttime soap operas were all really over-the-top and incredibly inflated.

Suffice it to say, the "Five Date Rule" has been around for a long time.

For those who may be unaware, the "Five Date Rule" simply means that you promise yourself to wait until at least five dates have transpired before entertaining any thoughts of intimacy. While there is certainly a lot of opinion, conjecture, and "wiggle-room" (no pun intended) concerning the "Five Date Rule," I again state indisputably that if you are not ready to become intimate after five dates (or after ten dates or after twenty-eight dates), then you are not ready. It's that simple. Furthermore, anyone who tries to guilt, cajole, or otherwise badger you into taking a step for which you are not ready is not worth your time and certainly does not deserve your heart (or any other part of you).

All of that said, and acknowledging that only you can set the rules when it comes to intimacy, the one thing that I am dead set against is a breach of the "*First* Date Rule."

The "First Date" Rule

After a first date, the *only* thing that you should be going to bed with is a teddy bear and a magazine or a cup of hot chocolate or a fabulous late-night snack and a wonderful old movie. No falling into bed after a first date, and I don't care if he's Prince Charming complete with a white horse and flags-a-flying.

The only thing that a wonderful first date should lead to is a fantastic second date. It should not lead to breakfast in bed the next morning. Not yet.

TAKING CARE OF A DIFFERENT KIND OF "BUSINESS"

> *"What if you're 'physically' ready for a relationship, but not emotionally?"*
>
> *"I don't think I'm ready to get involved with someone else yet, but I sure miss being 'close' with a man, if you know what I mean."*
>
> *"While my husband was sick, he kept saying that I should go out and just have a 'fling' to get it out of my system before I get involved with someone else. Now that [my husband] is gone, what do you think?"*
>
> *"Do you think you can just have sex without the 'complications' of a relationship?"*
>
> *"I've been tempted to just 'get it [intimacy] over with' and I'm wondering if that's a good idea."*

As stated earlier, my opinion is truly immaterial because I am not you, but I am delighted to share my own thoughts and decision-making processes when it comes to taking this most important step.

Get it "over with"? Are we talking about undergoing a root canal again? Intimacy is supposed to be a wonderful and beautiful experience between two committed people, not something to "get over with" or otherwise approach with the same attitude as you might have at the thought of scrubbing toilets or undergoing a tax audit. If this is how the thought of intimacy strikes you, you're not quite ready yet.

As much as we might wish it were different and despite what some women's magazines and saucy television shows may tell us (and I'm certainly a fan of both), most women cannot separate physical and emotional intimacy. This is somewhat confounding and enigmatic to a lot of men out there, but the fact remains that we tend to combine the emotional with the physical (immensely more satisfying if you ask me), while some men seem to be far more adept at separating the two.

If you're wondering if entering into an intimate relationship absent emotional involvement is a good idea, you've just answered your own question. Personally speaking, if I wasn't ready emotionally, I knew that I wasn't ready. Period.

I am just not the kind of woman who wanted a "friend with benefits," or who would answer a "booty call" or a "hit and quit" or whatever we're calling it these days, nor could I simply "hook up" with a man to make myself feel better. Did that make the *four years* between the cessation of intimacy during my husband's illness and the beginning of a new relationship after his death any easier (not to mention the three *additional* years that ensued after ending *that* relationship and meeting my beloved)? Of course not. Was it frustrating? Of course it was. I'm a woman and I naturally missed intimacy, closeness, and that wonderful feeling of being desired by a man, but not so much that I was willing to sacrifice my heart, my emotions, and my self-esteem.

I know myself well enough to understand that a strictly physical involvement would never have been enough for me. I was not willing to compromise my heart and my own self-worth in the interest of "taking care of business." The cost would have been far too high. It's rather like doing fabulous hair and makeup and then getting all dressed up in a cocktail dress, shoulder-sweeper earrings, and five-inch heels to go out for a fine dining experience, but rather than having filet mignon with béarnaise sauce, baby roasted potatoes, a brut champagne, and berries and whipped cream for dessert (my favorite meal), you instead go to the 24-hour Splash-and-Dash convenience store for a bag of Doritos and a Diet Coke. True, it tastes OK and it's momentarily filling, but not exactly what you would call deliciously satisfying.

And by the way, if you think for one minute that entering into a strictly sexual relationship doesn't carry the potential for emotional "complication," you are being just a little bit naïve.

Although you may believe that your needs are strictly limited to the physical, in reality, what you are truly longing for is *closeness*. That closeness, which is *true* intimacy, takes emotional involvement. If you're not ready emotionally and you jump in and get involved with someone physically, you're going to wind up feeling pretty empty after the fact. I know that it's difficult; I went through that lack of physical companionship for very long time, but if you're willing to wait for what you really want *and* wait until you're ready in all respects, it is *so* worth it.

It's A "Wrap"... Stiletto-Style!

There is absolutely no doubt that the decision to become physically involved again with anyone on any level is a decision potentially fraught with fear, doubt, and trepidation (rather like the Nordstrom Half-Yearly Sale).

This is once again a time of listening to that "little voice" inside of you that will tell you when, how, and with whom this decision should be made. Although there are likely as many opinions on the subject as there are shoes in the world: *the decision is yours!*

Trust in yourself and in that little voice inside. Don't allow yourself to be influenced, pressured, or goaded into making any moves for which you might not be ready just yet. Believe me, my sweet friends, both the right person and the right time will arrive!

chapter eight

Children—Their "Today" And Your Family's "Tomorrow"

When you are a widow with young or adolescent children, yours is truly a dual responsibility. You must see to your needs as a grieving widow, and at the same time, you must help your children with their grief and their eventual transition into new lives of their own.

Children of all ages not only need time and space to grieve, they need to have an environment created for them where they understand that they can be sad or angry or quiet or reflective. They need to know that it's not only OK to be feeling this way, but they will not be criticized or told to move on or otherwise be forced to stuff their feelings in a side pocket and paste a phony smile on their faces, crumbling inside all the while. Is it hard to watch your children in pain? It's horribly difficult as we know but this is part of parenthood. Allowing your children ample time and room to grieve is a vital part of helping your children take their first steps on their healing journey.

When Breaking the News Means Breaking a Heart

"I lost my husband to leukemia. We have a [young] son who loved his daddy dearly. It's still really hard to explain to my son how his daddy died. He knows Daddy got sick and is in Heaven now, but from time to time he still thinks his daddy will come home. It breaks my heart to see my son break down and it's even harder now that he's in school and all the other kids talk about their fathers."

"My daughter keeps asking when Daddy is coming home. When I try to explain to her that he's not coming home and why, she asks why he left us."

It is so difficult to grow up in a world where "everybody has a daddy except me." In fact, even though it has been many years since his death, Kendall still has times when she will break down and cry because Daddy isn't here. It doesn't happen as often as it once did, but she absolutely still feels his absence acutely, and she's an adult. There is little more that can break your heart as easily as the sight of your child in unbelievable emotional pain.

It's not at all unusual that a younger child doesn't truly understand why Daddy is gone and why he isn't coming home. When they ask if Daddy is coming back, you must answer honestly, but let them know that Daddy still loves them and always will. Be sure that they understand that Daddy did not willingly "leave" you. In other words, death does not equal abandonment.[8]

When the breakdowns occur, and they will, hold your children tight, let them know how much you love them, and that you understand how badly they are hurting. Do *not* discourage them from crying or from feeling pain; they need to know that theirs is an environment where expression of these emotions is absolutely acceptable, no matter how difficult it is on you.

---

8 I once again remind those of you who are the courageous survivors of a suicide that your husband was likely not thinking in terms of abandoning you or your children. I highly encourage spouses and children of suicides to seek counseling in this very specialized area of grief.

There are going to be those times when there truly is no substitute for Daddy. Examples include the father-child activities that take place at school and with clubs or sports organizations. On those occasions, when your child might be feeling the absence of their father just a little bit more acutely, you may want to design your own Big Night Out and go elsewhere. I have been asked many times if it wouldn't be better to just take a male relative and attend the event or just be Mommy and go to the event anyway. While I acknowledge that different ideas work for different families, under our own set of circumstances, this would have only served to magnify Mike's absence rather than mollify Kendall's feelings of sorrow. The establishment of special nights out on our own worked especially well in lieu of the annual father-daughter dance at school or the other father-daughter events that periodically came up on the calendar. To this day, Kendall speaks affectionately of those special nights that we shared.

> *"My husband was recently killed [in the line of duty]. My daughter just turned one year old and I am pregnant with our second child. How do I help them [understand that] their father is gone and convey to them that he loved them more than anything in the world?"*

> *"My husband became ill when our son was three years old and died right after our son turned six years old. How do I help our son to know his father without making him sad?"*

Don't be afraid to keep your husband's memory alive for your children in an age-appropriate manner. Encourage school-age children to display a framed picture or two of Dad in their bedrooms and keep a few mementos of Dad close at hand (which Kendall continues to this day and eventually wound up extending her displays and mementos to include her apartment and her car). Enjoy reminiscing through family photo albums and videotapes with your children. You might consider creating a "storybook" about their father, complete with how and when you met, and sweet, funny, embarrassing stories about your family that can be used during your healing journey and saved as a precious heirloom for your child to treasure as they grow into adulthood.

Most of all, don't be afraid to remember "out loud" by talking about him. Many parents make that error and not only does that fail to erase the memory, but oftentimes a child *wants* to talk or ask questions about their father but thinks that it's a taboo subject. Create an environment where your child understands that talking about their daddy is always going to be encouraged and welcomed.

BEING STRONG IS GREAT—BEING "WEAK" IS EVEN BETTER

> *"I feel that I cannot break down [because] I have to provide and care for my [child]."*
>
> *"I don't feel strong enough for my children."*
>
> *"How can I be strong for my children when I can't even be strong for myself?"*
>
> *"In addition to losing my husband, our children's lives are dramatically altered."*
>
> *"I know I have to be strong for my [children], but I've never felt so terrible in my entire life."*

It is perfectly acceptable for your children to see that Mommy is hurting. How on earth will they know that it's OK to be sad if Mommy isn't sad? Don't be worried about losing control; it's OK for your children to realize that you are a human being as well as their mother.

We know that our children take their cues from us. So what do you think is going through their heads if Mom hasn't cried or feels like everyone should be "over it" and moving on or if Mom doesn't want to talk about it anymore? Your children are going to think that they too must put their grief away someplace; if Mom isn't sad, then "Grief Time" must be officially finished.

As before, it is up to you to create the kind of environment that automatically lets your child know that sadness is a normal part of the healing process and that Mommies get sad too. This also opens the door to continued dialogue between you and your children, helping to ensure that your child will not consciously or otherwise choose more destructive methods with which to cope with their loss.

HELPING THE GRIEVING CHILD (UNDER THE AGE OF TEN YEARS)

> *"My children are two years old and four years old and they are really misbehaving lately. Do you think this is because of all that has happened?"*

> *"I thought that my [child] was dealing with things, but he has been acting up at school. He is so sweet and amazing at home, so I had no idea. I feel like I am not protecting my [child] from feeling this pain."*

> *"My [child] began wetting the bed shortly after my husband died. I'm really worried about this because [the child is] eight years old and we never had this problem before. Because of this, [the child] doesn't want to go to sleepovers or church camp. I think it may be related to the trauma of losing Dad, but maybe it's just a phase."*

> *"My ten-year-old always used to be so easygoing, but [since the death] everything is a fight. He refuses to do his chores and has become very defiant."*

Try as we might, not only can we not protect our children from the pain of grief or from their own healing journeys, it is a mistake to try. As discussed before, protecting or "shielding" a child from grief is tantamount to sending the message that grief should be denied or otherwise ignored, which is impossible.

Go back to the previous questions and answers concerning the creation of an environment where your child will feel comfortable talking about Dad. Is your child talking to you about his feelings, whatever those feelings happen to be at the moment? In the guise of protecting your child, do you discourage crying or other healthy and normal expressions of grief? These feelings have to come out somewhere and sometime and if grief is not coming out verbally or with healthy expression, it is going to manifest in other ways.

You are wise to take any signs of trauma seriously, rather than brush them off using that well-worn cliché that "It's just a phase and it will pass." All of these symptoms are classic symptoms of reaction to trauma and none should be ignored. Consult immediately with your child's pediatrician for assistance, so that these problems can be promptly addressed and resolved.

HELPING THE GRIEVING CHILD (ADOLESCENTS, TEENAGERS, YOUNG ADULTS)

> *"My husband, who had always been in perfect health, died suddenly. It is still such a shock. My [adult child] is dealing [with alcohol]. I haven't had time to think about my own grief because I'm so worried about [the] destructive activities. What can I do?"*

> *"I thought that my husband's death would bring our family closer. Instead, it has ripped us apart. [One child] won't talk about it and the other [child] only wants to know what's 'in it' [i.e., money] for her."*

> *"What do you do when your child's idea of coping is going out and partying nonstop and they quit caring about family, school, and their friends?"*

Your children are transitioning into a world where "everyone has a dad except me" and as you have discovered, that's a tough transition. Going through a depression of sorts is to be expected and to this day, Kendall still experiences those times when she struggles with her dad's absence, even though she too is an adult and it's been many years since her daddy died.

However, when the behavior starts to take a toll on the family or becomes destructive in *any* respect, that's when Mom has to get tough. I know that this is the last thing that you feel like doing; however, being a parent means that sometimes you are not going to be the most popular person in the room. This is one of those times.

Here comes the tough love part. Your children are either teenagers or adults and they need to behave accordingly. You have suffered a loss too and they should be just as concerned with you as you are with them. This would be an excellent time to remind them that you love them and would love to talk about the horrible tragedy of their fathers' death with them, but that destructive behavior is not acceptable—any of it. Excessive drinking, drugging, partying, irresponsible behaviors, etc., is not now, nor will it ever be OK. They need to be strongly reminded that they are *not* the only ones who have suffered a loss and that they are *not* the only ones in pain. Sometimes older children need to be reminded that the world does not completely revolve around them.

One more important point: If you feel that your child's behavior is an endangerment to him, to you, or to anyone else, intervention is necessary and I don't care how old the child is. Don't hesitate to confront the situation. I'd rather have a child here to "hate" me in the short run, than suffer dire consequences because I didn't interfere. Get any and all professional help that you need to get and do not let harsh words from your child deter you.

Most of all, please don't feel as though you are the only one to whom something like this has happened. I have coached many widowed mothers in the same way for the same reasons with excellent results.

"How can you tell the difference between grief and depression?"

I recently heard a statement that I thought was absolutely spot-on:

> Sadness is when you care about *everything;*
> depression is when you care about *nothing.*

Is it normal to feel depressed after what you and your children have experienced? Without question. However, there is a huge difference between depression that lasts for a finite period of time in reaction to traumatic events (situational depression) and depression that takes over, permeates, and dominates your entire life (clinical depression). It is incredibly vital that you distinguish between situational depression and a depression that is causing an inability to not only function in daily life, but to thrive as well.

Does your child show a general reluctance to return to normal daily activities and to their life as a whole? I'm not talking about going back to school the day after the funeral or not feeling like going to *a* slumber party or *one* football game, but rather, a general lack of engagement with life, be it with your family at dinnertime and/or with their close friends that despite your encouragement, does not seem to be improving. Most importantly, are they now or have they ever sat down and talked to you about their feelings?

If you feel that your child may be depressed, this is again a great time to get your family physician involved, as well as a school counselor or school psychologist. Tell them that you suspect that your child may be suffering from depression and don't be afraid to share all of the circumstances that exist in your household. Show your child that you are taking their pain seriously and remember that as with you, loss is a wound. Just because it doesn't show does not mean that it doesn't hurt all the same.

People Say the Dumbest Things, the "Junior" Version

> *"People have told my children, 'Stay close to your mom [because] she needs you.' Why do people say this? I feel like my children need as much support as I do."*

> *"When my [child] went back to school [after the death], the teacher actually said, 'You have to be strong for your mom.' Can you believe that?"*

*"Everyone (even relatives) tell my son 'You're the 'man of the house'
now.' Some of them made this comment right after the funeral.
And he's only seven years old!"*

*"My [adolescent child] came home from school crying because
another child told her, 'You're half an orphan.' I didn't know how
to respond [or provide comfort], which made me feel even worse."*

There was once a time that I naively thought that I had seen it all. And then I
started receiving letters like these, and worse.

When I read letters such as these (and I receive a lot of them), the one
thought that echoes through my head is: "Are you *kidding* me?"

We have all been the collective recipients of some pretty ridiculous statements, generally said in the guise of attempting to comfort us during our time
of bereavement and falling woefully short. Unfortunately, our children are
not immune to the whole "Some People Say the Most Insanely Ridiculous
Things Imaginable" phenomenon and are even less likely to know how to
deal with such statements. Imagine one widowed mother's horror when her
son approached her, asking where he could get a job as he had been told that
since his father was gone, he was now the "man of the house," at the age of
eight years.

Who in the *world* would say such things (and worse) to children?

Answer: Many of the same people that say some pretty ridiculous things
to widows.

The most regrettable thing about people who make such statements is that
unlike adults, who can learn how to rise above insensitivity (or even outright
stupidity), children are quite likely to actually believe that they are "orphaned"
or are now expected to be "in charge" or otherwise expected to become the
"head of the house." Here's where you need to jump in with both feet Mom!

If your child shares that statements like these (or similar) were made to
him, immediately stop *whatever* it is that you are doing (and that includes
pulling over if you are in the car and it is safe to do so) to reassure them that:

1. *No* child is expected to be in charge of a household or otherwise act in a parental role.

2. *No* child is expected to be "strong" because Mom is grieving.

3. There is *no such thing* as "half an orphan."

If and when your child protests (i.e., "But Aunt Mary said that…," "But my teacher says…," "All the kids say…"), feel free to tell them that even though Aunt Mary, or Teacher, or All The Kids may have meant well (and you may choke on those words but say them anyway), they are wrong nonetheless. Let them know that while it's true that you are grieving Dad's loss, you do not need them to "be strong" on your behalf or otherwise make any attempt to shield their feelings from you. In fact, this is a great time to actually encourage them to let their feelings out, particularly if you feel as though they might have actually given credence to any of these horribly inappropriate statements.

If you are able to ascertain who said these or any similar statements to your child, it is not out of line to take the person or people aside and *gently* let them know that this is not the sort of thing that your child needs to hear and that these statements can actually cause a great deal of harm in the long run. Let them know that your child needs support just as much as you do and that such statements actually deprive a child of their freedom to grieve.

If your child is being told these sorts of things by their peers, such as the "half an orphan" observation, then remind your child that their friends are also children and are not in the same position to help them as you or another trusted adult. For example, you might explain to your child that there is no such thing as "half an orphan" and perhaps their friends don't realize that because they are kids too.

It's almost impossible to fathom that children who have lost their fathers have to endure comments such as these; however, you must remember that the key here is *reassurance*. Reassure your child that while it is a difficult time right now, things are going to get better (and they will) and that most of all, they are the child, you are the parent, and you are the one who will be taking care of them, not the opposite.

"OVERFOCUS" ON YOUR CHILDREN; "UNDERFOCUS" ON YOU

> *"My friend lost her husband and has two young children. She is having a really hard time and she mentioned that she would like to find a place to 'get away' and deal with some of the issues that are unresolved. I think she is having trouble because she has to focus on her kids so much and has been putting her needs aside. I am worried about her."*

> *"I make time for my children, but I have zero time for me; between work and the kids, there's nothing left over for me."*

> *"My kids and their activities keep me distracted a lot of the time, but I need time to myself to figure things out too."*

Focusing on children is all well and fine and certainly necessary, particularly at this critical time in your lives. However, if you do not make time for you, whether it's to grieve or to go out and enjoy yourself, there isn't going to be any "you" left for anything or anyone else.

Furthermore, using children's activities or your career as distractions is not going to help you get through and past your grief, rather, these distractions will only serve to postpone the inevitable. There is no shortcutting or circumventing grief and no amount of diversion will change that fact. We all know that we are more productive as parents when we take the time to pay attention to ourselves, without guilt and without regret.

It's always been interesting to me that we make appointments with doctors and dentists, manicurists and massage therapists. We schedule parent-teacher conferences, soccer matches, and piano lessons. Why then can't we also schedule time for *us*—to soak in a tub, to visit the gym, to have lunch with a dear friend, or whatever it is that might bring us pleasure, peace, or at least a well-deserved break?

As much as we love our children, we cannot be the mothers that we want to be or that they need us to be if we are not caring for ourselves, in every respect and in the best way that we possibly can. Commit to making those appointments for and with yourself, not the "have to" kind of appointments, but the "Yippee, I get to pay attention to me!" kind of appointments.

You know what else? There's absolutely *nothing* wrong with wanting to "get away" from it all, if just for a little while, perhaps for an "overnight" or a weekend. If your children are not yet old enough to stay on their own, ask a relative or a close friend to host them for a day or two; chances are great that they will enjoy a getaway themselves! Then pack a bag and *go*—on a church or synagogue retreat, to a women's conference or tennis camp, or perhaps to a mountain resort or a beachside hotel.

Go someplace where you can refresh, renew, and revive yourself and your spirit. In fact, there are many conferences and retreats designed just for widows (I appear at a number of them) and although these conferences may not initially seem like you are getting away (since it involves widowhood), there also exists the chance to make new and lifelong friends who are traveling the identical road as you are, along with the opportunities to learn about everything from financial transition to what to wear on a first date.

Remember that you are no good to the people that need you the most until and unless you are good to you first and that you can be good to yourself absent any guilt. It's an *entitlement*, not a luxury.

> *"How do you get a 'new' life when your children need to stay in the 'old' life?"*

Don't confuse "routine" with "old life." Children are perfectly entitled, and generally delighted, to return to their familiar routines, such as school, extracurricular activities, time spent with friends, and so forth. In fact, it's one of the primary things that I recommend, especially for the newly widowed and their families. To a child (and to most of us), "routine" equals "security" and security is what a child of any age needs at this critical point in time.

When Kendall was in middle school, her highly anticipated cheerleading tryouts were scheduled to take place four months after her dad's death and while her grandfather (my father) was in a coma and not expected to live much longer (which he didn't). Although she desperately wanted to go ahead with tryouts, her first inclination was to forego them altogether because of both the immediately past and current situation in our family, yet I knew that skipping those tryouts would have been incredibly painful for her.

Keeping this in mind and realizing that my father's death was imminent, I let Kendall know that she was to absolutely participate in tryouts; the rationale being that missing those tryouts would neither bring her dad back, nor would it change the situation with her grandfather. I also knew that come autumn, it would have caused her additional pain in watching the new squad, knowing that she forfeited the opportunity to try out.

Kendall went ahead with tryouts, made the squad, and subsequently won two state championships that year. Was going ahead with her "routine" the right thing to do? Without a doubt. Furthermore, while supporting Kendall in her pursuits and activities and getting her from one end of the state to another for practices and competitions and whatnot, I too was simultaneously, slowly and surely moving forward into my new life, a life that eventually included changes in homes and careers.

As you can see, sticking to familiar routines while moving forward is not mutually exclusive; on the contrary, it is completely doable and desirable.

"I have been a widow for several years. Before their son died, we spent every holiday and a lot of time with [my in-laws]. I often resented it when my husband was alive, but went along with it for my husband's and children's sakes. Since he has been gone, I feel less comfortable with [my in-laws]. When I'm at their house, I feel really out of place without my husband there. I have continued to see them every holiday because they are my children's grandparents. My children are young adults now and live on their own. But increasingly, I feel more resentful that my mother-in-law expects it. [She] 'guilts' me if I have other plans. My children think I am

> *being unkind when I don't want to join in every time they are*
> *together. It feels like they want some sort of control over my loyalty.*
> *How much time should I spend with my in-laws in order to honor*
> *them as my husband's parents and my children's grandparents?"*

Girlfriend, you are a hero. You not only did the right thing by your in-laws when your husband was alive and your children were young, but you continue to do what is perceived to be the "right thing" by everyone in the world even *years* after your husband's death.

Now here are my questions to you: What about *you*? What do *you* want?

This is where we need to help you find your "inner voice," starting with the kids. Children can sometimes lose sight of the fact that Mom isn't just "Mom," she is a *person* as well. By your own description, your children are now young adults who live on their own. You need to have a calm, sit-down discussion with them and explain that far from being "unkind" for not spending every single special occasion with their grandparents, it is perfectly normal and natural for you to explore other avenues, adventures, or whatever it is that you feel like doing, even if it means just sleeping in on Christmas Day because *you* want to!

You are well within your rights to say, "I'm going to pass on this…" (holiday, weekend, special occasion) and offer an alternative time to get together as a family if you feel like doing so. Furthermore, your children are adults—what is preventing them from spending time with their grandparents on their own?

You may want to think about having the same kind of sit-down with your in-laws and gently explain that while you will always love and appreciate them and that you will never stop loving your late husband, your life is moving in a forward direction and that you are *entitled* to move in that forward direction. You are not destined to live your life in permanent mourning, nor would your husband have wanted that for you. Staying in a place of mourning will not bring him back.

While you may not necessarily want to flaunt the fact that you are dating, it's certainly not something that you have to keep secret either. If they ask you if you have dated or if you are dating, answer honestly. If they say something akin to, "How could you do that to him?", politely answer, "I'm not doing anything to him; he's not here anymore." It's hard to hear, it hurts, but it is also a fact.

As to "loyalty," your loyalty has been more than evident, not only throughout your marriage but since becoming a widow as well. It has been years since your husband's death and as I continue to teach:

YOU CAN HONOR YOUR PAST.
YOU CAN TREASURE YOUR PAST.
YOU CAN LOVE YOUR PAST.
YOU DO NOT HAVE TO *LIVE* IN YOUR PAST.

There are people who might prefer that you live in the past. The problem with that is that if you live in the past, you're missing out on something called life, and that is the most unfair part of this entire scenario. It's time for you to listen to that inner voice. It's time for you to honor *you*. It's time for you to help others realize that it has been years since you lost your husband and that while you will always love and miss him and no one could ever replace him, you are nonetheless entitled to move forward with life in the ways that you see fit. There is no "should" in the equation (as in, "How much time 'should' I spend with my in-laws?"), except to say that you *should* start paying attention to yourself first because you deserve it.

STEPS—THE ONES IN YOUR HEART

> *"Now that my husband is gone, what is the 'technical' relationship between me and his children? I have been a part of their lives for most of their lives, but I don't know how I fit in now."*
>
> *"Am I still 'mom' to my stepchildren [after their father's death]?"*

If you were married at the time of your husband's death, you are still stepmother to his children. It would be my fondest wish for you that whatever relationship(s) you established with your husband's children would continue after his death. If yours was a loving, productive relationship with your stepchildren, there is no reason at all why that should not continue, and in fact, you are likely to be of great help and comfort to one another as you move through your grief together.

> *"My husband had sole physical custody of my stepdaughter and she has lived with us since she was [a toddler]. She is now [a teenager] and her [biological] mother is planning to seek legal custody. This is kind of weird, since the mother has never been involved in her daughter's life. I feel like she is my own daughter and she doesn't want to leave the only home she remembers. Not to mention the fact that she has been through enough [because of her father's death]. Do I have any rights at all? Can her mother just come in and take her away? We're both really afraid."*

It is vital that you immediately seek counsel and guidance from an attorney specializing in family law matters. Depending upon where you live, teenagers often have the opportunity to express their custodial wishes to the commissioner, arbitrator, judge, or magistrate presiding over such custody cases. In deciding custody, the court takes all mitigating factors into consideration, including what sort of interference might occur with the child's education (i.e., a change of schools), as well as the biological parent's overall involvement in the child's life and the trauma that the child has already suffered as a result of the loss of her father. Counsel will not only be able to knowledgeably and wisely advise you, they will most importantly act as advocate for you, should the case proceed to court.

> *"I am so lucky [that I have] the best relationship with my [adult] stepchildren in the world. But since their dad passed away, I don't see or hear from them as much. Should I still seek them out and try to have a relationship with them? I would really miss it if I wasn't a part of their lives anymore."*

If you had a great relationship with your stepchildren prior to your husband's death, the fact that you are not hearing from them as much is probably not a reflection on you. Rather, it may be everyone trying to resume a "normal" life and trying to determine what that normal life entails.

As lousy a cliché as this is, life does, in fact, go on and your adult stepchildren likely have jobs, households, and children of their own that also require attention and the ensuing result is that you get, well, "forgotten." It may also be that they feel as though they are a sad reminder of your husband's absence and they may be slightly reluctant to contact you because of your grieving processes. In other words, they could be waiting to hear from *you* and if they don't hear from you, they are assuming that you may not *want* to hear from them.

If you are not hearing from your stepchildren as much as you would prefer, get proactive. Pick up the phone to find out how everyone is doing. Let them know that you would love to see them and that you miss them dearly. Plan a dinner or a get-together that doesn't involve a national holiday.

In other words, you are the "mom." Make the effort to remain the close-knit and loving family that you were prior to your husband's death and chances are excellent that you will find your efforts reciprocated in kind.

It's A "Wrap"...Stiletto-Style!

Remember that the key to helping your children recover and move forward from the death of their father is to always and forever continue to create an environment where your children know that not only is it OK to miss him, but it's also OK to talk about him, laugh about him, and cry about him. No matter what turns your lives take, no matter with whom you may become involved in the future, your children must always be given this freedom and you must be the person facilitating that freedom. When a child knows that he is free to remember in constructive ways, the tears of grief can eventually turn to smiles of remembrance and those are smiles that are wonderful to behold.

chapter nine

REMARRIAGE AND
RECOMMITMENT REVIEW

TELL THE TRUTH—DID YOU EVER THINK IT POSSIBLE?

Did you ever think that you would come to a point in your life where you would even *entertain* the thought of remarriage? The answer is likely, "You have *got* to be kidding me."

Guess what? The authors of the following letters felt the same way. However, as life progresses, so then does your healing.

As happy a time as it may be, the matter of remarriage is not quite as "cut-and-dried" as it likely was when you married your husband. There are many factors, both practical and emotional, that you must take into careful consideration before taking this major step forward in your life and we're here to help.

"I THOUGHT I WAS READY AND I'M NOT"

"I lost my husband after complications from surgery. I thought that my life was over, but with the help of my faith, my family and friends I started a new life. I met a widower, fell in love, and

> *he asked me to marry him. I thought that I was over losing my*
> *husband, but found myself comparing everything about my fiancé*
> *to my late husband. We broke off our engagement and this opened*
> *up the wounds of losing my husband all over again. I need some*
> *advice on starting over again."*

You are to first be congratulated for having the determination to move forward with your life. As we all know, this takes great courage, as does making yourself emotionally available to another in order to fall in love once again.

What happened to you is not at all uncommon. You have already learned about the "fog" that we're in after our husband's death—an anesthesia of sorts against the shock that we have sustained and the pain that we are suffering as a result. Sometimes, it's not until the introduction of a new person into our lives that we allow the "anesthesia" to truly wear off. The "fog" then begins to lift and the pain of the *reality* of the loss sets in.

Let's also address another common phenomenon, one that I addressed earlier, write about extensively, and have lovingly entitled, the "Ghost of Husband Past." I have found one very common denominator among widows: our late husbands never did anything wrong—ever! The Ghost of Husband Past was perfect in every way and anyone who comes along after the Ghost of Husband Past will never really measure up.

Now we all know that's not exactly accurate. Of course you want to remember the good qualities and the wonderful times that you had with your late husband but you must also remember that he wasn't without flaw or fault. Of equal importance is realizing that it is unfair to expect anyone to "compete" with the Ghost of Husband Past because it is impossible.

Have you ever compared yourself to women in the fashion magazines? When we do that, we are once again comparing our alleged weaknesses with what we perceive to be their "strengths." The same train of thought applies here. When we do the comparison making between "New Man" and "Past Life," we are comparing New Man's *weaknesses* to our late husband's *strengths*. As natural as it may seem to be and as we discussed earlier, you simply can't use your late husband as the "yardstick" against which everyone else will be measured. Not only is it unfair to the new person in your life, but you'll also be missing out on the strengths that this new person brings to your life as well.

You were wise in calling off your engagement for now, in order to take the time that you need to truly recover from the loss of your husband. This doesn't mean that at some point in the future you won't remarry. It simply means that right now was not the right time for you and you are smart to acknowledge that. I will always teach and remind that if you feel as though you've moved too quickly in *any* part of your recovery, back up and take the time off that you need for *you.*

> *"I am a recent widow and have been dating a man for six months. We've decided to marry next year. I thought [that] I was OK with it because he makes me so happy. Tonight the issue of taking his name came up and I'm having a hard time. It's not that I don't want to take his name; it's that I'm having trouble 'losing' my [late] husband's name. Maybe all this is too soon."*

Let's start with the very last sentiment: "Maybe all this is too soon." If the "little voice" inside is causing you to question the timing of a remarriage or your potential remarriage in general, then step back. Take an honest reexamination of the reason(s) that you are getting married. While he may make you very happy and that is wonderful, are you remarrying for the right reasons? Or is it because it's just too hard or hurts to be alone?

I have received literally hundreds of letters like these, where widows find themselves in relationships or engaged to be married or even already remarried and too late they feel that they may have "jumped" too soon. It is perfectly acceptable (and very smart) to wait awhile to make absolutely sure that this is the right person for you and that your reason(s) for remarrying are the right reasons.

As to the question of your last name, consider hyphenating your current last name with your new married name. Many widows have done this, especially when there are children involved. Let your intended know how you feel about potentially having to choose between your late husband's name and his and that you are thinking of hyphenating the two. Hopefully, you will be received with an attitude of compassion and understanding.

These are not at all uncommon situations. For whatever reason, you are not ready to recommit right now and the fact that you realize this is a huge step toward healing. I'm also proud of the fact that you recognize and welcome the opportunity to get to know yourself, as many women are afraid of facing that prospect.

Why can't you commit right now? It could be because you didn't grieve as much as you should have initially, or perhaps you felt like at some point, you "should" be over it and got reinvolved before you were really ready in your heart to do so. This does *not* mean that you will never find love again or be ready to commit. It just means that now is not the time.

Here's another thought—perhaps this isn't the right man for you and in your deepest heart of hearts, you know it. Remember that every single person on the planet has that "little voice" inside of them. So do you. That little voice is telling you something—listen to it!

You may have to just sit down and tell your man that now is not the right time for you to be seriously involved and that you need time to find your own way. Will this be a difficult conversation? Of course it will. Will he try and talk you into staying with him? Probably. Will he tell you that you should be "over" losing your husband by now? I'd be willing to bet on it. However, you will need to be strong for you and insist on having the life that you want and deserve.

Before you can be a full and complete partner to anyone, you need to first grieve your late husband properly. You next need to make sure that you are not comparing a new man's weaknesses to your late husband's strengths. You already know that we all tend to have selective amnesia when it comes to our late husbands and it's not fair to expect a new man to "measure up" to the Ghost of Husband Past. It won't happen.

For example, Mike had been gone for about two years, when I became

involved with and pursued a two-year relationship with the man who ultimately turned out to be not such a great partner for me. Was it because he
wasn't Mike? No. Was it because he didn't "measure up" to the very high
standard that was Mike Fleet? No. Did I once compare him to Mike? No. He
simply was not the right man for me.

Finally, remember that you're in charge here. Don't let anyone bully,
manipulate, or "guilt" you into staying where you can't be right now. Get to
know the awesome woman that you have become. Grieve your loss in the way
that perhaps you did not allow yourself when your husband died. In other
words, take time off and time out for you. Just as I encourage widows to take
their time in the grief recovery process, I also encourage you to really take
your time regarding this most important step in your life and I wish you every
happiness as you move forward.

> *"I've been in a relationship that I thought was the answer to my
> prayers [and] I could find love again. However, I find myself in a
> position that this isn't so. I can't move forward with this new person
> for many reasons. I don't want to hurt anyone, but I don't know how
> to handle this. I've told him that I am just not ready, but he would
> do anything for me and he wants to be with me '24/7.' I want to
> 'find me' and I guess I wasn't ready for this relationship."*

You can see that yours is not an unusual situation. For whatever reason, you
are not yet ready to recommit right now and the fact that you realize this is
a huge step toward healing. I'm also proud of the fact that you want to "find
you," as you say. This means that you recognize and welcome the opportunity
to get to know yourself and many women are afraid of facing that prospect.

Another point of concern is your comment that he wants to be with you
"24/7." Anyone who wants to wrap himself around your ankle needs to be
shaken loose. You need to have your own life, your own friends, your own
pursuits, your own interests, and your own time apart from a man and this is
advice that I would give to *any* woman, regardless of marital status.

Remember, you need to *insist* on having the life that you deserve and if it is a life that does not include this man, whether for the time being or forever, then that is the way it must be.

"I Think I Can—or Can I?"

> *"My husband and I always talked about the fact that we enjoyed our marriage so much that should one of us die, the other would definitely marry again but so far there has been no opportunity! I have children and my parents who love and support me, but I'm alone. I don't know what to do with the longing and the pain."*
>
> *"I would love to be married again. But I'm afraid that instead of marrying [because it is] the right person, I'll get married just because I miss being married so much."*

I understand that feeling because I truly love being married too. However, I am also able to distinguish between the love of a *person* and wanting to be with the *person* from merely "wanting to be married." In order to be able to make that distinction, you really need to know yourself; otherwise, you stand to make one whale of a mistake. I have always said and will always stand by the opinion that it is far preferable to actually *be* alone than to be with the wrong person and *wish* you were alone.

How to make the distinction? Go back and carefully review Chapter Six (Love Is All Around You...Really!) and answer the following questions: 1) How much time has passed since the death of my husband? 2) Am I happy on my own? 3) Do I go or have I gone out *by myself* and did I *enjoy* myself?

You need to know who *you* are before you can be a complete partner to anyone else. The fact is that you are not the same woman that you were when you first married your late husband because the experience of widowhood forever changes you. Even though you loved being married (and most of us did), be sure that you can distinguish between loving a person and simply loving the institution of marriage. Remember that while remarriage is certainly possible for you, we want it to be for all of the right reasons.

> *"It's been [many] years since my husband died. I've been involved*
> *with a man for [several] years and I would love to marry him but*
> *he thinks that it's just because I miss my husband. He even calls*
> *himself the 'substitute.' I can't seem to convince him that I love*
> *him for him. Any thoughts?"*

It's interesting to me that your man refers to himself as the "substitute" when judging by the tone of your letter you have not been at all treating him that way.

Assuming that you do not begin your sentences with "When Joe was alive, he used to…" or "Joe always…" or "Joe never…" (or any other preface that would infer or invite comparison), and that your beloved is not surrounded by shrines to your late husband, his clothes still hanging in the closet or dozens of pictures of him gracing your walls, my educated guess would be that your new love feels threatened by or as though he is standing in the shadow of a "ghost."

The reality is that your late husband is now and will always be a part of your life. Your new love needs to understand that the heart truly does have capacity enough for all kinds of love, the love that you will always have for a husband that you had a life with many years ago, as well as the love that you have for *this* man today, in *this* life. Enough time has passed to where you are hardly leaping from one marriage headlong into another.

The two of you might benefit from couples' counseling, as your new love may need to hear these words from someone other than you. Otherwise, there is little that you can do. Insecurity is a difficult opponent to conquer when it comes from within us, let alone when it is another person's demon. Your beloved is going to have to either find a way to trust you when you tell him that you love him based on *his* merits or take the very real chance of eventually losing you to someone who "gets it" and is not constantly questioning your love and your loyalties.

> *"It's been [a short time] since my husband died. My boyfriend has asked me to marry him, but I'm not sure I can."*

The "quick 'n' easy" answer here is, "If you're not sure, you're not ready." While that is certainly a true statement and it sounds simple enough, in this case, it's not exactly the appropriate response.

The bigger question here is *why* do you feel unsure? Is it because only a short time has passed since the loss of your husband? Or perhaps it's because of the man himself? You may be unsure as to whether or not he is the right person for you. Maybe you don't think you can marry him because deep down, you're worried about what other people may do, say, or think, should you decide to remarry within such a short period of time. In other words, you need to examine the "why" in your uncertainty and answer yourself honestly.

As said before, I generally recommend against remarriage after only a short period of time following your husband's passing, having nothing to do with any of the reasons set forth above. It bears repeating: You are not the same woman that you were prior to the experience that was losing your husband. You need ample opportunity to recover from the loss experience and to get to know the person that you are, independent of being Mr. and Mrs. One-Half-of-a-Couple. It's challenging and it's not always a fun process but it is a fundamental part of grief recovery. Go back and reread the letters from the women in the "I Thought I Was Ready and I'm Not" section and then choose to wait a bit, rather than wind up in their extremely difficult situations.

CONSIDER THIS...

> *"I am getting benefits [from the government]. What will happen to my benefits if I get married again?"*
>
> *"I am thinking about getting married to my boyfriend [but] I receive [various] benefits for my [minor] children since their father's death. I want to marry my boyfriend, but I really don't want to lose [my children's benefits]. What should I do?"*

"I don't mean to sound like money matters more than love, but wouldn't it be kind of foolish to get married and maybe give up money that I'm entitled to?"

Ah, the eternal question: "Is money more important than love?"

In this particular situation, the answer is an emphatic *yes.*

No, I'm not shallow or superficial. I have never requested financial statements from *anyone* with whom I have ever been involved (although there were a few times I probably should have), nor is that how I measure any human being's value. While I did choose to involve myself with a man who does not either need me to or look to me to pay all of the bills and pick up all of the tabs (having made gross errors in judgment in the not-too-distant past in that regard), a bulging bank account and owning a bunch of high-priced "stuff" is not now, nor has it ever been a prerequisite for me to fall in or be in love.

That having been said, this is not what we're talking about here. We're talking about the potential forfeiture of financial benefits that, depending on the issuing entity, can last for the rest of your life. These are benefits that are meant to help secure you and your children financially. Once those benefits are forfeited, that's it. They're gone. No going back and saying, "Well, I was in love and now I'm not, so please crank up the benefit machine again."

Prior to making any decisions concerning marriage, it is absolutely vital that you contact each and every entity, company, or organization from whom you receive monetary benefits, as well as any company through whom you might be medically insured or have a life insurance policy. Ask them what their specific policies are concerning survivor benefits and remarriage and whatever the response, note with whom it was that you spoke and get their response in writing.

Do not let the person with whom you are involved bully, "guilt," or otherwise make you feel like a horrible person for conducting financially responsible investigations and making financially responsible choices. Years ago, I was accused of "loving money" by someone who thought I was putting the importance of my financial security (as well as that of my child) before a relationship. I was acting responsibly on behalf of myself and my child and he either couldn't handle it or didn't get it. Whichever was the case with him, and interestingly enough, the relationship soon fizzled after that conversation, clearly demonstrating that I had made a very wise decision indeed.

There are millions of people today who would love to remarry but can't because of benefits that they are receiving as they flat-out need the money (who among us doesn't?). Do your homework, get everything in writing, and do *not* feel guilty for choosing benefits over betrothal.

> *"[My fiancé and I] both have substantial savings [and other assets].*
> *Any advice on our financial and legal concerns?"*

You are very wise to each examine your finances and make preparations accordingly. I am of the very strong opinion that each of you should maintain your own finances separate of the other, so that if anything happens, you are both adequately protected. There is also the matter of the legacies that you each wish to leave to your own children and you will need to take that into consideration as well.

You may wish to establish one joint checking account together and have one major credit card together. These might take care of the day-to-day household bills, household emergencies, vacations, etc. However, for your own financial protection, you will want to maintain separate credit cards and do *not* merge your existing bank or credit accounts.

Remember, if either one of you are receiving any kind of benefits as widow or widower, you may forever forfeit these benefits upon remarriage. These benefits may include those paid through an employer (including medical insurance) or Social Security. This requires careful investigation, as there is no such thing as a "do over" when it comes to forfeiture of these benefits.

BLENDING FAMILIES: STIR TOGETHER AND MIX WELL?

"After spending [many] years as a widow, I am thrilled to be getting married to a fantastic man. He is divorced with two children and I have three children of my own. They all range in age from [very young] to [late teens]. Right now everyone is happy and excited but I know that there are still going to be adjustments. How do we make those adjustments as simple as possible?"

"I'm engaged to a widower and we are expecting our first child. He has no children and I have one [young child] by my late husband. I know that getting married and having a baby right away is a lot for a child to deal with all at once. How do we make it so that my [child] doesn't feel left out in all of this?"

"I have two [children] and so does my husband-to-be. But [some of] the kids aren't really happy with the idea of us getting married. Have you ever heard of 'staying single for the children' because [my fiancé and I have] talked about doing that."

"I am a widow [with two young children] and I am remarrying a widower in six months. Can you give any advice on remarriage?"

When you are remarrying after death or divorce, you are inevitably going to deal with the "Ghosts of Spouses Past," be they good (as is generally the case with a late spouse) or bad (as may be the case with an ex-spouse). While continuing to remember and paying honor to the past that each of you have, it is also up to you to put the past in its proper perspective, by making no comparisons between a past spouse and a future spouse (inwardly or outwardly) and taking steps to create the formation of a new family dynamic.

No matter how much they profess to love the new person, somewhere, in the back of the children's minds lurks the question, "Is Mommy replacing Daddy?" and vice versa. The parent must sit down with the child or children and discuss this very important step honestly and in an age-appropriate manner, being prepared to listen to and discuss all of the children's fears and concerns in-depth with an open mind, and taking care not to trivialize the children's genuine feelings.

You must remember that regardless of age, children are still children when it comes to Mom or Dad. The parent should gently and lovingly advise their child that while they will always treasure the time that they had with the absent parent, that period of their life has come to an end. While no one will ever truly "replace" the absent parent, it is absolutely acceptable for a single adult to seek love and companionship with another. In other words, no, you do not have to "stay single for the children."

Children of all ages can also be encouraged to continue to display pictures or other mementos of the absent parent if they wish, in their room at home, in their locker at school, etc. As discussed earlier, my daughter has always displayed pictures of her dad in her room, at school, in her car, and now, in her own apartment and does so with my continued and wholehearted support and blessing. In this manner, the parent is reassuring the child that the absent parent is not being "replaced," and that the child is neither dishonoring nor being disloyal to the absent parent by loving and creating a relationship with a stepparent.

It's also important to remember that in any successful family dynamic, there are several "lives" involved: each spouse's life individually, their life as a couple, life as a family, and each parent individually with the children. Even though there may be the addition of a new spouse, the parent must continue to make the time for spending with just the children and the prospective spouse will need to understand this. At the same time, the parent might encourage the new spouse to also spend time alone with the children. Without forcing things, it can also be a fun and important time of bonding, where they can start their own traditions and outings.

IT'S A "WRAP"... STILETTO-STYLE!

Make no mistake: While a very exciting moment in your life, the matter of remarrying is a serious matter indeed, as you have many more considerations this time than you likely had when you married your late husband. However, this is also a time of celebration—a celebration of your new life, a celebration of new love, and a celebration of a renewed spirit—*yours*! For that and for reaching this moment in time, whether you eventually remarry or not, you are to be sincerely and truly congratulated.

chapter ten

THE "AFTERLIFE"—YOURS!

"I lost my husband [several years ago]. I am since remarried (to a widower I met online), but I saw [Widows Wear Stilettos] and wanted to say great job!"

"Why is it that being widowed brings out the free spirit in women? I know it's not just me, I've seen it often. I took up [tap and jazz] dancing at forty [years old], and became a 'shoe girl'!"

"It's been a year since my husband passed away and the one thing that really hit me the day after his passing was, 'Oh, my God, I'm a widow at [my age]!' I thought I would be well into my seventies or eighties [before] that would happen. It's been a journey, but I am coming out the 'other end.' The positive 'twist' is my husband taught me to use tools and I use those skills by volunteering my time to Habitat for Humanity in his honor. You are right; we need to move on."

"I've been a widow for a few years now and have a reached a point in my life where I'm enjoying life again. And it feels good."

"I have recently met a widower and I have allowed myself to experience joy and happiness again. I am so scared, yet thrilled to learn about yet another part of this journey, that you can live again and perhaps even love again!"

"I am doing so much better. I have a purpose in my life that for the first time in a long time is positive. I know that I 'got lost' for a while, but I am rediscovering [myself] a little more each day."

"I have felt so raw inside. I now feel like maybe tomorrow won't be so painful. It just helps knowing that I can come to my 'safe place' [at Widows Wear Stilettos] and relate to all my 'widow sisters.'"

As much as I love every single letter that I receive, it's letters like these that I treasure the most. Letters of triumph, of hope, and of optimism. Letters that tell me of travels through the dark times and moving forward into a place of happiness, peace, and abundance. Letters that say, "It hasn't been easy and it surely hasn't always been fun but I can do this. I can live again, I can laugh again, and maybe one day, I'll even love again."

You might not be exactly where the authors of these letters are right now, at this moment in time and that's OK. Your healing journey isn't a race and it isn't a competition against other widows to see who can heal the fastest. Focus on the important things that you have learned thus far.

You have learned that by making the conscious *choice* to heal (because it is a choice), by surrounding yourself with the necessary tools to facilitate your healing (books, CDs, and websites), and by acknowledging that you can honor and love your past without being destined (or "sentenced") to live in the past, you are taking vital steps to move in the right direction and that direction is *forward*.

You will have days or moments in time or certain periods that test you, the days that you might be tempted to use words like "setback" and "lost ground."

Remember that moving forward is not synonymous with "never feeling bad again." You may still have those days—choose to embrace them. Permit yourself the tears, the quiet, the anger, whatever it is that you are feeling at that moment. Embrace it, make it a part of you, and then continue to move on.

Being on a mission of service to others in need is one of the greatest missions that anyone can undertake. If you don't feel as though you are yet in a position to help others, believe me, there are plenty of others that are in a position to help *you,* if only by something as simple as writing a note that says, "I've been *exactly* where you are." How wonderful to hear those words from people who actually *have* been exactly where you are!

Keep this book handy to use as a reference, to answer your questions, calm your concerns, and most importantly, to help you actually *see* your recovery in progress. As you move forward, you also need to be able to look back and celebrate how far you have come, regardless of how little or how much time has passed since your husband's passing. Remember that *any* step forward is a STEP *FORWARD!*

My fondest wish is that one day soon, I will receive a letter from you that sounds similar to the letters in this closing chapter, a letter that says, "I'm doing it! I'm overcoming grief, I'm overcoming pain and hurt, and I'm jumping back into life." Lastly, never forget:

We are *going.* We are *growing.*
We *are* Widows Wear Stilettos and we *will* be heard.

Stay strong my friend—and I know you will.

epilogue

I wish you
Blue skies and green lights,
Blessings abundant,
Burdens few.
Family and friends to forever love and laugh with,
Wisdom to guide you,
A spirit that has freed you,
And a heart that will always embrace the past,
While loving today,
and with a passion for the possibilities that make up all of
your tomorrows.

—Carole Brody Fleet

afterthoughts

S<small>EVERAL YEARS AFTER</small> M<small>IKE'S DEATH,</small> I <small>WROTE MY FIRST BOOK,</small>
Widows Wear Stilettos: A Practical and Emotional Guide for the Young Widow,
for one simple reason. I figured that if I had all of these questions and experiences, trials and errors, ups, downs, moods, and "madnesses," there had to be
one or two (or millions of) others who'd had similar experiences and might
need a little bit of help and guidance or maybe just needed something as
simple as hearing one other person say, "Yeah, I've been there."

However, what started out as one book turned into so much more than
what I had ever envisioned. Widows Wear Stilettos quickly evolved into a
global support network, bringing together widows of all ages, from all
walks of life and from all over the world at www.widowswearstilettos.com. I
began receiving literally thousands of letters through the website, letters that
continue to this very day. The CD, *Widows Wear Stilettos: What Now?* soon
followed and proved to be an immediate hit. Before we knew it, we were
forming Widows Wear Stilettos in-person support groups throughout the
United States. We then formed a nonprofit foundation and thereafter began

offering Widows Wear Stilettos merchandise to support the foundation.

All of it—the books, the CD, the support groups, the merchandise, and everything that Widows Wear Stilettos has become—was designed for and is intended to educate, support, and create a community among the widowed. Widows Wear Stilettos is meant to teach the widowed how to grow *through* their loss experience to a place of peace, rather than feel compelled to skulk about in quiet grief, needless shame, or worse yet, feel as though they aren't entitled to speak about their widowhood at all.

What started as just one book has indeed become a movement.

Most importantly, realize that you are not alone in your journey of healing and your journey of learning. Widows Wear Stilettos's motto has always been, "We're Here and We Care," because it's a fact. We are here to answer your questions compassionately and honestly, ease your way, reassure your mind, bolster your spirit, and most especially, we are here to help you return to a life that is whole, healthy, and happy, a life that you can live happily *even* after!

acknowledgments

No AUTHOR ENJOYS ANY KIND OF SUCCESS WITHOUT A HOST OF PEOPLE making sure that she crosses the finish line. The author lovingly and gratefully acknowledges the following, without whom success would have been impossible:

I begin with a group that has talent, imagination, and "possibility thinking" that is unparalleled. My agent, Dr. Sidney Harriet, and Agents Ink: through the ups, downs, sidesteps, detours, and ultimate triumphs of this journey called writing, you have all been unwavering in your belief, both in me and in the mission of Widows Wear Stilettos. You'll never know how much that means to me and the people we serve. My editor and champion, Brenda "Don't Stop Believin'" Knight, you are not only the most amazing visionary, you are also an incredible "widow warrior," who is equally dedicated to bringing education and healing to the widowed community. Many thanks to Nancy Fish, Felice Newman, Kat Sanborn, Kara Wuest, Jennifer Privateer, and everyone at Viva Editions for being those special visionaries, for believing in this project as passionately as all of you do, and for being the very special hands into which I could place both this project and my trust.

Steve Harrison, Bill Harrison, Gail Snyder, Nick Summa, Ginny Shepard, and the entire team at Bradley Communications: I seriously doubt that Widows Wear Stilettos would be what it has become had it not been for all of you. Last, but never ever least, is the "Glam Squad" (because it *does* take a village!): Teddie Tillett, Ashley Elkins Hoffman, Jenn Beaver, Nicole England; and Anna, Lisa, and everyone on the "Princess Team": Thank you all for working so hard to make me the best "me" possible (and that *is* hard work!). My deepest gratitude and thanks go out to each and every one of you.

No matter how important or attention-worthy a message may be, nothing can be accomplished without the people who are committed to sharing the message of help and hope. For allowing us to reach and ultimately give a voice to an audience who so badly needs to be heard, I give my sincerest thanks to the many members of the media with whom I've had the privilege of working through the years, with very special thanks to: Deborah Roberts, Angela Hill, Cherry Key (who started the ABC "ball" rolling for us), and everyone at ABC News and *Good Morning America*; Cynthia Butler, Guy Farris, Jodi Moreno, and everyone at ABC News 10; Kristi Kline, Allison Scheetz, Alex Miranda, and Ann Lauricello; along with the amazing crew at ABC/KGUN; Elaine Ledesma, Stacy Butler, Michael "MJ" James, and everyone at CBS2/KCAL9 News; the entire crew at *Woman's World* Magazine, especially my superstar buddy and eternal optimist, Kristin Higson-Hughes; Carol Pereyra and the entire staff of *Going Bonkers?* Magazine; Kim Iverson, Jill Crapanzano, Casey Acevedo, and Ron Freshour; Mary Jones and Tony Borelli; Bonnie D. Graham; Victoria Davis; Lolis Garcia-Babb; Nick Lawrence; Linda Franklin; Bill McCleod; Mike Schikman; Stacey Gualandi; Lisa Bradshaw; Gary Pozsik; Jenifer Goodwin; Melody Ballard; Richard Asa; and every single member of the media in all forms with whom we've worked over the years, as well as all of the wonderful literary critics who have been so complimentary and kind to us. Thank you many times over for taking the time and the heart to listen to and deliver our message to the millions that need to hear it over and over again.

Lee and Bob Woodruff: You are both a continual inspiration, and Lee, you know you're my comic relief and "Go-To Girl" who is never ever too busy to lend your talent, your heart, and your wit to my life. You guys just rock!

Lenore Skenazy and Marci Shimoff, you are not only two of the most gifted authors on the planet, you are also always there for me and for Widows Wear Stilettos. I can't thank you enough for all you have done for us, and all that you do in the name of educating and empowering others as well.

State Farm Insurance and the *Embrace Life* program: With education, motivation, and inspiration, you changed my life, you are changing the lives of others who have been affected by loss, and most importantly, you are changing the way that society views loss—what a fantastic mission. Special thanks to Susan Waring, Carol Carey-Odekirk, Colleen Phillips, and to all of my fellow State Farm *Embrace Life* Honorees. Most especially, I thank State Farm Agent Dan Marshall, Huntington Beach, California, and the Marshall Crew for being there 24/7, "Like a good neighbor."

The Ritz Restaurant and Garden, Newport Beach, California: For well over twenty years, you have given me and our entire family many of our happiest memories and helped to get us through some of our darkest times with your caring, your humor, and your steadfast support. For that and so much more, you have my love and gratitude; with very special thanks and love to our sweet Beccy "Official Dinner-Timer and Clock-Keeper" Rogers, Judy Simpson, Sharon "Planner Extraordinaire" Virtue, Jim Roberts, Stacy Beech, Taylor "Tay-Tay" Gibson, Moises Mejia, the incomparable Arthur "Where the Hell Did the Ring Go?" Shegog, and, of course, our adorable Walter "Uncle Stretchy" Yong.

Taryn Davis and the American Widow Project and everyone at Soaring Spirits Loss Foundation: I thank you for allowing me the privilege of working alongside you toward achieving our common goals of healing in the widowed community. My thanks and love especially to Michele Neff Hernandez, Founder and Executive Director of Soaring Spirits Loss Foundation, as well as the creative genius behind the one, the only, and the original Camp Widow™ International Conferences, for your generosity, wisdom, completely fabulous sense of humor, and for the zillions of very-late-night-emails, text messages, hours-long phone conversations, lemon-drop martinis, and Saturday night dinners that we share.

Lisa Kline and Manisha Thakor: You stand as shining examples of what can be if one refuses to give up or give in. I never stop learning from you and your occasional tough love and I am a better person for knowing each of you. You have my love always.

Marni Gaylord Bernstein of Euphoria and Kerri Zane and crew at Kerri Zane Enterprises: Not only do you take vision and creativity to new levels, you both have the ability to take what exists and make it so much better than I ever dreamed it could be. Working with both of you is both a privilege and beyond fantastic, plus the laughter, friendship, and "girlfriend time" is really cool!

Walter Gobas: For the gift of being able to put a smile on my face, as well as always and forever giving me a healthy dose of perspective, I love you madly. Always have. Always will. And to Eleanor Gobas of blessed memory, we love you so much and we miss you endlessly.

To the entire team that comprises Widows Wear Stilettos: If you didn't do what you do, it would be impossible for me to do what I do. From our Board of Directors to our in-office support, to every single Widows Wear Stilettos support group facilitator and Widows Wear Stilettos Media Group member throughout the United States and Canada, each one of you has made this mission your mission as well, helping to grow and expand our organization to reach people that might still be suffering without all you. My special thanks and love to Shannon Bell, Kathy McGill, Martha Rodriguez, Jennifer Arches, Patricia Shuman, Lynn Dolegala, Jill Neff, Lisa Wagner, Celeste Ledesma, Amanda "Mandie" Felgenhauer, Sandy Hinesly, Jodi Hettergott, Kendall Brody, and Dave Stansbury for generously sharing your personal stories of tragedy and healing with our membership and with the media, fielding late night phone calls, facilitating our social media presence, handling website production crises, answering emails, quashing panic situations, jumping in whenever the words "last minute" came into play, keeping the behind-the-scenes machine moving, and generally keeping me organized and in one piece.

To my high school journalism advisor, Gene Genisauski, who coined the line, "Milk Drinkers Make Better 'Clinkers,'" who once told a wide-eyed, fifteen-year-old girl with a big dream, "Yes, you can" when everyone else was saying, "No, you can't," and who I am quite sure is dismayed that I now wield a pen (so to speak). Mr. "G," by throwing a sophomore into the "snake pit" of seniors on *The Lance* newspaper staff, you also became one of the first people who taught me how to dream big. Although I still can't write a headline to save my soul, you were a huge influence as an educator, to me and to countless others. For all this and more, you have my thanks and undying gratitude.

Part of the joy of reaching this season in my life is being able to look back and smile warmly at the precious friendships that have endured through several decades of both geographical and life changes. I give my love to the friends of my past who many years later, remain the friends and support of my present: Nanci (Doran) Alderson-Cooley; Karen (Anderson) Cooper; Laura (Billingsley) Evink; Susan (Venuti) Hampton; Lisa Guest; Taryn Whiteleather; Kathy (Green) Schutt; Donna (Salvitti) Nagle (who is also responsible for facilitating our liaison with the American Widow Project); Sharla Sanders; Mark and Tina Armijo; Gary and Elissa Wahlenmaier; and Debra Boyd (Deb, please meet me on the mezzanine with chicken enchiladas). I had the privilege of being a kid with all of you and it's even more fabulous to be "all grown up" with you as well. Thank you all for the love, encouragement, and support that you have given me through the years and especially with Widows Wear Stilettos.

Bobby Slayton, you keep me laughing (especially on the days when I don't feel like laughing) and you keep me reaching for the "skull within," even when I feel like it has deserted me. Thank you not just for the gift of laughter, but also for teaching me that it's always going to be OK to laugh, no matter what. Thank you also for the best pistachio pizza on earth. Teddie Tillett Slayton, it's difficult to find words to express what you mean to me. Through thick and thin, 405-freeway traffic, impossible schedules, seemingly overwhelming obstacles, and various dramas and crises, you have always been and continue to be by my side, without fail and regardless of whatever else is going on. From the bottom of my heart, thank you for being such a phenomenal "sister" to me and for keeping this "Deep Fried Poodle" on the ground; I love you so much. Natasha Slayton, my sweet Tashie-Girl, to have been a part of your growing up, to have you standing next to me on my wedding day, and now watching all of your years of hard work culminating in your own dreams coming true is a genuine joy. Don't ever forget how much your "Mommy C" loves you and how proud I am of you.

I firmly believe that without family ardently supporting you, loudly cheering for you, and constantly lifting you, there can be no real success. My family regularly sacrifices time spent together, decent nutrition, and a normal life in general and does so happily and without complaint (most of the time). It is with all my love and heart that I again thank my partner in life and in love, my husband, Dave "Spinner" Stansbury; my beautiful daughters, Kendall and Michelle; and the sage behind many of my "Mom Quotes," my mother, Eilene Clinkenbeard, as well as Kenneth "The Boss" Stansbury, David Clinkenbeard, Barbara Hedrick, Joan, Ronnie, Ken, Rick and Laurie Adler (P.S. to Rick—a major thank you for all of your help!), Russell Gilbert, M.D. and Kiyomi Gilbert; Max and Linda Ciampoli; Chuck Collins and Randy George; and every single member of the Berman/Spielman, Williamson, Bobinsky, and Zimmer families. I love you all so very much.

Finally, to Uncle Harry Williamson of blessed memory, I love you endlessly and will miss you forever.

We encourage you to continue your healing journey by visiting the following organizations for assistance**:

1) Widows Wear Stilettos, Inc. at www.widowswearstilettos.com: An award-winning nonprofit organization, Widows Wear Stilettos provides additional support, education, and information to that which is included in the books, including information regarding support groups, the charitable foundation, and various other products and services that are offered.

2) "Fleet-ing Thoughts" at www.widowswearstilettos.blogspot.com: Carole Brody Fleet, Chief Executive Officer and Founder of Widows Wear Stilettos, Inc., shares thoughts and messages of hope for the widowed community.

3) Soaring Spirits Loss Foundation at www.sslf.org: An award-winning nonprofit organization that operates several programs for the widowed community, including the annual Camp Widow™ International Confer-

ences (www.campwidow.org) and Widowed Village (www.widowedvillage.org).

4) The American Widow Project at www.americanwidowproject.org: An award-winning nonprofit that provides resources, products, services, and special outings and gatherings for widows and families of military personnel.

5) Social Security Administration at www.ssa.gov: Provides specific instructions and directions on obtaining survivor benefits for the widowed and for their children and also provides information on various programs and assistance available to survivors and their families.

6) Department of Veterans affairs at www.va.gov: Provides specific instructions and directions on obtaining benefits for survivors of military personnel (active, inactive, retired, or deceased) and also provides information on various programs and assistance available to survivors and their families.

7) Paralyzed Veterans of America at www.pva.org: Advocating on behalf of all military veterans and their surviving families regardless of current military status, the PVA assists survivors with questions regarding and the obtaining of military benefits from the government and does so free of charge.

**Please note that all aforementioned resources can also be located via Facebook, Twitter, and various other social media sources.

CAROLE BRODY FLEET IS THE AWARD-WINNING AUTHOR OF *WIDOWS Wear Stilettos: A Practical and Emotional Guide for the Young Widow*, (New Horizon Press) as well as the author and executive producer of the bestselling CD, *Widows Wear Stilettos: What Now?* She is the Founder and Chief Executive Officer of Widows Wear Stilettos, Inc.

Using a fresh approach and putting a unique twist on her topics, Ms. Fleet is a popular motivational speaker to those who have been touched by the pain and challenge of loss, regardless of age. With her own inimitable message of "What Now and What Next?" Ms. Fleet educates, motivates, inspires, enlightens, and offers practical, emotional, and even humorous guidance to the millions who have experienced loss, tragedy, or a challenge in their lives.

Ms. Fleet also speaks to general audiences of all ages, addressing such issues as goal-setting and achievement; overcoming obstacles; time management; stress management; work and life balance; leadership or "leaner-ship"; giving back/effecting change; and "finding the powerful voice within," and does so in an uplifting, witty manner.

Ms. Fleet makes guest appearances on national, regional, and local television; she appears as a regular guest on numerous radio programs in the United States and Canada; and she is a featured expert in many well-known international and national magazines, newspapers, and websites in the United States, Canada, and the United Kingdom. She addresses a wide variety of topics, including, but not limited to: caregiving, illness, and loss/post-loss issues; matters relating to financial transition after loss or divorce; raising children who have lost a parent; reentering the world of dating and love; and most importantly, making a return to a fulfilling and abundant life after the loss of a spouse; as well as after any kind of loss, tragedy, challenge, or life difficulty.

Photograph by Jun Juong/Star Image.

To Our Readers

Viva Editions publishes books that inform, enlighten, and entertain. We do our best to bring you, the reader, quality books that celebrate life, inspire the mind, revive the spirit, and enhance lives all around. Our authors are practical visionaries: people who offer deep wisdom in a hopeful and helpful manner. Viva was launched with an attitude of growth and we want to spread our joy and offer our support and advice where we can to help you live the Viva way: vivaciously!

We're grateful for all our readers and want to keep bringing you books for inspired living. We invite you to write to us with your comments and suggestions, and what you'd like to see more of. You can also sign up for our online newsletter to learn about new titles, author events, and special offers.

Viva Editions
2246 Sixth St.
Berkeley, CA 94710
www.vivaeditions.com
(800) 780-2279
Follow us on Twitter @vivaeditions
Friend/fan us on Facebook